A DICTIONARY OF SELECTED VERBS FOR ALL AGES

ASHWANNIE HARRIPERSAUD

| JESSICA SEERAJ | ALLISON E. DANIELS | CLINTON WARDE |

BLUEROSE PUBLISHERS
India | U.K.

Copyright © Ashwannie Harripersaud, Clinton Warde,
Jessica Seeraj, Allison E. Daniels 2024

All rights reserved by author. No part of this publication may be reproduced, stored in a retrieval system or transmitted in any form or by any means, electronic, mechanical, photocopying, recording or otherwise, without the prior permission of the author. Although every precaution has been taken to verify the accuracy of the information contained herein, the publisher assume no responsibility for any errors or omissions. No liability is assumed for damages that may result from the use of information contained within.

BlueRose Publishers takes no responsibility for any damages, losses, or liabilities that may arise from the use or misuse of the information, products, or services provided in this publication.

For permissions requests or inquiries regarding this publication,
please contact:

BLUEROSE PUBLISHERS
www.BlueRoseONE.com
info@bluerosepublishers.com
+91 8882 898 898
+4407342408967

ISBN: 978-93-6783-964-5

Cover design: Daksh
Typesetting: Tanya Raj Upadhyay

First Edition: December 2024

Acknowledgement

We are indebted to all lexicographers that preceded us: from Samuel Johnson to Richard Allsopp and Walter Edwards. They led; we merely followed.

Thanks to Professor Daizal R. Samad. We are deeply grateful for your invaluable guidance and motivation throughout the completion of this dictionary. Your insights and encouragement were crucial to our development, and we truly appreciate the time and effort you dedicated to our progress.

A heartfelt thanks to Maylyn Amanda Bootoon. Your technological expertise made a significant difference towards the completion of this work.

About Our Dictionary

Background:

"A Dictionary of Selected Verbs for All Ages" is the fourth instalment in a carefully curated series of dictionaries, each focusing on essential aspects of language and communication that have shaped human expression across generations. The motivation behind this volume, dedicated to verbs, stems from the recognition that verbs are the core of any sentence, giving life to language by expressing actions, states, and occurrences. Verbs have the power to move, transform, and define experiences, making them indispensable in both written and spoken communication. The authors saw verbs as pivotal in connecting the past, present, and future of human interaction, and this dictionary seeks to highlight that enduring significance.

Aim:

The aim of **"A Dictionary of Selected Verbs for All Ages"** is to provide a thorough and accessible resource that enriches the vocabulary of readers across different age groups. This dictionary seeks to illuminate the variations of verbs through clear definitions, varied usage

Examples, and practical applications. By focusing on verbs that are versatile and impactful, it aims to strengthen language proficiency, encourage expressive communication, and support effective writing and speaking skills for individuals at any stage of their language learning journey.

Scope:

The scope of this work is not limited to a specific audience. However, students in Primary and Secondary schools that have English within their curricula will benefit in inestimable ways. The content comprises over 1000 verbs. These words are accompanied by their phonetic transcriptions, in line with the International Phonetic Alphabet, and their definitions. Each word is also accompanied by a simple sentence that provides exemplary usage.

Rationale:

"A Dictionary of Selected Verbs for All Ages" serves a crucial role in strengthening linguistic proficiency and understanding for individuals at every stage of their language development. The rationale for this dictionary stems from the importance of verbs in constructing meaningful sentences and conveying actions, states, and occurrences clearly and effectively.

Verbs are fundamental to language, driving communication and expression. However, the vast array of verbs in the English language can be overwhelming, especially for learners. This dictionary aims to address this challenge by selecting verbs that are not only common and useful but also versatile and impactful across a variety of contexts.

Concentrating on selected verbs, the dictionary helps users to understand the variations and connotations of each verb, facilitating more precise and varied use of language. It provides

Examples and definitions that illustrate how these verbs can be employed effectively, improving both written and oral communication skills.

Additionally, **"A Dictionary of Selected Verbs for All Ages"** is designed to be accessible to all ages, offering explanations and

Examples that are appropriate for young learners as well as adults. This makes it a valuable resource for educators, students, writers, and anyone interested in improving their language skills.

Definition of a Verb

A verb is a word that expresses an action, occurrence, or state of being. Verbs are essential to forming sentences because they typically indicate what the subject is doing or what is happening to the subject.

Types of Verbs

Action Verbs

An action verb is a verb that describes an action that a subject is performing. It expresses what someone or something is doing.

Example: They **built** a new house in the neighbourhood.

"Built" is the action verb showing the construction activity.

Transitive Verbs

A transitive verb is a verb that requires a direct object to complete its meaning. The action of the verb is directed towards the object, which is the recipient of the action.

Example: The teacher **graded** the papers.

"Graded" is the transitive verb, and "the papers" is the direct object.

Intransitive Verbs

Intransitive verbs are verbs that do not require a direct object to complete their meaning. These verbs express actions or states that do not transfer to a recipient or object.

Example: She **spoke** fluently.

"Spoke" is the intransitive verb, focusing on the action without a direct object.

Auxiliary Verbs

Auxiliary verbs, also known as helping verbs, are used alongside main verbs to help express tense, aspect, mood, or voice. They provide additional meaning to the main verb in a sentence. Common auxiliary verbs in English include forms of "be", "have", "do", "can", "shall", "will", "may", "might", "must", and "should."

Example: They **have** finished their homework.

"Have" is the auxiliary verb used to form the present perfect tense of "finished."

Stative Verbs

A stative verb is a verb that describes a state, condition, or situation rather than an action or process. Stative verbs often relate to thoughts, emotions, relationships, senses, or conditions that are static and unchanging.

Example: They **belong** to the same club.

"Belong" is a stative verb describing a relationship.

Modal Verbs

Modal verbs are auxiliary verbs that express necessity, possibility, permission, or ability. They are used with the base form of another verb and do not change according to the subject. Common modal verbs in English include "can", "could", "may", "might", "shall", "should", "will", "would", and "must."

Example: You **should** apologise for being late.

"Should" expresses advice or recommendation.

Phrasal Verbs

Phrasal verbs are combinations of a verb and one or more particles (such as prepositions or adverbs) that, when used together, have a meaning different from the original verb alone. These particles modify the meaning of the verb in significant ways.

Example: She **turned off** the lights when she left the room.

"Turned off" is a phrasal verb meaning to switch off.

Irregular Verbs

An irregular verb is a verb that does not follow the standard pattern of adding "-ed" to form the past tense and past participle. Instead, irregular verbs have unique forms for the past tense and past participle that must be memorised.

Example: She **went** to the market yesterday.

"Went" is the past tense of "go."

Regular Verbs

Regular verbs are verbs that follow a standard pattern when forming the past tense and past participle. In English, this typically involves adding "-ed" to the base form of the verb. Regular verbs do not change in spelling except for the addition of this suffix, making them relatively predictable in their conjugation.

Example: She **walked** to the store yesterday.

"Walked" is the past tense of "walk."

Preface

"A Dictionary of Selected Verbs for All Ages" is the fourth in a series of novel dictionaries done by Ashwannie Harripersaud and her Team. It follows the Dictionaries of Adjectives, Nouns, and Adverbs, and continues the trajectory of providing words and meanings in a focused manner, keeping with a target part of speech.

A dictionary of verbs proves to be very useful, as verbs are very important across all languages. As I would normally tell my students of Linguistics, the verb is the king of the sentence. Verbs must be in every sentence, and they have a way of determining what goes on in the sentence for the sentence to make sense. The choice of verb determines whether the subject should be an agent or an experiencer, or if the sentence requires a theme. Verbs are quite dynamic – they sometimes change their forms as they team up with tense to express actions in the present, past, and future; and with aspect to communicate whether actions will start shortly, are progressing currently, or have recently ended. They even change their forms to match the needs of the subject! The verb in a sentence operates like the heart in your body, you simply cannot do without it. The more verbs you know, the more advanced your grammatical skills will become. This Dictionary of Selected Verbs for All Ages will therefore help to increase your ability to express your ideas more precisely, whether you opt for simple words, or more complex alternatives, thus improving your overall communicative skills. Verbs are also important in setting the tone and the mood of your writing or speech, and the general appeal to your audience. Mastering verbs is therefore important, and this Dictionary of Verbs for All Ages provides a tool to do just that.

Perusing the dictionary of over 1000 verbs, I found myself paying great attention to not only the verbs listed, but to the

Examples, which were relatable, easy to understand, and picturesquely brought the words to life. The phonemic representations included provide a guide to the pronunciations, and would therefore be applicable to an international audience, especially learners of the English Language. As a Caribbean Linguist, I selfishly yearn for representations reflecting Caribbean English pronunciations, and hope that perhaps the authors may be inspired to consider doing a version of the dictionary for Caribbean students with Caribbean pronunciations! As an educator with over 20 years of experience, Ashwannie Harripersaud and her team of authors, all teachers of English, are so poised to guide us, and we thank them for providing this resource to assist us in improving our communication skills.

Regards,
Tamirand Nnena De Lisser, PhD.
Senior Lecturer of Linguistics
University of Guyana

Aa

abate /ɑbˈeɪt/
to become less intense or severe
Example: The storm began to abate after several hours of heavy rain.
to diminish
Example: Her anger abated as she listened to his explanation.
to reduce in amount or degree
Example: After the heavy rainfall, the floodwaters began to abate, allowing residents to return to their homes.

abbreviate /ɑbrˈiːvɪˌeɪt/
to shorten a word, phrase, or text by omitting letters or parts while retaining the essential meaning.
Example: We often abbreviate "Doctor" as "Dr."

abide /ɑbˈaɪd/
to accept or act in accordance with a rule, decision, or recommendation
Example: She promised to abide by the rules of the game.
to tolerate or endure
Example: He could not abide the constant noise from the construction site.
to remain stable or fixed in a state
Example: The paint abides on the walls.

abort /ɑbˈɔːt/
to terminate or end prematurely, especially a planned activity, process, or mission
Example: The pilot had to abort the landing due to poor visibility.

abscond /ɑbskˈɒnd/
to leave hurriedly and secretly, typically to avoid detection or arrest

Example: The thief absconded with the jewels in the dead of night.

absorb /ɑbsˈɔːb/
to take in or soak up something such as liquid, energy, or information
Example: The sponge can absorb a lot of water.
to assimilate or integrate something into oneself or something else
Example: She was deeply absorbed in her book.

abstain /ɑbstˈeɪn/
to refrain voluntarily from doing something, especially from indulging in a particular activity or behaviour
Example: He decided to abstain from drinking alcohol during the week.

abuse /ɑbˈuwus/
to use something or someone in a harmful, unjust, or improper way, often involving mistreatment, exploitation, or cruelty
Example: They abused the power they were given.

accede /ɑksˈiːd/
to agree to a request or demand, to consent or yield to a proposal
Example: The government acceded to the demands of the protesters.
to assume an office or position
Example: She acceded to the throne after her father's death.

accelerate /ɑksˈɛlərˌeɪt/
to increase in speed or to cause something to move faster
Example: The car accelerated quickly after the light turned green.
to increase the rate or pace of something, such as growth, development, or progress
Example: The company's growth accelerated after the new product launch.

accent /ɑkˈsnt/
to emphasise or stress a particular sound, syllable, word, or phrase in speech
Example: The teacher asked him to accent the second syllable in the word "banana."
to give prominence or importance to something
Example: The interior designer chose a red sofa to accent the room's modern theme.

accentuate /ɑksˈɛntʃuːˌeɪt/
to emphasise, highlight, or make something more noticeable or prominent
Example: The new lighting will accentuate the architectural details of the building.

accept /ɑksˈɛpt/
to agree to take or receive something that is offered, given, or presented
Example: She decided to accept the job offer after careful consideration.
to acknowledge the truth, validity, or existence of something
Example: He refused to accept that he had made a mistake.

accommodate /ɑkˈɒmədˌeɪt/
to provide lodging or space for someone
Example: The hotel can accommodate up to 300 guests.
to adapt or adjust to someone's needs or requests
Example: The school will do its best to accommodate students with special needs.
to make something suitable or convenient for a particular purpose
Example: The car was modified to accommodate the driver's disability.

accompany /ɑkˈʌmpəni/
to go somewhere with someone as a companion or escort, often for support, guidance, or company
Example: She asked her friend to accompany her to the doctor's appointment.
to go together with something else, such as music accompanying a performance or a side dish accompanying a main course
Example: A pianist will accompany the singer during the concert.

accost /ɑkˈɒst/
to approach someone boldly or aggressively, typically to confront, address, or speak to them, often in an intrusive manner
Example: A stranger accosted her on the street, demanding to know where she was going.

accuse /ɑkjˈuːz/
to charge someone with an offence or wrongdoing, typically by making a formal statement or allegation, claiming that they are responsible for a specific action or behaviour
Example: He was accused of stealing the money from the store.

ache /eɪk/
to experience a continuous, dull pain or discomfort in a part of the body, typically without severe intensity but persisting over time
Example: Her back began to ache after sitting for hours.
a lingering emotional or psychological discomfort
Example: He felt a deep ache in his heart after the breakup.

achieve /ɑtʃˈiːv/
to successfully reach or accomplish a desired goal, result, or outcome through effort, skill, or perseverance
Example: She worked hard to achieve her dream of becoming a doctor.

acknowledge /ɑknˈɒlɪdʒ/
to recognize, admit, or accept the existence, truth, or validity of something
Example: He had to acknowledge that he had been wrong about the project's potential.
to express gratitude or appreciation for something or someone
Example: She sent a thank-you note to acknowledge their support.

acquiesce /ˌɑkwɪˈɛs/
to yield or give in to a request, demand, or situation without expressing open resistance
Example: Despite his initial reluctance, he eventually acquiesced to their demands.

acquire /ɑkwˈaɪə/
to obtain, gain, or procure something, typically through effort, purchase, or experience
Example: She acquired a new skill by taking online courses.

act /ˈɑkt/
to take control or do something
Example: It is time to act on your plans and make them a reality.
to behave or conduct oneself in a particular way
Example: He tends to act nervously around strangers.
to portray a character or perform a role
Example: She loves to act in school plays.
to function or operate in a certain way
Example: The drug will act quickly to relieve pain.
to pretend or feign
Example: He decided to act surprised at the party, even though he knew about it in advance.

adapt /ədˈæpt/
to adjust or modify something to fit a new situation, environment, or purpose
Example: *The software was adapted to meet the needs of different users.*

add /ˈæd/
to combine or join something to something else, typically to increase the total amount, quantity, or value
Example: *She decided to add more spices to the recipe for extra flavour.*

address /ˈaˌdrɛs/
to deal with or attend to a specific matter, problem, or issue
Example: *The committee met to address the budget concerns.*
to speak to or communicate with someone, especially formally or publicly
Example: *The CEO will address the employees at the annual meeting.*
to write or print a name and address on an envelope, package, letter, etc. in preparation for sending it
Example: *She carefully addressed the invitation envelopes.*

adhere /ədhˈiə/
to stick or cling firmly to something, either physically or figuratively
Example: *The glue will adhere to most surfaces.*
to follow closely or remain loyal to a belief, principle, or rule
Example: *They adhere strictly to their traditions.*

adjust /ədʒˈʌst/
to change or alter something slightly to achieve better fit, function, or suitability
Example: *He adjusted the seat height for a more comfortable ride.*

administer /ɑdmˈɪnɪstɐ/
to manage, supervise, or oversee the implementation of something, such as a system, program, or medication
Example: *The nurse will administer the medication.*

admire /ɑdmˈaɪə/
to regard with respect, and approval for someone or something due to their qualities, achievements, or attributes
Example: *She admired his dedication and hard work.*

admit /ɑdmˈɪt/
to allow entry or access to someone or something, typically into a place or situation
Example: *The security guard admitted them into the restricted area.*
to acknowledge or confess to something, often something that is considered true, valid, or undesirable
Example: *She admitted her mistake and apologised sincerely.*

admonish /ɑdmˈɒnɪʃ/
to reprimand or scold someone mildly but earnestly, typically to correct a fault or wrongdoing
Example: *The teacher admonished the student for being late to class.*
to caution or advise against something
Example: *He admonished them not to play with fire.*

adore /əˈdɔː/
to love and admire someone or something deeply and with great affection
Example: *She adores her baby brother and spends hours playing with him.*

adorn /əˈdɔːn/
to decorate or embellish something, typically with beautiful or ornamental features
Example:　The bride adorned her hair with fresh flowers for the wedding.

advance /ədˈvɑns/
to move forward or progress in a particular direction, either physically or metaphorically
Example:　The army advanced toward the enemy's position.
to promote or further a cause, idea, or objective, often by taking action or making improvements
Example:　She advanced the theory that would revolutionise their field.
to provide or offer something, such as help, money, or knowledge, before it is requested or expected
Example:　He advanced her a loan to help with her business.

advertise /ˈadvərˌtaɪz/
to promote or publicise a product, service, event, or idea through various forms of media or communication channels
Example:　The company advertised their new product on television and social media.

advise /ədˈvaɪz/
to offer suggestions, recommendations, or guidance to someone, typically based on one's knowledge, expertise, or experience
Example:　She advised him to invest in real estate rather than stocks.

advocate /ˈadvəkət/
to publicly support or recommend a particular cause, policy, or course of action
Example:　She advocates for equal rights and opportunities for all.

affirm /əˈfɜːrm/
to state or assert something positively and firmly as true or valid
Example: She affirmed her commitment to finishing the project on time.
to provide emotional support or encouragement to someone
Example: He affirmed his daughter's decision to pursue her passion.

affix /əˈfɪks/
to attach or fasten something to something else, typically by means of adhesive, nails, screws, or other methods
Example: Please affix your signature at the bottom of the page.
to add a prefix, suffix, or other linguistic element to a word to alter its meaning or form
Example: The prefix "un-" can be affixed to many adjectives to indicate negation.

aggravate /ˈæɡrəˌveɪt/
to make a problem, situation, or condition worse or more severe
Example: His constant complaining only served to aggravate the situation.

agonise /ˈæɡəˌnaɪz/
to suffer mental anguish or intense emotional distress, often over a difficult decision, situation, or outcome
Example: She agonised over whether to accept the job offer or not.

agree /əˈɡriː/
to have the same opinion, view, or understanding as someone else
Example: We agreed on the best course of action for the project.
to be in accordance with or comply with a proposal, request, or condition
Example: She agreed to the terms and conditions of the contract.

aid /eɪd/
to provide assistance, support, or help to someone or something in need, typically in a tangible or practical way
Example: The volunteers aided the flood victims by delivering food and water.

aim /eɪm/
to point or direct something, such as a weapon, object, or effort, toward a particular target, goal, or objective
Example: She aimed the arrow carefully before releasing it.
to have a specific purpose or intention in mind when taking action
Example: They aimed to reduce carbon emissions by fifty percent within five years.

air /eər/
to ventilate or freshen by exposing to air
Example: She aired out the room to get rid of the musty smell.
to broadcast or transmit something, such as a program or information, through radio or television
Example: The news channel airs the latest updates every hour.
to express thoughts or feelings openly, often in a public manner
Example: He aired his grievances during the meeting.

alert /əˈlɜːrt/
to warn or notify someone of potential danger, threat, or problem, typically to prompt them to take action or be vigilant
Example: The lifeguard alerted the swimmers to the presence of a shark.
to make someone aware or attentive to something important or urgent
Example: She alerted him to the approaching deadline.

align /əˈlaɪn/
to arrange or position something in a straight line or in a parallel manner with something else

Example: He aligned the bookshelf with the wall for a neat appearance.
to bring into agreement, harmony, or conformity with a particular standard, goal, or belief
Example: Their interests and values aligned perfectly.

allege /əˈlɛdʒ/
to assert or claim something without providing definite proof or evidence
Example: He alleged that his neighbour was stealing his newspaper every morning.
to accuse someone of wrongdoing or making a specific statement without necessarily proving it to be true
Example: The defendant alleged that he was innocent of the charges.

allow /əˈlaʊ/
to give permission or consent for something to happen or be done
Example: His parents allowed him to stay out late on weekends.
to acknowledge or concede the truth or validity of something
Example: After reviewing the evidence, he had to allow that his initial assumptions were incorrect.

allude /əˈluːd/
to indirectly or subtly refer to something, typically without explicitly mentioning it
Example: She alluded to her difficult childhood without going into specifics.

alphabetize /ˈalfəbəˌtaɪz/
to arrange items, such as words, names, or objects, in alphabetical order according to the sequence of letters in the alphabet
Example: Please alphabetize the list of names before filing them.

alter /ˈɔːltər/
to change or modify something, typically in a relatively small or subtle way, often to adapt or adjust it to a different condition, state, or purpose
Example: She altered the dress to fit her perfectly.

alternate /ˈɔːltərˌneɪt/
to occur or happen in turns or succession, often in a recurring pattern
Example: Their meetings alternate between Monday mornings and Thursday afternoons.
to exchange or take turns between two or more options or possibilities
Example: They alternate the responsibility of taking care of their elderly parents.
to serve as a substitute or replacement for something else, typically in a cyclic or rotational manner
Example: We alternate driving duties on our weekly commute.
to modify or adjust to achieve variety or balance
Example: The chef alternates the menu every season to keep it fresh.

amble /ˈæmbəl/
to walk at a leisurely, relaxed pace, often characterised by a casual and unhurried manner
Example: They ambled along the beach, enjoying the sunset.

amend /əˈmɛnd/
to make changes or modifications to something, typically a document, law, agreement, or plan, to improve, correct, or update
Example: The committee voted to amend the constitution to include new rights.

amuse /əˈmjuːz/
to entertain or provide enjoyment or amusement to someone, typically by engaging their attention in a light-hearted or enjoyable manner
Example: The clown's antics never failed to amuse the children.

analyse /ˈanəlaɪz/
to examine something in detail, typically by breaking it down into its constituent parts or components to understand its structure, function, or meaning
Example: *She analysed the data to identify trends and patterns.*

angle /ˈaŋgəl/
to approach or present something from a particular perspective or standpoint, often with the intention of influencing or persuading others
Example: *The journalist angled her story to highlight the human impact of the policy.*
to position or direct something, such as a camera, at a specific direction
Example: *He angled the spotlight to illuminate the stage.*

animate /ˈanəˌmeɪt/
to give life or vitality to something, such as an object or character, often through movement or expression
Example: *The artist animated the characters in the film.*
to make lively, energetic, or spirited
Example: *The music at the party animated the guests, who started dancing enthusiastically.*
to encourage or inspire someone to take action or to have enthusiasm or motivation for something
Example: *Her speech animated the audience to volunteer for the community project.*

annotate /ˈanəʊtˌeɪt/ to add explanatory notes or comments to a text, document, or other written material
Example: *In academic research, scholars often annotate their sources to provide context.*

announce /əˈnaʊns/
to make a formal or public declaration or proclamation about something, typically to convey information or news to others

Example: *The CEO announced a new strategic initiative to expand the company's market reach.*

annoy /əˈnɔɪ/
to irritate, disturb, or provoke someone, typically by repeated or persistent actions, behaviours, or comments that cause frustration, inconvenience, or discomfort
Example: *Her constant tapping on the desk began to annoy her colleagues.*

anoint /əˈnɔɪnt/
to ceremonially apply oil or a similar substance to someone or something, often as a sign of consecration, blessing, or empowerment
Example: *The priest anointed the new-born with holy oil during the baptism.*

answer /ˈɑːnsə/
to respond to a question, request, or statement with a reply or explanation
Example: *He did not answer her question directly, which made her suspicious.*

antagonise /ænˈtæɡəˌnaɪz/
to provoke or cause hostility, opposition, or conflict with someone, typically by deliberately irritating, provoking, or upsetting them
Example: *He knew criticising her favourite team would antagonise her, but he did it anyway.*

anticipate /ænˈtɪsɪˌpeɪt/
to expect or foresee something happening, typically based on observation, experience, or reasoning
Example: *Investors anticipated a downturn in the market and began selling off stocks.*

apologize /əˈpɒlədʒaɪz/
to express regret or remorse for an action, statement, or behaviour that has caused harm, offence, or inconvenience to someone else
Example: *He apologised sincerely for forgetting her birthday.*

appeal /ɑpˈiːl/
to make a sincere request or plea for something, often to a higher authority or to the public, to gain support, assistance, or approval
Example: *The lawyer's appeal to the jury was emotional and compelling.*
to attract or be interesting or desirable to someone, often by having qualities or features that evoke interest, sympathy, or admiration
Example: *The idea of living abroad has a strong appeal to many young people.*
to apply to a higher court to review a decision made by a lower court, typically to seek a reversal or modification of the decision
Example: *They decided to appeal the court's decision in hopes of a more favourable outcome.*
to have a strong emotional impact or influence on someone, often by eliciting feelings of sympathy, empathy, or concern
Example: *Her story of struggle and perseverance appealed to the audience.*
to resort or turn to something or someone for help, guidance, or resolution of a problem or difficulty
Example: *In times of crisis, people often appeal to their faith.*

appear /ɑpˈiə/ to become visible or to be seen by others, typically in a particular place or situation
Example: *The sun appeared on the horizon at dawn.*
to come into existence or to become evident or apparent
Example: *Symptoms usually appear within a few days of infection.*
to present oneself formally in a public setting, such as in court or on stage
Example: *The actor appeared on stage to a round of applause.*

appease /ɑpˈiːz/
to pacify, soothe, or calm someone's feelings, typically by making concessions or fulfilling their demands
Example: *The agreement appeased the dissenters, restoring peace within the group.*

applaud /ɑplˈɔːd/
to express approval, admiration, or appreciation for someone or something by clapping one's hands together
Example: *The audience applauded enthusiastically at the end of the performance.*

apply /ɑˈplaɪ/
to make a formal request or submit an application for something, such as a job, program, or permission
Example: *She applied for admission to several universities.*
to use or implement something, such as a skill, technique, or method, in
a specific context or situation
Example: *He applied his knowledge of science to solve the problem.*
to place or spread something onto a surface or object, such as applying paint to a wall
Example: *She carefully applied the paint to the canvas.*
to exert or devote effort or attention to something, such as applying oneself to a task or study
Example: *He applied himself to learning a new language.*

appraise /ɑprˈeɪz/
to assess, valuate, or estimate the value, quality, or significance of something, often in a systematic or professional manner
Example: *The expert appraised the antique vase at several thousand dollars.*

appreciate /əprˈiːʃɪˌeɪt/
to recognize the value, worth, or significance of something or someone and to show gratitude for it
Example: *I really appreciate your help with the project.*
to increase in value over time, especially in terms of financial value
Example: *The property has appreciated significantly in the last decade.*
to enjoy or derive pleasure from something, such as art, music, or nature
Example: *She appreciates classical music deeply.*
to express or demonstrate admiration, respect, or affection for someone or something
Example: *He always appreciates it when you take the time to visit him.*

approach /əprˈəʊtʃ/
to move nearer to something or someone in distance, time, or quality, often with the intention of interacting or engaging with it/them
Example: *The cat cautiously approached the new visitor.*
to adopt a particular method, strategy, or attitude in dealing with a situation or problem
Example: *We need to approach this issue with great care.*
to make a request or proposal to someone in a friendly or persuasive manner
Example: *He approached the manager with a request for additional resources.*

appropriate /əˈprəʊpriˌeɪt/
to take or use something for a particular purpose, and usually in a way that is considered proper or suitable
Example: *Funds were appropriated for the new building project.*
to allocate or assign funds, resources, or responsibilities for a specific purpose or use
Example: *The government appropriated millions for disaster relief.*

to embody or display qualities, behaviours, or customs that are considered typical or suitable for a particular situation, context, or culture
Example: *His response was appropriate for the solemn occasion.*
to legally transfer or assign property or assets to someone else, typically by authority or by formal agreement
Example: *The rights to the invention were appropriately transferred to the company.*

approve /əpr'uːv/
to officially agree to or accept something as satisfactory, valid, or suitable
Example: *The committee approved the new policy unanimously.*
to express favourable opinion or support for something
Example: *Her parents approved of her decision to study abroad.*

arc /'ɑːk/
to move or follow a curved path, often in a graceful or sweeping manner
Example: *The basketball arced beautifully through the air into the net.*

arch /'ɑːtʃ/
to curve or bend
Example: *The cat arches its back when it gets scared.*

argue /'ɑːgjuː/
to present reasons or evidence in support of a position or viewpoint, often in a debate or discussion, with the aim of persuading others to accept one's perspectives
Example: *He argued that the policy would benefit the company in the long run.*
to engage in a verbal disagreement or dispute, often involving opposing

viewpoints or conflicting interests
Example: *They argued for hours but could not reach a consensus.*

arise /ɑrˈaɪz/
to come into existence, happen, or occur, often unexpectedly or spontaneously
Example: *Issues arise unexpectedly during the project.*
to originate or stem from a particular source or cause
Example: *Most of her fears arise from past experiences.*

arrange /ɑrˈeɪndʒ/
to organise or put things in a particular order, pattern, or configuration
Example: *She arranged the flowers in a beautiful pattern.*
to make preparations or plans for an event, meeting, or activity
Example: *He arranged a meeting between the stakeholders.*

arrest /ɑrˈɛst/
to seize or take into custody someone suspected of committing a crime
Example: *The police arrested the suspect near the crime scene.*
to halt or stop the progress or development of something
Example: *The new treatment effectively arrested the spread of the infection.*

articulate /ɑrˈtɪkjəˌleɪt/
to express or communicate thoughts, ideas, or feelings clearly and effectively
Example: *She articulated her objections to the plan with great clarity.*
to pronounce words or sounds distinctly and clearly
Example: *He articulated each word carefully during his speech.*
to join or connect in a way that allows for movement or flexibility, as in
the joints of the body

Example: *The robot's arm is articulated to mimic human movements.*
to delineate or specify the details or components of something clearly and precisely
Example: *The engineer articulated the steps involved in the process.*

ascend /ɑsˈɛnd/
to move or go upward
Example: *The balloon ascended into the sky.*
to reach a higher rank, status, or level of importance
Example: *She ascended to the position of CEO within five years.*

ascertain /ˌɑsətˈeɪn/
to find out or determine something with certainty
Example: *The detective worked to ascertain the truth behind the alibi.*

ask /ˈɑːsk/
to make a request or inquiry of someone
Example: *He asked her to close the door on her way out.*

assail /ɑsˈeɪl/
to attack violently or aggressively, either physically or verbally
Example: *The critics assailed the author's newest book.*
to be overwhelmed by something, such as problems or difficulties
Example: *She was assailed by doubts about her decision.*

assault /ɑsˈɒlt/
to physically attack or threaten someone violently or aggressively, causing harm or injury
Example: *The person was charged with assault after attacking a bystander.*
to launch a verbal or written attack on someone

Example: *The politician was frequently assaulted by criticism in the media.*

assay /ɑsˈeɪ/
to analyse or examine a substance to determine its composition, purity, or quality, especially in scientific or medical contexts
Example: *The lab technician assayed the blood samples for signs of infection.*
to attempt or try something, often with the aim of evaluating its effectiveness or success
Example: *She assayed a new technique to improve productivity.*
to test a sample of ore to determine its mineral content and value
Example: *The geologist assayed the rock for gold content.*

assent /ɑsˈɛnt/
to express agreement or approval
Example: *She nodded in assent to the proposed plan.*

assert /ɑsˈɜːt/
to state or declare something confidently and forcefully
Example: *He asserted his innocence throughout the trial.*
to demonstrate or display one's authority, power, or dominance in a situation
Example: *The leader asserted his control over the committee.*

assess /ɑsˈɛs/
to evaluate or appraise something systematically and thoroughly to determine its nature, quality, value, or significance
Example: *The expert assessed the painting to be worth thousands of dollars.*

assign /əsˈaɪn/
to designate or allocate someone or something to a particular role, task, duty, or position
Example: *The teacher assigned each student a topic for the presentation.*
to transfer ownership or rights of something to another person or entity
Example: *Rights to the software were assigned to the company.*

assist /əsˈɪst/
to help or aid someone in performing a task, achieving a goal, or overcoming a difficulty
Example: *She assisted him in completing the project on time.*

assume /əsˈuːm/
to take on or adopt a particular role, position, or responsibility
Example: *He assumed the role of the mediator in the negotiations.*
to believe or suppose something to be true without definite proof or evidence
Example: *She assumed that they would arrive on time without confirming.*
to undertake or begin to have control or possession of something
Example: *She assumed control of the company after her father's retirement.*
to accept or receive something willingly or readily, such as an obligation or debt
Example: *He assumed responsibility for the errors made by his team.*
to take for granted or accept something as a fact without question or inquiry
Example: *It's dangerous to assume the safety of the equipment without checking.*

assure /əʃjˈɔː/
to give someone confidence or certainty about something
Example: *He assured her that everything would be ready on time.*

astonish /ɑstˈɒnɪʃ/
to greatly surprise or amaze someone
Example: *The magician's trick astonished the crowd.*

attach /ɑtˈɑtʃ/
to fasten or join one thing to another
Example: *Please attach this document to your email.*
to associate or connect something closely with another thing, often in a figurative sense
Example: *He is closely attached to his family's traditions.*
to include or add something, such as a document or file, to an email, message, or correspondence
Example: *I attached the report for your review.*
to assign or allocate someone to a particular role, task, or responsibility
Example: *She was attached to the embassy in France.*
to ascribe or attribute certain qualities or characteristics to someone or something
Example: *Certain stigmas are often unfairly attached to mental health issues.*

attack /ɑtˈɑk/
to aggressively and forcefully assault or strike someone or something with the intent to cause harm, damage, or destruction
Example: *The army attacked at dawn.*
to launch a verbal or written criticism or assault on someone's character, reputation, beliefs, or ideas
Example: *The article attacked the politician's credibility.*

attempt /ɑtˈɛmpt/
to make an effort or endeavour to achieve or accomplish something
Example: *She attempted to climb the mountain despite the bad weather.*

attend /ɑtˈɛnd/
to be present at or participate in an event, meeting, class, or activity
Example: *He attended the conference last week.*
to pay attention to or focus on something
Example: *You must attend to the details if you want to succeed.*

audit /ˈɔːdɪt/
to conduct an official examination, review, or inspection of financial records, accounts, procedures, or systems to verify accuracy, compliance, or efficiency
Example: *The company conducts an annual audit to ensure financial transparency.*

authorise /ˈɔːθɔːrˌaɪz/
to grant official permission, approval, or consent for something to be done or to take place
Example: *The board authorised the new development plan.*

aver /ˈeɪvɚ/
to state or assert something confidently or firmly, often as if it were a fact
Example: *She averred that she had seen him at the scene of the crime.*

avert /ɑvˈɜːt/
to prevent or avoid something undesirable or harmful from happening, often by taking action to stop it or by diverting its course
Example: *Quick action averted a disaster.*
to turn aside or avoid something unpleasant or distressing
Example: *She averted her gaze when he approached.*

avoid /ɑvˈɔɪd/
to deliberately stay away from someone or something
Example: *She avoids the busy supermarket on weekends.*

to refrain from doing something or to take measures to prevent or escape from a particular situation or activity
Example: *He avoided the traffic because he took a different route to work.*

avow /ɑvˈaʊ/
to openly declare or acknowledge something
Example: *He avowed his commitment to the cause.*

await /ɑwˈeɪt/
to be in a state of readiness or expectation for a particular event, outcome, or action
Example: *They awaited the judge's decision with bated breath.*

awaken /ɑwˈeɪkən/
to rouse or cause someone to wake up from sleep or a state of unconsciousness
Example: *The alarm clock awakened her at dawn.*
to become aware or enlightened about something
Example: *He was finally awakened to the realities of climate change.*

Bb

babble /bˈabəl/
to talk rapidly and incoherently, often with little regard for making sense
Example: *The toddler babbled excitedly.*
the sound of a baby making nonsensical noises
Example: *Her baby's babble filled the room.*

backhand /bˈakhand/
(in tennis or other racket sports) to hit the ball with the back of the hand facing the direction of the stroke
Example: *She backhanded the ball skilfully during the match.*
to strike or hit someone or something with the back of one's hand
Example: *He backhanded the fly that landed on his arm.*

backpedal /bˈakˌpɛdəl/
to reverse one's previous position, opinion, or course of action
Example: *The politician backpedalled on his earlier statement.*

backtrack /bˈaktrak/
to retrace one's steps or to go back over a path or course of action previously taken
Example: *The crew backtracked after missing the correct trail.*

badger /bˈadʒɐ/
to repeatedly and persistently ask, persuade, or bother someone in an annoying or harassing manner
Example: *She badgered him until he agreed to go.*

badmouth /bˈadməθ/
to speak negatively or disparagingly about someone or something, often behind their back or in a derogatory manner
Example: *He's known to badmouth his competitors.*

baffle /bˈafəl/
to perplex or confuse someone completely
Example: *The puzzle baffled everyone who tried it.*

bait /bˈeɪt/
to deliberately provoke or lure someone into a reaction
Example: *She baited him into arguing.*
to use something as a lure or enticement to attract or trap someone or something
Example: *He baited the hook with a worm.*

bake /bˈeɪk/
to cook food by dry heat in an oven
Example: *She bakes fresh bread every Sunday.*

balance /bˈaləns/
to arrange or adjust something in such a way that it remains steady or level
Example: *He balanced the books on the shelf carefully.*
to offset or counteract one thing with another to maintain stability or equilibrium
Example: *She balanced her studies with leisure activities.*
to consider and weigh different factors or options to make a fair decision or judgement
Example: *The judge balanced the evidence before making a ruling.*
to ensure that income and expenses are equal or in harmony, or to reconcile accounts
Example: *He balanced his budget at the end of each month.*

to physically maintain one's equilibrium, often by keeping one's body upright and steady
Example: *She balanced on one foot during the yoga pose.*

ball /bˈɔːl/
to shape something into a spherical or rounded shape, such as rolling dough into shape
Example: *She balled the dough into small portions.*
to enjoy oneself or have a great time at an event or gathering
Example: *They really balled at the New Year's Eve party, dancing until sunrise.*
to curl into a rounded shape, often for warmth or comfort
Example: *The cat balled itself up in the corner.*

bang /bˈaŋ/
to hit or strike something with a sudden and loud impact
Example: *She banged the door shut as she left.*
to produce a loud, sharp sound, often associated with an explosion or a
sudden impact
Example: *The old car banged as it backfired on the road.*

banish /bˈanɪʃ/
to exile or expel someone from a place
Example: *The community banished him for his actions.*

banter /bˈɑːntɐ/
to engage in playful and light-hearted conversation or exchange
Example: *They bantered about their childhood memories.*

bare /bˈeə/
to expose something that was previously hidden or covered; to reveal one's innermost thoughts or feelings

Example: *He bared the truth during the meeting.*
to remove clothing or coverings, leaving something exposed or naked
Example: *She quickly bared her arm for the vaccine.*
to strip something of its contents or to make it empty or devoid of substance
Example: *The robbers bared the safe of all its contents.*

bargain /bˈɑːgɪn/
to negotiate or haggle over the terms of a transaction
Example: *He bargained with the vendor for a better price.*

barge /bˈɑːdʒ/
to push or move forward in a rough or clumsy manner
Example: *She barged past the others to get to the front of the line.*
to intrude or interrupt rudely and abruptly, without permission or consideration for others
Example: *He barged into the room without knocking.*
to transport goods or cargo on a flat-bottomed boat
Example: *They barged the heavy equipment down the canal.*

bark /bˈɑːk/
the sound made by a dog as a warning or to communicate
Example: *The guard dog barked loudly at the strangers.*
to speak or shout angrily or aggressively
Example: *The manager barked instructions to the team during the emergency.*

barrage /bˈɑrɑːʒ/
to bombard someone or something with a rapid and continuous series of something, such as questions, criticisms, or attacks
Example: *The defence barraged the witness with question after question.*

barter /bˈɑːtɐ/
to exchange goods or services for other goods or services without using money
Example: *The villagers bartered grain for cloth.*

bash /bˈaʃ/
to hit something or someone forcefully
Example: *He bashed the door open with his shoulder.*
to criticise or verbally attack someone or something harshly and relentlessly
Example: *The critics bashed the new movie for its poor plot.*

bask /bˈɑːsk/
to enjoy and take pleasure in something, often in a relaxed or contented manner
Example: *She basked in the sunshine on the beach.*

bat /bˈat/
to hit a ball or another object with a bat
Example: *He batted the ball straight into the outfield.*
to move or strike something rapidly and repeatedly
Example: *The cat batted at the dangling string playfully.*

bathe /bˈeɪð/
to wash or immerse oneself in water for cleanliness, relaxation, or refreshment
Example: *She bathed in the warm waters of the spring.*

bawl /bˈɔːl/
to cry or sob loudly and unrestrainedly
Example: *The child bawled when he dropped his ice cream.*

bay /bˈeɪ/
the deep, prolonged barking sound made by dogs, particularly hounds or hunting dogs
Example: *The hounds bayed as they chased the fox.*
to persistently demand or pursue something, often with determination or insistence
Example: *The crowd bayed for an encore after the concert.*

beam /bˈiːm/
to shine brightly, radiate light, or emit energy
Example: *The lighthouse beamed across the bay.*
to smile with happiness or satisfaction
Example: *She beamed with pride at her graduation.*

bear /bˈeə/
to carry or support the weight of something, either physically or metaphorically
Example: *He bore the weight of the heavy boxes up the stairs.*
to endure or tolerate a difficult or unpleasant situation
Example: *She bore the pain without complaint.*
to give birth to offspring
Example: *The cat bore four kittens.*
to exhibit or show a particular quality or characteristic
Example: *The testimony bore evidence of his honesty.*

beat /bˈiːt/
to strike something or someone repeatedly
Example: *He beat the drum rhythmically.*
to defeat or overcome someone or something
Example: *She beat her opponent in the final round.*
to pulsate or throb with a regular rhythm
Example: *His heart beat rapidly with excitement.*
to mix or stir ingredients together vigorously, often to incorporate air or

create a smooth consistency
Example: *She beat the eggs and sugar together for the cake.*

beautify /bjˈuːtɪfˌaɪ/
to enhance the beauty or appearance of something
Example: *They beautified the neighbourhood by planting flowers.*

beckon /bˈɛkən/
to make a gesture with the hand, arm, or head to encourage someone to come closer or follow
Example: *He beckoned her to join him at the table.*

become /bɪkˈʌm/
to undergo a change or transformation leading to a new or different status
Example: *He will become the next president of the club.*

befall /bɪfˈɔːl/
to happen to someone or something, especially in a negative or unexpected way
Example: *A misfortune befell the expedition.*

beg /bˈɛg/
to earnestly request something
Example: *He begged for forgiveness.*

begin /bɪgˈɪn/
to start or initiate something
Example: *The meeting will begin at noon.*

behave /bɪhˈeɪv/
to conduct oneself in a particular way, especially in terms of manners, actions, or reactions

Example: *The children behaved well at the dinner party.*

behold /bɪhˈəʊld/
to see or observe something, typically with a sense of wonder, awe, or admiration
Example: *We beheld the stunning array of modern art on display after we entered the gallery.*

belch /bˈɛltʃ/
to expel gas loudly and noisily from the stomach through the mouth
Example: *He belched loudly after the meal.*

believe /bɪlˈiːv/
to accept something as true, genuine, or real
Example: *She believes in the power of education.*

belittle /bɪlˈɪtəl/
to make someone or something seem less important, valuable, or worthy
Example: *He belittled her achievements.*

bellow /bˈɛləʊ/
to shout or roar loudly, usually expressing anger, frustration, or strong emotion
Example: *The coach bellowed instructions from the side-lines.*

bemoan /bɪmˈəʊn/
to express sorrow, grief, or disappointment about something
Example: *She bemoaned the loss of her favourite book.*

bend /bˈɛnd/
to curve or flex something to change its shape or direction
Example: *He bent the wire into a circle.*

to lean or stoop downwards
Example: *She bent down to pick up the coin.*
to yield or adapt to a particular situation or circumstance, often implying a sense of flexibility or willingness to compromise
Example: *The company bent its rules to accommodate him.*

berate /bɪrˈeɪt/
to scold or criticise someone angrily and forcefully
Example: *The manager berated the staff for their mistakes.*

beseech /bɪsˈiːtʃ/
to urgently and fervently request or implore someone for something
Example: *She beseeched him to stay.*

bestow /bɪstˈəʊ/
to give or present something to someone as a gift or honour
Example: *The university bestowed an honorary degree on her.*

bet /bˈɛt/
to wager or gamble on the outcome of an event or situation
Example: *He bet $50 on the horse to win the race.*

betray /bɪtrˈeɪ/
to deceive or act disloyally towards someone's trust or confidence
Example: *She betrayed her best friend when she shared her secrets.*

bicker /bˈɪkɐ/
to argue or quarrel about petty or trivial matters, often in a repetitive or irritating manner
Example: *The siblings bicker over who would get the last slice of pizza.*

bid /bˈɪd/
to offer a specific amount of money for something, typically in a competition with others
Example: *He bid $200 at the auction for the vintage clock.*
to make a formal offer or proposal for something, such as a contract
Example: *The company bid for the government contract.*
to command or invite someone to do something
Example: *He bid his guests to enter.*
to say farewell or goodbye to someone
Example: *She bid farewell to her colleagues on her last day.*

bind /bˈaɪnd/
to tie or fasten something tightly, such as with rope or string, to hold it in place
Example: *She bound the package with strong twine.*
to create a legal or moral obligation or commitment, such as by contract or oath
Example: *The agreement binds them to complete the project by March.*
to enclose something in a covering or wrapper, such as binding a book with a cover
Example: *The craftsman bound the old book in new leather.*

bite /bˈaɪt/
to grip or cut with the teeth
Example: *The dog bit the intruder.*
to be harsh or incisive in speech or writing
Example: *Her words bit sharply during the debate.*

blame /blˈeɪm/
to hold someone responsible for a fault, mistake, or wrongdoing
Example: *She blamed him for the failure of the project.*

blanch /blˈɑːntʃ/
to turn pale or become whitened, often because of shock, fear, or surprise
Example: *She blanched when she heard the news.*
to scald food briefly in boiling water, often to remove the skin or to prepare it for freezing
Example: *He blanched the almonds to easily peel them.*

blare /blˈeə/
to emit a loud, harsh, and usually unpleasant sound that can be heard over a considerable distance
Example: *The ambulance sirens blared through the night.*

blaspheme /blɑːsfˈiːm/
to speak irreverently or disrespectfully about sacred things, deities, religious beliefs, or religious practices
Example: *He blasphemed against the church.*

blather /blˈɑːðɐ/
to talk excessively and nonsensically, often in a rambling or incoherent manner
Example: *He blathered on about nothing in particular.*

bleat /blˈiːt/
to make the characteristic sound of a sheep or goat, typically a high-pitched or plaintive cry
Example: *The lost lamb bleated for its mother.*

bleed /blˈiːd/
to emit blood from the body, either internally or externally, often due to injury or trauma
Example: *He bled profusely from the cut.*
to intentionally draw blood from someone for medical purposes, such

as testing or donation
Example: *The nurse bled the patient for a blood sample.*
for a substance to flow or seep out slowly, often in a continuous or uncontrolled manner
Example: *The ink bled through the paper.*
to lose money or resources gradually or consistently because of poor management or excessive spending
Example: *The company was bleeding money due to inefficient processes.*

blend /blˈɛnd/
to mix or combine different substances or elements together thoroughly to create a uniform or homogeneous mixture
Example: *She blended the fruits to make a smoothie.*
to harmoniously combine different styles, flavours, or ideas
Example: *The chef blended Asian and European cuisines in his new dishes.*

bless /blˈɛs/
to confer or invoke divine favour, protection, or guidance upon someone or something
Example: *The priest blessed the congregation during the service.*

blind /blˈaɪnd/
to deprive someone of their sight, either temporarily or permanently, often as a result of injury, disease, or a deliberate action
Example: *The accident blinded him in one eye.*
to block or obstruct someone's vision, preventing them from seeing something clearly or entirely
Example: *The bright lights blinded her momentarily.*
to deceive or mislead someone, typically by withholding or distorting information or by leading them to false conclusions
Example: *He was blinded by his ambition.*

blink /blˈɪŋk/
to close and reopen one's eyes quickly
Example: *She blinked rapidly to clear her vision.*
to flicker or flash briefly
Example: *The neon sign blinked on and off.*

block /blˈɒk/
to obstruct or hinder movement, progress, or access by placing an obstacle in the way
Example: *The fallen tree blocked the road.*
to shield or protect something or someone from harm, danger, or unwanted influence
Example: *The firewall blocks unauthorised access to the network.*
to halt the execution of a computer program until certain conditions are met
Example: *The software blocks until data is received.*
to deny access to or communication with someone
Example: *She blocked him on social media.*

blossom /blˈɒsəm/
to develop or mature into a more advanced or desirable state
Example: *Her talent for music blossomed as she grew older.*

blot /blˈɒt/
to absorb or soak up liquid
Example: *He blotted the spill with a paper towel.*
to make a mess or stain something, typically by spilling or smudging a liquid or substance
Example: *Ink blotted the document, ruining it.*

blow /blˈəʊ/
to expel air forcefully from the mouth
Example: *He blew out the candles on his birthday cake.*

to move or be moved by wind
Example: *The strong wind blew the leaves off the trees.*

blubber /blˈʌbɚ/
to cry noisily and incoherently
Example: *The child blubbered uncontrollably after falling.*

bludgeon /blˈʌdʒən/
to hit someone multiple times with a heavy object
Example: *The robber bludgeoned the safe with a sledgehammer.*
to attack or overcome someone with an aggressive argument
Example: *She bludgeoned her opponent in the debate with relentless arguments.*

bluff /blˈʌf/
to deceive someone by pretending to do something with no intention to actually do it
Example: *He bluffed about leaving the job to get a raise.*

blunder /blˈʌndɚ/
to move around unsteadily or confusedly
Example: *He blundered through the dark room, knocking over a lamp.*
to speak thoughtlessly
Example: *She blundered by revealing the surprise party.*
to make a mistake through ignorance or carelessness
Example: *The scientist blundered in his calculations and had to start over.*

blurt /blˈɜːt/
to utter impulsively
Example: *He blurted out the answer before raising his hand.*

blush /blˈʌʃ/
to become red in the face from shame, modesty, or confusion
Example: *She blushed when her crush complimented her.*

bluster /blˈʌstɐ/
to speak or act with noisy threats
Example: *The boss blustered about firing everyone, but no one took him seriously.*
to blow in stormy noisy blasts of air
Example: *The wind blustered all night, rattling the windows.*

boast /bˈəʊst/
to praise oneself excessively in speech
Example: *He boasted about his achievements at every opportunity.*

bob /bˈɒb/
to move up and down quickly or repeatedly
Example: *The boat bobbed on the waves.*
to make a sudden movement so as to appear or disappear
Example: *He bobbed his head in agreement.*

boggle /bˈɒgəl/
to become overwhelmed with surprise or fright
Example: *The complexity of the situation boggled his mind.*

bolster /bˈəʊlstɐ/
to give support or a boost
Example: *She bolstered his confidence with her encouragement.*

bolt /bˈəʊlt/
to move suddenly or nervously
Example: *The cat bolted out of the room when the dog entered.*

bond /bˈɒnd/
to form a close relationship with someone through frequent interactions
Example: *The teammates bonded during the weekend retreat.*
to hold together firmly
Example: *The glue bonded the pieces of wood together.*

bonk /bˈɒŋk/
to hit someone or something
Example: *He accidentally bonked his head on the low ceiling.*
to have sexual intercourse with someone
Example: *They bonked after several dates.*

boo /bˈuː/
to express disapproval or displeasure
Example: *The audience booed the performer off the stage.*

boom /bˈuːm/
to make a deep hollow sound
Example: *The sound of the cannon boomed across the valley.*
to increase in size or importance
Example: *The tech industry boomed in the early 2000s.*

boost /bˈuːst/
to push up from underneath
Example: *He boosted her over the fence.*
to promote a cause
Example: *They boosted awareness for the charity event.*
to raise the voltage of or across something
Example: *The technician boosted the voltage to get the machine working.*

bop /bˈɒp/
to go somewhere unceremoniously

Example: *Let us bop over to the café for a coffee.*
to dance or move along to pop music
Example: *She was bopping along to her favourite tune.*

bore /bˈɔː/
to make a hole by twisting or turning a tool
Example: *He bored a hole in the wall for the screw.*
to make one's way steadily especially against resistance
Example: *The ship bored through the heavy ice in the Arctic.*

boss /bˈɒs/
to exercise control or authority over someone or something
Example: *She bossed the team efficiently, ensuring deadlines were met.*

bounce /bˈaʊns/
to rebound or reflect after striking a surface
Example: *The ball bounced off the wall.*
to eliminate from a competition by defeating
Example: *They bounced their rivals from the tournament early.*
to present something to someone to obtain comments about it
Example: *He bounced his ideas off his mentor for feedback.*

bound /bˈaʊnd/
to move by leaping
Example: *The deer bounded across the field.*

bow /ˈbaʊ/
to cease from competition or resistance
Example: *The challenger bowed out of the race due to personal reasons.*
to bend the head, body, or knee in reverence, submission, or shame
Example: *He bowed deeply before the queen.*

to play a stringed instrument
Example: *She bowed the violin expertly during the concert.*

box /bˈɒks/
to enclose in or as if in a box
Example: *They boxed the leftovers for takeout.*
to fight with one's fists
Example: *He boxed competitively in college.*

brace /brˈeɪs/
to make stronger
Example: *The engineer braced the structure with extra beams.*
to get ready in the case of an attack
Example: *The soldiers braced for the incoming assault.*
to fasten tightly
Example: *She braced her backpack before hiking.*

brag /brˈag/
to talk boastfully, such as assertions
Example: *He bragged about winning the poker game.*

braid /brˈeɪd/
to do up the hair by interweaving three or more strands
Example: *She braided her daughter's hair for school.*
to ornament especially with a ribbon or braid
Example: *They braided the ceremonial staff with colourful ribbons.*

brandish /brˈandɪʃ/
to shake or wave something in an aggressive way, such as a weapon
Example: *The warrior brandished his sword in defiance.*

brawl /brˈɔːl/
to quarrel or fight noisily

Example: *The fans brawled in the stands after the game.*
to make a loud confused noise
Example: *The machinery brawled as it operated.*

bray /brˈeɪ/
to make a sound similar to the loud cry of a donkey
Example: *The donkey brayed loudly at dawn.*
to crush or grind finely
Example: *The mill brayed the grain into flour.*
to spread thinly
Example: *The painter brayed the paste across the canvas.*

break /brˈeɪk/
to separate into parts
Example: *The vase broke into pieces when it fell.*
to force entry into or from somewhere
Example: *Burglars broke into the house last night.*
to exhaust in health, strength, and capacity
Example: *The marathon broke her physically and mentally.*
to bring an end suddenly
Example: *He broke off the relationship.*
to make something known such as news
Example: *The media broke the news of the celebrity scandal.*
to exceed or surpass something such as a record
Example: *She broke the world record in the 100-metre dash.*

breathe /brˈiːð/
to draw air into and expel it from the lungs
Example: *He breathed deeply to calm his nerves.*
to pause or rest before continuing
Example: *The speaker breathed heavily before delivering the final part of the speech.*

breed /brˈiːd/
to mate or produce offspring either by hatching or gestation
Example: *The fish breed in shallow waters.*
to propagate plants or animals
Example: *Farmers breed cattle for both milk and meat.*
to instil training by frequent instruction
Example: *The academy breeds its students to be leaders.*

breeze /brˈiːz/
to move or progress swiftly and airily
Example: *She breezed through the exam with ease.*

bribe /brˈaɪb/
to influence the judgement or conduct of someone with offers of money or favour
Example: *He bribed the official to speed up the permit process.*

bridle /brˈaɪdəl/
to restrain, check, or control with or as if with a harness for a horse
Example: *She bridled her impatience during the long meeting.*
to show resentment or hostility especially by drawing back one's head and chin
Example: *He bridled at the suggestion that he was not qualified.*

brighten /brˈaɪtən/
to intensify the brightness
Example: *New lamps brightened the formerly dim room.*
to enhance the flavour of food especially by adding acidic ingredients
Example: *A squeeze of lemon brightened the flavour of the grilled fish.*

bring /brˈɪŋ/
to cause to be, act, or move in a special way

Example: *Music brings joy to everyone.*
to convey, lead, carry, or cause to come along with one toward the place from which the action is being regarded
Example: *My mom always brings a present for me whenever she goes shopping.*

bristle /brˈɪsəl/
to furnish with short stiff coarse hairs or filaments
Example: *The brush was bristled with tough fibres.*
to make aggressive or angry
Example: *He bristled at the accusation.*
to rise and stand stiffly erect
Example: *The cat's fur bristled when it saw the dog.*
to be full of something specified
Example: *The forest bristled with sounds of wildlife.*

broach /brˈəʊtʃ/
to pierce something in order to draw the contents
Example: *She broached the barrel of cider for the party.*
to make known for the first time or open up a topic for discussion
Example: *He broached the sensitive topic at the meeting.*
to break the surface from below
Example: *The submarine broached the ocean surface.*

broadcast /brˈɔːdkɑːst/
to scatter or sow over a broad area
Example: *They broadcast seeds over the field.*
to make widely known
Example: *The network broadcast the news of the royal wedding.*
to transmit using a radio, television, or stream over the internet
Example: *The event was broadcasted live worldwide.*

broaden /brˈɔːdən/
to make wider or larger
Example: *The company broadened its product range to include electronics.*

brood /brˈuːd/
to produce by or as if by incubation
Example: *The hen brooded her eggs until they hatched.*
to think anxiously or gloomily
Example: *He brooded over the mistake he had made.*

browbeat /brˈaʊbiːt/
to intimidate or disconcert by a stern manner or arrogant speech
Example: *The manager browbeat the staff into agreeing with his plan.*

browse /brˈaʊz/
to feed on leaves of trees and tender shoots
Example: *The deer browsed on the bushes.*
to look over casually
Example: *She browsed the bookstore for the latest releases.*
to access a network using a browser
Example: *He browsed the internet for information on his topic.*

brush /brˈʌʃ/
to move lightly over or across in passing
Example: *He brushed the dust off his jacket.*
to dismiss in an offhand way
Example: *She brushed off the criticism and continued her work.*

buck /bˈʌk/
to move or charge against something
Example: *The horse bucked unexpectedly.*

to pass from one person to another
Example: *The responsibility bucked from one team member to another.*
to move or load especially with mechanical equipment
Example: *They bucked the bales of hay onto the truck.*

buckle /bˈʌkəl/
to fasten especially with a buckle
Example: *He buckled his belt tightly.* to prepare oneself with vigour
Example: *The team buckled down for the tough game ahead.*
to cause to bend, give way, or crumple under the influence of an external agency
Example: *The bridge buckled under the weight of the heavy trucks.*

buff /bˈʌf/
to give a velvety surface to especially leather
Example: *He buffed the leather shoes to a high shine.*

buffet /bəˈfeɪ/
to strike sharply and/or repeatedly especially with the hand
Example: *The wind buffeted the ship during the storm.*
to make one's way especially under difficult conditions
Example: *He buffeted through the crowds to reach the stage.*

bug /bˈʌg/
to plant a concealed microphone in, especially objects
Example: *The spies bugged the embassy room.*
to lose one's composure
Example: *She bugged out when she saw the spider.*

build /bˈɪld/
to form by ordering and uniting materials by gradual means into a composite whole

Example: *They built the house over the course of a year.*

bulge /bˈʌldʒ/
to become swollen or filled to overflowing
Example: *His pockets bulged with coins.*
to bend outward
Example: *The wall bulged under the pressure of the water.*

bully /bˈʊli/
to use language or behaviour that is cruel, insulting, threatening, and aggressive
Example: *The older students bullied the younger ones.*
to cause someone to do something using force or coercion
Example: *He bullied his way into the crowded room.*

bumble /bˈʌmbəl/
to proceed unsteadily, such as speech
Example: *He bumbled through his presentation nervously.*

bump /bˈʌmp/
to strike or knock with sudden force or violence, such as using a body part
Example: *She bumped her head on the low ceiling.*
to move someone or something to a different level, position, or rank
Example: *He was bumped to first class due to an overbooked flight.*

bunch /bˈʌntʃ/
to form a group or cluster
Example: *The tourists bunched together for safety.*

bundle /bˈʌndəl/
to hustle or hurry unceremoniously
Example: *They bundled the kids into the car.*

to tie or roll up a number of things into a package
Example: *She bundled up all her old clothes for donation.*

burble /bˈɜːbəl/
to make a bubbling sound
Example: *The stream burbled gently in the background.*

burn /bˈɜːn/
to consume fuel and give off heat, light, and gases
Example: *The campfire burned brightly under the stars.*
to use freely without limits
Example: *They burned through their savings quickly.*
to produce or undergo an uncomfortable or painful sensation like that of being injured by fire
Example: *He burned his hand on the hot stove.*
to become emotionally excited or agitated
Example: *She burned with anger when she heard the news.*
to record digital data or music
Example: *He burned the files onto a CD.*

burp /bˈɜːp/
to help expel gas from the stomach especially by patting or rubbing the baby's back
Example: *She gently burped the baby after feeding.*

burrow /bˈʌrəʊ/
to progress by or as if by digging
Example: *The rabbit burrowed into its hole.*

burst /bˈɜːst/
to break open, apart, or into pieces usually from impact or from pressure from within
Example: *The balloon burst when it was pricked.*

to give way from an excess of emotion
Example: *She burst into tears after winning the award.*

bury /bˈɛɹi/
to cover from view, such as in the earth
Example: *They buried the treasure in the backyard.*
to have done with someone or something
Example: *He buried his past and started anew.*
to defeat overwhelmingly, such as in a sport
Example: *The team was buried under a landslide of goals.*

buss /bˈʌs/
to kiss someone in a friendly rather than sexual way
Example: *She bussed her grandfather on the cheek.*

bust /bˈʌst/
to break or smash especially with force
Example: *He busted the door open during the raid.*
to ruin financially
Example: *Excessive spending finally busted the once-thriving company.*

bustle /bˈʌsəl/
to move quickly and often showily
Example: *She bustled around the office preparing for the meeting.*

butcher /bˈʊtʃɐ/
to slaughter and dress for market
Example: *The farmer butchered the chicken for the market.*
to kill in a barbarous manner
Example: *The dictator was accused of butchering his own citizens.*

button /bˈʌtən/
to pass an item such as a button through a buttonhole or loop
Example: *She buttoned her coat as the wind picked up.*
to close the lips to prevent speech
Example: *He buttoned his lip before he could say something regrettable.*

buy /bˈaɪ/
to acquire possession, ownership, or rights to the use or services of by payment especially of money
Example: *She bought a new car with her first pay- check.*
to believe that something is true
Example: *I do not buy that explanation for one second.*

buzz /bˈʌz/
to make a low continuous humming sound like that of a bee
Example: *The old refrigerator buzzed quietly in the corner of the kitchen.*
to go quickly
Example: *He buzzed past me on his scooter.*
to feel high, especially from a drug
Example: *After the medication, he buzzed with a strange energy.*
to summon or signal with a buzzer
Example: *She buzzed her assistant into the office.*

Cc

cackle /kˈɑkəl/
to laugh especially in a harsh or sharp manner
Example: She cackled wickedly at the joke.

cajole /kɐdʒˈəʊl/
to persuade with flattery or gentle urging especially in the face of reluctance
Example: He cajoled her into agreeing to the deal.
to deceive with soothing words or false premises
Example: She cajoled him into believing it was all just a misunderstanding.

calculate /kˈɑlkjʊlˌeɪt/
to determine by mathematical processes
Example: She calculated the total expenses for the trip.
to design or adapt for a purpose
Example: He calculated his speech to appeal to a broad audience.
to judge to be true or probable
Example: She calculated the likelihood of success before proceeding.

call /kˈɔːl/
to speak in a loud distinct voice so as to be heard at a distance
Example: He called out to his friends across the street.
to make a request or a demand
Example: She called for a change in the regulations.
to make a brief visit
Example: I'll call at your house this evening.
to generate signals in order to reach the party to whom the number is assigned

Example: *He called the wrong number by mistake.*
to describe correctly in advance of or without knowledge of the event
Example: *The analyst called the election results accurately.*
to speak of or address by a specified name
Example: *They called him a hero for his actions.*

calm /kˈɑːm/
to make or become still
Example: *She calmed the anxious crowd.*

canvass /kˈɑnvəs/
to examine in detail
Example: *They canvassed the document for any errors.*
to seek orders or votes
Example: *The politician canvassed the neighbourhood ahead of the election.*

caper /kˈeɪpɐ/
to leap or prance about in a playful manner
Example: *The children capered around the garden, full of joy.*

capitulate /kɐpˈɪtʃʊlˌeɪt/
to cease resisting or surrender often after negotiation of terms
Example: *The suspect finally capitulated after hours of negotiation.*

capture /kˈɑptʃɐ/
to gain control of someone or something especially by force
Example: *The police captured the fugitive near the border.*
to record in a permanent file such as in a computer
Example: *The camera captured a stunning image of the sunset.*
to emphasize, represent, or preserve something such as a scene in a permanent form
Example: *The film captured the essence of the novel perfectly.*

care /kˈeə/
to feel trouble or concern
Example: *She cares deeply about environmental issues.*
to have a liking, fondness, or taste
Example: *He cares for classical music above all.*
to have an inclination
Example: *They do not care to discuss politics.*

careen /kɚˈin/
to put a ship or boat on a beach specially to clean, caulk, or repair the hull
Example: *They careened the vessel during the low tide.*
to sway from side to side
Example: *The car careened down the road, out of control.*

caress /kərˈɛs/
to treat with tokens of fondness, affection, or kindness
Example: *He caressed the baby's cheek gently.*
to touch or stroke lightly in a loving or endearing manner
Example: *She caressed the fabric, appreciating its smoothness.*

carol /kˈɑrəl/
to sing especially in a joyful manner
Example: *They carolled through the streets during the holiday season.*

carry /kˈɑri/
to move while supporting
Example: *He carried the groceries up the stairs.*
to wear or have on one's person
Example: *She always carries a book in her bag.*
to have or bear especially as a mark, attribute, or property
Example: *The device carries a one-year warranty.*

to hold or comport in a specified manner, such as oneself
Example: *She carries herself with dignity.*

cartwheel /kˈɑːtwiːl/
to move like a turning wheel
Example: *The gymnast cartwheeled across the floor.*

carve /kˈɑːv/
to cut with care or precision
Example: *He carved a beautiful sculpture from a block of marble.*
to cut up and serve meat
Example: *She carved the turkey for Thanksgiving dinner.*

cash /kˈaʃ/
to pay or obtain cash for
Example: *He cashed a check at the bank.*

cast /kˈɑːst/
to cause to move or send forth by throwing
Example: *She cast the stone into the river.*
to dispose or arrange into parts or into a suitable form or order
Example: *He cast the documents into piles.*
to assign the parts to actors, such as in a dramatic production
Example: *The director cast her in the lead role.*

castle /kˈɑːsəl/
to establish in a castle
Example: *The king castled his family for safety during the war.*
to move a chess king two squares toward a rook and in the same move the rook to the square next past the king
Example: *He castled early in the game to protect his king.*

catalogue /ˈkatəlɔg/
to classify something descriptively, such as books or information
Example: *She catalogued all the articles for the research project.*
to become listed in a catalogue at a specified price
Example: *The new book will catalogue at fifteen dollars.*

catapult /kˈatɐpˌʌlt/
to throw or launch by as if by a catapult
Example: *The engineers catapulted the payload into space.*

catcall /ˈkatˌkɔl/
the act of shouting, harassing and often sexually suggestive, threatening, or derisive comments at someone publicly.
Example: *Fans cat-called the referee for the bad call.*

catch /kˈatʃ/
to capture or seize especially after pursuit
Example: *The police finally caught the runaway thief.*
to discover or affect suddenly
Example: *She caught the mistake just in time.*
to check oneself suddenly and momentarily
Example: *He caught himself before revealing the secret.*

categorise /kˈatɪgərˌaɪz/
to put into a category, such as by type
Example: *The librarian categorised the books by genre.*

caterwaul /ˈkatɝwal/
to make a harsh cry
Example: *The cat caterwauled outside all night.*
to protest or complain noisily
Example: *The citizens caterwauled about the new policy.*

cause /kˈɔːz/
to serve as a cause or occasion of
Example: *The icy roads caused multiple accidents.*
to compel by command, authority, or force
Example: *The judge caused the witness to testify.*

caution /kˈɔːʃən/
to advise warning to
Example: *The sign cautioned hikers about the steep trails.*

cavort /kɐvˈɔːt/
to leap or dance about in a lively manner
Example: *The children cavorted in the park, laughing, and playing.*
to engage in extravagant behaviour
Example: *Celebrities often cavort at extravagant parties.*

caw /kˈɔː/
to utter the harsh raucous natural call of the crow or a similar cry
Example: *The crow cawed loudly from the treetop.*

cease /sˈiːs/
to cause to come to an end especially gradually
Example: *The rain ceased toward evening.*

celebrate /sˈɛləbrˌeɪt/
to observe an occasion such as a holiday, perform a religious ceremony, or take part in a festival
Example: *They celebrated the new year with fireworks.*

centre /sˈɛntɐ/
to place or fix at or around a central area
Example: *She centred the vase on the table.*
to give a central focus or basis

Example: *The debate centred on the issue of climate change.*
to be at the middle point or part
Example: *The discussion centred around the main topic.*

certify /sˈɜːtɪfˌaɪ/
to attest as being true or as represented or as meeting a standard
Example: *The document was certified by the notary.*

challenge /tʃˈalɪndʒ/
to dispute especially as being unjust, invalid, or outmoded
Example: *She challenged the outdated policy.*

change /tʃˈeɪndʒ/
to make a difference in some way
Example: *He changed the layout of the room.*
to replace with another
Example: *She changed her shoes after the hike.*

chant /tʃˈɑːnt/
to make melodic sounds with the voice, especially to sing a chant
Example: *The monks chanted during the ceremony.*
to recite something in a monotonous repetitive tone
Example: *The crowd chanted the team's anthem.*

chaperone /ʃˈapərˌəʊn/
to act as a chaperone or escort, such as for an event
Example: *She chaperoned the students on the field trip.*

charge /ˈtʃɑrdʒ/
to fix or ask as a fee or payment
Example: *The restaurant charged for the water.*
to give an electric charge to
Example: *He charged the battery overnight.*

to rush against
Example: *The bull charged at the red flag.*
to make an assertion against especially by ascribing guilt or blame
Example: *The prosecutor charged the suspect with theft.*
to impose a task or responsibility on
Example: *The manager charged her with leading the project.*

chase /tʃeɪs/
to follow rapidly
Example: *The cat chased the mouse across the yard.*
to follow regularly or persistently with the intention of attracting or alluring
Example: *He chased fame his whole life.*
to cause to depart or flee
Example: *The dog chased the intruders away.*
to ornament by indenting with a hammer and tools without a cutting edge
Example: *The artisan chased designs into the metal plate.*

chasten /ˈtʃeɪsən/
to correct by punishment or suffering
Example: *The experience chastened his reckless attitude.*
to prune something of excess, pretence, or falsity, such as a work of art
Example: *The editor chastened the manuscript by removing redundant passages.*
to cause to be more humble or restrained
Example: *Failure chastened his perspective on success.*

chastise /tʃɑːstaɪz/
to censure severely
Example: *The teacher chastised the student for cheating.*
to inflict punishment on, such as by whipping or beating
Example: *The law forbids chastising children physically.*

chat /tʃɑt/
to talk in an informal or familiar manner
Example: *They chatted about their weekend plans over coffee.*
to take part in an online discussion in a chat room
Example: *She chatted with her fans during the livestream.*

chatter /tʃɑtɐ/
to utter rapid short sounds suggestive of language but inarticulate and indistinct
Example: *The baby chattered happily in her crib.*
to talk idly, incessantly, or fast
Example: *He chattered away during the entire car ride.*
to click repeatedly or uncontrollably
Example: *Her teeth chattered in the cold.*

cheat /tʃiːt/
to deprive of something valuable by the use of deceit or fraud
Example: *He cheated investors out of millions of dollars.*
to influence or lead by deceit, trick, or artifice
Example: *She cheated at cards to win the game.*
to be sexually unfaithful
Example: *He cheated on his partner.*
to position oneself defensively near a particular area in anticipation of a
play in that area
Example: *The player cheated towards the left to cover more ground.*

check /tʃɛk/
to inspect, examine, or look at appraisingly or appreciatively
Example: *The mechanic checked the engine for issues.*
to compare with a source, original, or authority
Example: *She checked her receipt against the store's records.*
to look at something to obtain information
Example: *He checked the scoreboard during the game.*

to slow or bring to a stop
Example: *The boulder checked the rolling tire's progress.*
to leave or accept for safekeeping
Example: *They checked their coats at the door.*

cheer /tʃˈiə/
to utter a shout of applause or triumph
Example: *The crowd cheered when the team scored a goal.*
to make glad or happy
Example: *Her kind words cheered him up.*

cherish /tʃˈɛrɪʃ/
to keep or cultivate with care and affection
Example: *She cherished the time spent with her grandparents.*
to entertain or harbour in the mind deeply and resolutely
Example: *He cherished the memories of his childhood.*

chew /tʃjˈuː/
to crush, grind, or gnaw something with or as if with the teeth, such as food
Example: *She chewed her food carefully.*
to injure, destroy, or consume as if by chewing
Example: *The machine chewed up the paper.*

chide /tʃˈaɪd/
to speak out in angry or displeased rebuke
Example: *She chided him for being late.*
to scold in a usually mild and constructive manner
Example: *The coach chided the players for their lack of effort.*

chill /tʃˈɪl/
to make cold or chilly
Example: *The sudden breeze chilled the air.*

to shiver or quake with or as if with cold
Example: *He chilled at the thought of facing his opponent.*

chime /tʃ aɪm/
to make a musical and especially a harmonious sound
Example: *The clock chimed at midnight.*
to utter repetitively
Example: *She chimed in with her opinion repeatedly during the meeting.*
to call or indicate by chiming
Example: *The bell chimed the hour.*

chip /tʃ ɪp/
to cut or hew with an edged tool
Example: *He chipped the wood to fit the space.*
to cut or break a small piece from something
Example: *She chipped a piece off the block of ice.*
to hit with backspin, such as a return in tennis
Example: *He chipped the ball over the net.*

chirp /tʃ ɜːp/
to make a chirp or a sound resembling a chirp, such as from a bird
Example: *The birds chirped cheerfully in the morning.*
to utter something with a cheerful liveliness
Example: *She chirped a greeting as she entered.*
to make sharply critical, complaining, or taunting remarks
Example: *He chirped at the referees after the game.*

chisel /tʃ ɪzəl/
to cut or work with or as if with a chisel
Example: *The sculptor chiselled the marble with precision.*
to employ shrewd or unfair practices on to obtain one's end

Example: *He chiselled his way into the deal through cunning negotiation.*

chitter /tʃˈɪtɐ/
to make high-pitched sounds, as if birds
Example: *The small birds chittered excitedly at dawn.*

choke /tʃˈəʊk/
to check or block normal breathing of by compressing or obstructing the trachea or by poisoning or adulterating available air
Example: *The smoke from the fire choked the room.*
to obstruct by filling up or clogging
Example: *Leaves choked the drain, causing the sink to overflow.*
to lose one's composure and fail to perform effectively in a critical situation
Example: *He choked during his presentation and forgot his lines.*

chomp /tʃˈɒmp/
to chew or bite on something
Example: *The dog chomped on his bone contentedly.*

choose /tʃˈuːz/
to select freely and after consideration
Example: *She chose the red dress over the blue one.*
to prefer something
Example: *I always choose coffee over tea.*

chop /tʃˈɒp/
to cut into or sever usually by repeated blows of a sharp instrument
Example: *He chopped wood for the fireplace.*
to strike something with a short quick downward stroke
Example: *She chopped the onion quickly and efficiently.*

chortle /tʃˈɔːtəl/
to sing or chant exultantly
Example: *He chortled with joy at the news.*
to laugh or chuckle especially when amused or pleased
Example: *She chortled at the clever joke.*

chuck /tʃˈʌk/
to throw, such as without a thought
Example: *He chucked the ball to his dog in the park.*

chuckle /tʃˈʌkəl/
to laugh inwardly or quietly
Example: *She chuckled to herself when she thought of the funny moment.*
to make a continuous gentle sound resembling suppressed
Example: *The stream chuckled along its path through the woods.*

cinch /sˈɪntʃ/
to fasten tightly, such as a belt
Example: *He cinched the strap to secure the load.*
to make certain
Example: *Winning the last game cinched the championship for them.*

circle /sˈɜːkəl/
to move or revolve around
Example: *The moon circles the earth.*

cite /sˈaɪt/
to quote by way of example, authority, or proof
Example: *The student cited three sources in her essay.*

claim /klˈeɪm/
to ask for especially as a right

Example: *She claimed her luggage at the carousel.*
to take as the rightful owner
Example: *He claimed ownership of the abandoned property.*

clamber /klˈambɐ/
to climb awkwardly or with effort especially by using both the hands and the feet
Example: *The children clambered over the rocks at the beach.*

clamour /klˈamɐ/
to become loudly insistent
Example: *The crowd clamoured for the singer to return to the stage.*

clamp /klˈamp/
to fasten with or as if with a clamp
Example: *She clamped the papers together.*
to place by decree
Example: *The government clamped new restrictions on trade.*

clang /klˈaŋ/
to make a loud metallic ringing sound
Example: *The gate clanged shut behind them.*

clap /klˈap/
to strike two things together to produce a sharp percussive noise, such as two flat, hard surfaces
Example: *The audience clapped their hands in applause.*

clarify /klˈarɪfˌaɪ/
to make it understandable or clear
Example: *The teacher clarified the complex topic with a simple explanation.*

clash /klˈaʃ/
to come into conflict or collide
Example: *Their ideas clashed during the meeting, leading to a heated argument.*

clasp /klˈɑːsp/
to enclose and hold with the arms
Example: *She clasped her friend in a warm hug.*

classify /klˈasɪfˌaɪ/
to consider someone or something as belonging to a particular group
Example: *The librarian classified the new books according to genre.*

claw /klˈɔː/
to rake, seize, dig, or progress with or as if with claws
Example: *The cat clawed at the curtains, trying to climb them.*

clean /klˈiːn/
to rid of dirt, impurities, or extraneous matter
Example: *She cleaned the kitchen thoroughly.*
to deprive of money or possessions
Example: *The scam artist cleaned out their bank accounts.*

cleanse /klˈɛnz/
to rid of impurities by or as if by washing
Example: *He cleansed his face with warm water.*

clear /klˈiə/
to free from pollution or cloudiness
Example: *The wind cleared the sky of clouds.*
to free from accusation or blame
Example: *The evidence cleared him of any wrongdoing.*
to give insight to

Example: *The explanation cleared up all confusion.*
to free from what obstructs or is unneeded
Example: *They cleared the debris from the road.*
to submit for approval
Example: *She cleared her plans with management before proceeding.*
to go over, under, or by without touching
Example: *The bird cleared the fence effortlessly.*

cleave /klˈiːv/
to adhere firmly and closely or loyally and unwaveringly
Example: *She cleaved to her beliefs despite criticism.*
to divide by or as if by a cutting blow
Example: *The butcher cleaved the meat with a sharp knife.*
to separate into distinct parts and especially into groups having divergent views
Example: *The issue cleaved the community into two opposing camps.*

clench /klˈɛntʃ/
to hold fast
Example: *He clenched the rope tightly during the rescue.*
to set or close tightly
Example: *She clenched her teeth in determination.*

click /klˈɪk/
to strike, move, or produce with a click
Example: *He clicked the pen on and off nervously.*
to select especially in a computer interface by pressing a button on a control device, such as a mouse
Example: *She clicked on the link to open the webpage.*
to turn something on or off by pushing a button or moving a switch
Example: *He clicked off the light as he left the room.*
to fit or agree exactly
Example: *Their personalities clicked at the very first meeting.*

climb /klˈaɪm/
to go upward with gradual or continuous progress
Example: *The hikers climbed the mountain slowly.*
to go about or down usually by grasping or holding with the hands
Example: *She climbed down the ladder carefully.*
to get into or out of clothing usually with some haste or effort
Example: *He climbed into his suit for the interview.*

clinch /klˈɪntʃ/
to turn over or flatten the protruding pointed end of a driven nail
Example: *The carpenter clinched the nail to secure the beam.*
to make final or irrefutable
Example: *She clinched the argument with undeniable facts.*
to hold fast or firmly
Example: *He clinched the rope during the tug of war.*

cling /klˈɪŋ/
to hold together
Example: *The wet clothes clung together in the washing machine.*
to have a strong emotional attachment or dependence
Example: *The child clung to his mother on the first day of school.*
to remain or linger as if resisting complete spreading or scattering
Example: *The fog clung to the valley in the early morning.*

clink /klˈɪŋk/
to give out a slight sharp short metallic sound
Example: *Glasses clinked during the toast at the wedding.*

clip /klˈɪp/
to hold in a tight grip
Example: *She clipped the papers together with a binder clip.*
to clasp, fasten, or secure with a clip
Example: *He clipped his ID badge to his shirt.*

clop /klˈɒp/
to make or move along with a sound as of a horse's hooves striking the ground
Example: *The horse clopped down the cobblestone road.*

close /ˈkloʊz/
to contract, fold, swing, or slide to leave no opening
Example: *She closed the book and sighed.*
to block against entry or passage
Example: *He closed the gate behind him.*
to bring to an end
Example: *The manager closed the meeting with a few announcements.*

clothe /klˈoʊð/
to cover with or as if with cloth or clothing
Example: *They clothed the statue to protect it from damage.*
to express or enhance by suitably significant language
Example: *The author clothed her sentiments in poetic language.*
to endow especially with power or a quality
Example: *The role clothed him with unprecedented authority.*

club /klˈʌb/
to beat or strike with or as if with a club
Example: *The character in the novel clubbed the attacker in self-defence.*
to unite or combine for a common cause
Example: *Several organisations clubbed together to raise funds.*

cluck /klˈʌk/
to make a clicking sound with the tongue
Example: *She clucked her tongue in disapproval.*
to express interest or concern
Example: *The mother clucked over her children warmly.*

clutch /klˈʌtʃ/
to grasp or hold with or as if with the hand or claws usually strongly, tightly, or suddenly
Example: *He clutched the railing as he slipped.*

coach /kˈəʊtʃ/
to train intensively as by instruction and demonstration
Example: *She coached the debate team to victory.*

coax /ˈkoʊks/
to influence or gently urge by caressing or flattering
Example: *He coaxed the cat down from the tree.*
to manipulate with great perseverance and usually with considerable effort toward a desired state or activity
Example: *She coaxed the engine to life on a cold morning.*

cobble /kˈɒbəl/
to mend or patch coarsely
Example: *He cobbled his shoes to last another season.*
to make or put together roughly or hastily
Example: *The team cobbled together a prototype overnight.*

cock /kˈɒk/
to turn, tip, or stick up
Example: *He cocked his hat at a jaunty angle.*
to draw or bend back in preparation for throwing or hitting
Example: *She cocked her arm back to throw the ball.*
to position the hammer of a firearm for firing
Example: *He cocked the gun carefully.*

coddle /kˈɒdəl/
to cook something, such as eggs, in liquid slowly and gently just below the boiling point

Example: *She coddled the eggs for breakfast.*
to treat with extreme or excessive care or kindness
Example: *His grandmother coddled him whenever he was ill.*

coerce /kˌoʊˈɜːs/
to compel to an act or choice
Example: *They coerced him into signing the document.*
to achieve by force or threat
Example: *The thief coerced compliance with a threatening gesture.*
to restrain or dominate by force
Example: *The regime coerced the population into obedience.*

coil /kˈɔɪl/
to wind into rings or spirals
Example: *She coiled the rope neatly in the boat.*
to move in a circular or spiral course
Example: *The snake coiled itself around the branch.*

collapse /kəlˈɑps/
to fall or shrink together abruptly and completely
Example: *The chair collapsed under his weight.*
to suddenly lose force, significance, effectiveness, or worth
Example: *The company's strategy collapsed under market pressure.*
to fold down into a more compact shape
Example: *She collapsed the stroller before putting it in the car.*

collect /kəˈlɛkt/
to bring together into one body or place
Example: *She collected the students for the assembly.*
to gain or regain control of
Example: *He collected his thoughts before speaking.*
to receive payment
Example: *The cashier collected the money from customers.*

to get and bring with one
Example: *He collected his belongings from the office.*

collide /kəlˈaɪd/
to come together with solid or direct impact
Example: *The two cars collided at the intersection.*

colour /kˈʌlɐ/
to change the colour of something as if by dyeing, staining, or painting
Example: *She coloured the fabric with natural dyes.*
to fill in a shape or picture outlined on a piece of paper using markers, crayons, or coloured pencils
Example: *The children coloured pictures during art class.*

comb /kˈəʊm/
to draw a comb through for the purpose of arranging or cleaning
Example: *He combed his hair in the morning.*
to pass across with a scraping or raking action
Example: *The archaeologist combed the site for artifacts.*
to search or examine systematically
Example: *Detectives combed the area for evidence.*

combine /kəmˈbaɪn/
to unite into a single number or expression
Example: *The ingredients were combined to make the cake.*
to bring into such close relationship as to obscure individual characters
Example: *The twins' personalities were combined in the eyes of their friends.*
to unite to form a chemical compound
Example: *Oxygen and hydrogen combine to form water.*

comfort /kˈʌmfət/
to give strength and hope to

Example: *She comforted her friend during a difficult time.*
to ease the grief or trouble of
Example: *Music comforted him after his loss.*

command /kəm'ɑːnd/
to order or request to be given
Example: *The officer commanded his troops to advance.*
to dominate as if from an elevated place
Example: *The castle commands the valley below.*

commence /kəm'ɛns/
to enter upon
Example: *She commenced her new job with enthusiasm.*
to have or make a beginning
Example: *The ceremony will commence at noon.*
to take a degree at a university
Example: *He commenced with honours in engineering.*

commend /kəm'ɛnd/
to entrust for care or preservation
Example: *She commended her valuables to the bank's safe.*
to recommend as worthy of confidence or notice
Example: *The author commended the book to young readers.*
to mention with approbation
Example: *His performance was commended by all.*

comment /k'ɒmɛnt/
to explain or interpret something by comment
Example: *She commented on the unusual design of the building.*

commentate /k'ɒmənt,eɪt/
to comment in a usually expository or interpretive manner

Example: *He will commentate during the live broadcast of the parade.*

commiserate /kəmˈɪsərˌeɪt/
to feel or express sympathy
Example: *They commiserate with her after hearing about her job loss.*

commit /kəmˈɪt/
to carry into action deliberately
Example: *He committed to completing the project by the deadline.*
to put into charge or trust
Example: *She committed her finances to a trusted advisor.*

commune /kəmˈjun/
to talk over or discuss
Example: *They communed about their shared goals for the community.*

communicate /kəmjˈuːnɪkˌeɪt/
to convey knowledge of or information about
Example: *He communicated the risks involved in the procedure.*
to cause to pass from one to another
Example: *The teacher communicated her enthusiasm to her students.*
to receive Communion
Example: *They communicate at the church service every Sunday.*

compare /kəmpˈeə/
to represent as similar
Example: *She compared the growth of the plant to a child's development.*
to examine the character or qualities of specially to discover resemblances or differences

Example: *We compared the two products to determine the better one.*
to inflect or modify an adjective or adverb according to the degrees of comparison
Example: *In grammar class, we learned how to compare adjectives.*

compel /kəmpˈɛl/
to drive or urge forcefully or irresistibly
Example: *The situation compelled him to act immediately.*
to cause to do or occur by overwhelming pressure
Example: *She felt compelled to apologize.*
to drive together
Example: *The farmers compelled the sheep into the pen.*

compete /kəmpˈiːt/
to strive consciously or unconsciously for an objective, such as position, profit, or a prize
Example: *Teams will compete for the championship this weekend.*

complain /kəmplˈeɪn/
to express grief, pain, or discontent
Example: *He complained about the noise coming from upstairs.*
to make a formal accusation or charge
Example: *She complained to the company about the poor service.*

compliment /kɑmpləmɛnt/
to express esteem, respect, affection, or admiration to
Example: *He complimented her on her excellent presentation.*

comply /kəmplˈaɪ/
to conform, submit, or adapt as to a regulation or to another's wishes as required or requested
Example: *She complied with the rules of the game.*
to be ceremoniously courteous

Example: *He complied with her request to leave.*

comport /kəmpˈɔːt/
to be fitting
Example: *His behaviour comports with the standards set by the school.*
to behave in a manner conformable to what is right, proper, or expected
Example: *She comported herself with dignity throughout the ceremony.*

compose /kəmpˈəʊz/
to form by putting together
Example: *She composed a beautiful bouquet for the wedding.*
to create by mental or artistic labour
Example: *He composed a new poem for the occasion.*
to deal with or act on so as to reduce to a minimum
Example: *The negotiator composed the tensions in the room.*
to arrange in proper or orderly form
Example: *The teacher composed the students into groups.*
to free from agitation
Example: *He took a deep breath to compose himself.*

comprehend /kˌɒmprɪhˈɛnd/
to grasp the nature, significance, or meaning of
Example: *She quickly comprehended the complex concept explained in class.*
to contain or hold within a total scope, significance, or amount
Example: *The lecture series comprehends all topics related to environmental science.*
to include by construction or implication
Example: *The rule comprehends all forms of misconduct.*

compress /kəmˈprɛs/
to press or squeeze together
Example: *He compressed the clothes into the suitcase.*
to reduce in size, quantity, or volume as if by squeezing
Example: *The software compressed the video files to save space.*

compromise /ˈkɒmprəmˌaɪz/
to come to agreement by mutual concession
Example: *They finally compromised after a lengthy discussion.*
to make a shameful or disreputable concession
Example: *He compromised his ethics to win the contract, a decision he later regretted.*
to reveal or expose to an unauthorised person and especially to an enemy
Example: *The data breach compromised the personal information of thousands.*

conceal /kənsˈiːl/
to prevent disclosure or recognition of
Example: *He concealed the evidence before the police arrived.*
to place out of sight
Example: *She concealed the gift under the bed.*

concede /kənsˈiːd/
to acknowledge grudgingly or hesitantly
Example: *He finally conceded that she was right.*
to relinquish grudgingly or hesitantly
Example: *She conceded her position in the debate.*
to grant as a right or privilege
Example: *The company conceded a bonus to its employees.*

concentrate /ˈkɒnsəntrˌeɪt/
to bring or direct toward a common centre or objective

Example: *The team concentrated their efforts on finishing the project.*
to express or exhibit in condensed form
Example: *The report concentrated on the main findings.*

conclude /kənkl'uːd/
to bring to an end especially in a particular way or with a particular action
Example: *The author concluded the chapter with a cliff-hanger.*
to reach as a logically necessary end by reasoning
Example: *From the evidence, the detective concluded that the butler was innocent.*
to bring about as a result
Example: *His hard work concluded in a well-deserved promotion.*
to shut up
Example: *They concluded the animals in the barn for the night.*

concur /kənk'ɜː/
to express agreement
Example: *The committee concurred with the decision to increase funding.*
to act together to a common end or single effect
Example: *All departments must concur to achieve the company's goals.*
to happen together
Example: *The events concurred to produce an unexpected outcome.*
to come together
Example: *Experts from various fields concurred at the conference.*

condemn /kənd'ɛm/
to declare to be reprehensible, wrong, or evil usually after weighing evidence and without reservation
Example: *The judge condemned the act as a clear violation of law.*
to pronounce guilty

Example: *She was condemned by the jury.*
to adjudge unfit for use or consumption
Example: *The building was condemned after failing the safety inspection.*

condescend /ˌkɒndɪsˈɛnd/
to assume an air of superiority
Example: *She condescended to their level of understanding.*
to descend to a less formal or dignified level
Example: *He condescended to explain the process in simple terms.*

condone /kəndˈəʊn/
to regard or treat something bad or blameworthy as acceptable, forgivable, or harmless
Example: *The school does not condone bullying in any form.*

conduct /ˈkɑndəkt/
to direct or take part in an operation
Example: *She conducted the meeting with great efficiency.*
to cause oneself to act or behave in a particular and especially in a controlled manner
Example: *He conducted himself professionally despite the provocation.*
to bring by or as if by leading
Example: *The tour guide conducted us through the ancient ruins.*
to act as a medium for conveying or transmitting
Example: *The metal rod conducts electricity.*

confer /kənfˈɜː/
to compare views or take counsel
Example: *The department heads conferred to finalise the budget.*
to bestow from or as if from a position of superiority
Example: *The university conferred an honorary degree upon her.*

to give something, such as a property or characteristic, to someone or something
Example: *The humid climate confers a lush greenness to the landscape.*

confess /kənfˈɛs/
to tell or make known something, such as something wrong or damaging to oneself
Example: *He confessed his mistakes to his team.*
to acknowledge sin to God or to a priest
Example: *She confessed her sins before the holiday.*
to declare faith in or adherence to
Example: *He confessed his faith during the ceremony.*
to give evidence of
Example: *The suspect confessed during the interrogation.*

confide /kənfˈaɪd/
to have confidence
Example: *She confided in her ability to resolve the issue.*
to show confidence by imparting secrets
Example: *He confided his plans only to his closest advisers.*
to give to the care or protection of another
Example: *They confided their pets to a neighbour while they travelled.*

confine /kənˈfaɪn/
to hold within a location
Example: *The animals are confined to their habitats at the zoo.*
to keep within limits
Example: *She confined her remarks to the topic at hand.*

confirm /kənfˈɜːm/
to give approval to

Example: *The board confirmed the decision to proceed with the new strategy.*
to make firm or firmer
Example: *His support confirmed her resolve.*
to remove doubt about by authoritative act or indisputable fact
Example: *The tests confirmed the diagnosis.*

confiscate /kˈɒnfɪskˌeɪt/
to seize as forfeited to the public treasury
Example: *Customs officials confiscated the smuggled goods.*
to seize by or as if by authority
Example: *The school confiscated cell phones during the exam.*

confront /kənfrˈʌnt/
to face especially in challenge
Example: *She confronted her opponent in the debate.*

confuse /kənfjˈuːz/
to disturb in mind or purpose
Example: *The contradictory advice confused him.*
to make indistinct
Example: *The fog confused the outline of the building.*
to make embarrassed
Example: *His question confused her during the presentation.*

congratulate /kəngrˈatʃʊlˌeɪt/
to express vicarious pleasure to a person on success or good fortune
Example: *They congratulated her on her recent promotion.*

conjecture /kəndʒˈɛktʃɐ/
to arrive at or deduce by surmise or guesswork
Example: *Based on the evidence, he conjectured that the lost hikers might have taken the wrong path.*

connect /kənˈɛkt/
to become joined
Example: *The two roads connect at the highway.*
to meet for the transference of passengers
Example: *The local bus connects with the train at the station.*
to make a successful hit, shot, or throw
Example: *She connected the bat to the ball perfectly.*
to have or establish a rapport
Example: *He connects well with his clients.*
to establish a communications connection
Example: *She connected her phone to the Wi-Fi network.*

connote /kəˈnoʊt/
to convey in addition to exact explicit meaning
Example: *The word "home" connotes feelings of safety and warmth.*
to be associated with or inseparable from a consequence or concomitant
Example: *The term "pirate" connotes danger and lawlessness.*

conquer /kˈɒnkɐ/
to gain or acquire by force of arms
Example: *The general conquered the enemy territory.* to gain mastery over or win by overcoming obstacles or opposition
Example: *She conquered her fear of public speaking.*
to overcome by mental or moral power
Example: *He conquered his desire to react angrily.*

consecrate /kˈɒnsɪkrˌeɪt/
to induct a person into a permanent office with a religious rite
Example: *They consecrated the new bishop in a solemn ceremony.*
to make or declare sacred
Example: *The community consecrated the ancient tree as a natural monument.*

to make inviolable or venerable
Example: *The treaty consecrated the peace between the two nations.*

consent /kəns'ɛnt/
to give assent or approval
Example: *She consented to the terms of the agreement.*

conserve /kən'sɝv/
to keep in a safe or sound state
Example: *He conserved his energy for the final part of the race.*
to preserve with sugar
Example: *They conserved the fruit to make jam.*
to maintain a quantity constant during a process of chemical, physical, or evolutionary change
Example: *The process conserved the material's properties despite the high temperatures.*

consider /kəns'ɪdɚ/
to think about carefully
Example: *She considered her options before deciding.*
to regard or treat in an attentive or kindly way
Example: *He considered his guests' needs carefully.*
to gaze on steadily or reflectively
Example: *He considered painting for a long time.*
to come to judge or classify
Example: *They considered the film a masterpiece.*

consign /kəns'aɪn/
to give over to another's care
Example: *She consigned her antique furniture to her children.*
to give, transfer, or deliver into the hands or control of another
Example: *The manufacturer consigned the goods to the distributor.*
to send or address to an agent to be cared for or sold

Example: He consigned his paintings to the gallery for the upcoming exhibition.

console /ˈkɑnsoʊl/
to alleviate grief, sense of loss, or trouble, such as of a person
Example: She consoled her friend who was grieving the loss of a pet.

consort /kənˈsɔrt/
to keep company
Example: She consorted with famous writers.
to make harmony
Example: The new policies consort with the company's principles.

conspire /kənspˈaɪə/
to join in a secret agreement to do an unlawful or wrongful act or an act which becomes unlawful because of the secret agreement
Example: They conspired to rig the election.
to act in harmony toward a common end
Example: The team members conspired to surprise their boss with a party.

constrain /kənstrˈeɪn/
to force by imposed stricture, restriction, or limitation
Example: The regulations constrain their options.

constrict /kənstrˈɪkt/
to make narrow or draw together
Example: The snake constricts its prey.
to stultify, stop, or cause to falter
Example: Fear constricted his ability to respond.

construct /kənˈstrəkt/
to make or form by combining or arranging parts or elements

Example: *They constructed a new bridge.*
to draw a geometrical figure with suitable instruments and under specified conditions
Example: *The students constructed a triangle using a compass and ruler.*

consult /kənˈsəlt/
to have regard to
Example: *She consulted her own feelings before deciding.*
to ask the advice or opinion of
Example: *He consulted a lawyer about the legal implications.*

contemplate /kˈɒntɪmplˌeɪt/
to view or consider with continued attention
Example: *She contemplated the painting for a long time.*
to view as likely or probable or as an end or intention
Example: *He contemplated moving abroad for work.*

contend /kənˈtɛnd/
to strive or vie in contest or rivalry or against difficulties
Example: *She contended for the gold medal in the Olympics.*

contest /kənˈtɛst/
to make the subject of dispute, contention, or litigation
Example: *He contested the inaccurate charges on his bill.*

continue /kəntˈɪnjuː/
to maintain without interruption a condition, course, or action
Example: *The show will continue after a short break.*
to resume an activity after interruption
Example: *She continued her studies after taking a year off.*

contort /kənt'ɔːt/
to twist into or as if into a strained shape or expression
Example: *His face contorted in pain.*

contract /kən'trækt/
to bring on oneself, inadvertently or on purpose
Example: *She contracted a cold during her travels.*
to reduce to smaller size by or as if by squeezing or forcing together
Example: *The fabric contracts when it is exposed to heat.*

contradict /ˌkɒntrəd'ɪkt/
to imply the opposite or deny
Example: *His actions contradict his earlier statements.*

contribute /k'ɒntrɪbjˌuːt/
to give or supply as a part or share
Example: *Each employee contributed ideas to the project.*
to supply for a publication
Example: *She contributed articles to the magazine regularly.*
to play a significant part in making something happen
Example: *His quick thinking contributed to the success of the rescue mission.*

control /kəntr'əʊl/
to exercise restraining or directing influence over
Example: *She controls the company's finances.*
to incorporate controls in an experiment or study
Example: *The researcher controlled for variables affecting the data.*

convene /kənv'iːn/
to come together in a body
Example: *The committee will convene at noon.*

converge /kənˈvɜːdʒ/
to tend or move toward one point or one another
Example: *The protestors converged at the square.*
to come together and unite in a common interest or focus
Example: *Different disciplines converged to address the issue.*
to approach a limit as the number of terms increases without limit
Example: *The sequence converges to zero.*

converse /kənˈvɜ˞s/
to exchange thoughts and opinions in spoken words or sign language
Example: *They conversed about politics.*
to have acquaintance or familiarity
Example: *He converses with several celebrities.*

convert /kənˈvɜ˞t/
to bring over from one belief, view, or party to another
Example: *He converted to a new religion.*
to alter the physical or chemical nature or properties of, especially in manufacturing
Example: *The plant converts raw materials into finished products.*
to succeed in an attempt for a point, field goal, or free throw
Example: *He converted the free throw into points.*

convey /kənˈveɪ/
to bear from one place to another
Example: *The conveyor belt conveys boxes into the truck.*
to impart or communicate by statement, suggestion, gesture, or appearance
Example: *Her smile conveyed her happiness.*

convict /kənˈvɪkt/
to find or prove to be guilty
Example: *The jury convicted him of robbery.*

to convince of error or sinfulness
Example: *His arguments convicted her of her mistakes.*

convince /kənvˈɪns/
to bring to belief, consent, or a course of action
Example: *He convinced her to join the project after outlining its benefits.*
to overcome by argument
Example: *She convinced the board with her compelling presentation.*

convulse /kənvˈʌls/
to shake or agitate violently
Example: *The earthquake convulsed the city.*

coo /kˈuː/
to make the low soft cry of a dove or pigeon or a similar sound
Example: *The pigeons cooed softly on the rooftop.*
to talk fondly, amorously, or appreciatively
Example: *She cooed over the new-born baby.*

cook /kˈʊk/
to prepare food for eating by a heating process
Example: *He cooked dinner for the family.*
to alter with the intention of deceiving or misleading
Example: *They cooked the books to hide the financial problems.*
to perform, do, or proceed well
Example: *The band cooked up an amazing performance last night.*

cool /kˈuːl/
to lose heat or warmth
Example: *The soup cooled quickly on the windowsill.*
to lose ardour or passion
Example: *Her enthusiasm cooled after the initial excitement.*

cooperate /kəʊˈɒpərˌeɪt/
to act or work with another or others, such as for mutual benefit
Example: *The team members cooperated to complete the project on time.*

coordinate /koʊˈɔːrdəˌneɪt/
to put in the same order or rank
Example: *She coordinated the tasks according to priority.*
to bring into a common action, movement, or condition
Example: *The manager coordinated the efforts of various departments.*

cope /kˈəʊp/
to deal with and attempt to overcome problems and difficulties
Example: *She coped with the stress by meditating.*
to maintain a contest or combat usually on even terms or with success
Example: *He coped well in the highly competitive industry.*

copy /kˈɒpi/
to make a duplicate
Example: *She copied the document for the meeting.*
to model oneself on
Example: *He copied his mentor's negotiation tactics.*
to acknowledge receipt and understanding of a message
Example: *"Copy that," the pilot responded to the control tower.*

corner /kˈɔːnɐ/
to catch and hold the attention of, especially to force an interview
Example: *The reporter cornered the celebrity for an exclusive interview.*
to meet or converge at a corner or angle
Example: *Two streets corner at an acute angle in the old part of the city.*

correct /kərˈɛkt/
to make or set right
Example: *He corrected the errors in the report before submission.*
to discipline or punish for some fault or lapse
Example: *The teacher corrected the students when they misbehaved.*

correspond /ˌkɒrɪspˈɒnd/
to be in conformity or agreement
Example: *His actions do not correspond with his words.*
to communicate with a person by exchange of letters
Example: *She corresponded with her pen pal for several years.*

corrode /kərˈəʊd/
to eat away by degrees as if by gnawing
Example: *Rust corroded the metal fence.*
to weaken or destroy gradually
Example: *Doubt corroded his confidence.*

corrupt /kərˈʌpt/
to change from good to bad in morals, manners, or actions
Example: *Power corrupted the leader over time.*
to alter from the original or correct form or version
Example: *The file was corrupted and could not be opened.*

cosset /kˈɒsɛt/
to treat as a pet
Example: *She cosseted her cat, spoiling it with gourmet treats.*

cough /kˈɒf/
to expel air from the lungs suddenly with a sharp, short noise
Example: *He coughed loudly during the concert.*

counsel /kˈaʊnsəl/
to give advice or guidance
Example: *She counselled the students on their career options.*

count /kˈaʊnt/
to indicate or name by units or groups to find the total number of units involved
Example: *She counted the tickets to ensure everyone had one.*
to rely or depend on someone or something
Example: *You can count on me for support.*
to have value or significance
Example: *Every vote counts.*

counter /kˈaʊntɐ/
to meet attacks or arguments with defensive or retaliatory steps
Example: *He countered the accusations with proof of his whereabouts.*
to assert in answer
Example: *She countered that the approach would not work.*

counteract /kˌaʊntərˈakt/
to make ineffective or restrain or neutralise the usually ill effects of by means of an opposite force, action, or influence
Example: *The medication counteracted the symptoms.*

court /kˈɔːt/
to seek to gain or achieve
Example: *He courted success with his innovative approach.*
to engage in social activities leading to engagement and marriage
Example: *They courted for two years before getting married.*

cover /kˈʌvɐ/
to guard from attack

Example: *The soldiers covered each other during the retreat.*
to hide from sight or knowledge
Example: *He covered the surprise party plans from his wife.*
to lay or spread something over
Example: *She covered the table with a cloth.*
to act as a substitute or replacement during an absence
Example: *I will cover for you while you are on vacation.*

covet /kˈʌvɪt/
to wish for earnestly
Example: *He coveted the latest model of the smartphone.*
to feel inordinate desire for what belongs to another
Example: *She coveted her neighbour's new car.*

cower /kˈaʊɐ/
to shrink away or crouch especially for shelter from something that menaces, domineers, or dismays
Example: *The child cowered in the corner during the thunderstorm.*

cozen /kˈəʊzən/
to deceive, win over, or induce to do something by artful coaxing and wheedling or shrewd trickery
Example: *He cozened the old man into signing the dubious contract.*

crack /krˈak/
to make a very sharp explosive sound
Example: *The whip cracked loudly in the air.*
to break, split, or snap apart
Example: *The vase cracked when it hit the floor.*
to lose control or effectiveness under pressure
Example: *He cracked under the intense stress of the job.*
to go or travel at good speed
Example: *She cracked down the highway in her new sports car.*
to tell or do especially suddenly or strikingly

Example: *He cracked a joke that made everyone laugh.*

crackle /krˈakəl/
to make small sharp sudden repeated noises
Example: *The fire crackled in the fireplace.*
to show animation
Example: *Her eyes crackled with excitement.*

cradle /krˈeɪdəl/
to place or keep in or as if in a cradle
Example: *She cradled the baby in her arms.*

cram /krˈam/
to pack tight
Example: *She crammed her suitcase with clothes.*
to prepare hastily for an examination
Example: *He crammed all night for the final exam.*
to eat greedily or to satiety
Example: *He crammed himself with pizza at the party.*

crane /krˈeɪn/
to stretch toward an object of attention
Example: *She craned her neck to see the parade.*
to raise or lift by or as if by a crane
Example: *They craned the heavy machinery into place.*

crash /krˈaʃ/
to break violently and noisily
Example: *The car crashed into the wall.*
to cause to make a loud noise
Example: *He crashed the cymbals together.*
to enter or attend without invitation or without paying
Example: *They crashed the wedding party.*

to move toward aggressively
Example: *The bull crashed through the fence.*
to suffer a sudden major failure usually with attendant loss of data
Example: *Her computer crashed, losing all her work.*
to go to bed or fall asleep
Example: *After the long trip, he crashed on the couch.*

crave /krˈeɪv/
to ask for earnestly
Example: *She craved his forgiveness.*
to want greatly
Example: *He craved some peace and quiet.*

crawl /krˈɔːl/
to move on one's hands and knees
Example: *The baby crawled across the floor.*
to move slowly in a prone position without or as if without the use of limbs
Example: *The injured soldier crawled to safety.*
to move or progress slowly or laboriously
Example: *Traffic crawled during rush hour.*
to advance by guile or servility
Example: *He crawled his way to the top.*
to be alive or swarming with or as if with creeping things
Example: *The old log was crawling with ants.*
to reprove harshly
Example: *She crawled him for his careless mistakes.*

crease /krˈiːs/
to wound slightly, especially by grazing
Example: *The bullet creased his arm.*
to make a wrinkle in or on
Example: *He creased the paper when he folded it.*

create /kriːˈeɪt/
to bring into existence
Example: *She created a beautiful sculpture.*
to produce or bring about by a course of action or behaviour
Example: *His comment created an awkward silence.*
to produce through imaginative skill
Example: *He created a vivid setting in his novel.*

creep /krˈiːp/
to move along with the body prone and close to the ground
Example: *The cat crept silently towards the bird.*
to go very slowly
Example: *Time seems to creep when you are waiting.*
to slip or gradually shift position
Example: *The table slowly crept across the floor due to the vibrations.*
a distressing sensation like a feeling of apprehension or horror
Example: *A creep of fear crawled up her spine.*

crimp /krˈɪmp/
to cause to become wavy, bent, or pinched
Example: *She crimped her hair for the party.*
to be an inhibiting or restraining influence on
Example: *Lack of funds crimped our vacation plans.*

cringe /krˈɪndʒ/
to recoil in distaste
Example: *He cringed at the bitter taste.*
to shrink in fear or servility
Example: *The dog cringed when scolded.*
to behave in an excessively humble or servile way
Example: *She cringed before her boss.*
to draw in or contract one's muscles involuntarily
Example: *He cringed as the dentist started drilling.*

crinkle /krˈɪŋkəl/
to form many short bends or ripples
Example: *The leaves crinkled underfoot.*
to give forth a thin crackling sound
Example: *The wrapping paper crinkled as she opened the gift.*

criticise /krˈɪtɪsˌaɪz/
to consider the merits and demerits of and judge accordingly
Example: *She criticised the proposal for lacking detail.*
to find fault with
Example: *He frequently criticises his own work.*

critique /krɪtˈiːk/
to examine critically
Example: *The professor critiqued the student's thesis.*

croak /krˈəʊk/
to make a deep harsh sound
Example: *The frog croaked loudly by the pond.*
to speak in a hoarse throaty voice
Example: *He croaked his disapproval.*

crook /krˈʊk/
to bend the arm or finger
Example: *She crooked her finger to signal him discreetly.*

croon /krˈuːn/
to sing or speak in a gentle murmuring manner
Example: *He crooned a lullaby to the baby.*

crop /krˈɒp/
to remove the upper or outer parts
Example: *She cropped the photo to emphasise the sunset.*

to yield or make a crop
Example: *The field crops twice a year.*
to appear unexpectedly or casually
Example: *He cropped up at the party unexpectedly.*

cross /krˈɒs/
to lie or be situated across
Example: *A bridge crosses the river.*
to cancel by marking a cross on or drawing a line through
Example: *She crossed out the error in the document.*
to place or fold crosswise one over the other
Example: *He crossed his arms in frustration.*
to extend across or over
Example: *The road crosses several counties.*
to meet in passing especially from opposite directions
Example: *We crossed paths at the grocery store.*

crouch /krˈaʊtʃ/
to lower the body stance especially by bending the legs
Example: *He crouched down to pick up the coin.*
to bend or bow servilely
Example: *She crouched before the tyrant.*
to stand at a low height
Example: *The shed crouched under the old oak tree.*

crow /krˈəʊ/
to make the loud shrill sound characteristic of a cock
Example: *The rooster crowed at dawn.*
to utter a sound expressive of pleasure
Example: *He crowed with delight at the news.*
to exult gloatingly especially over the distress of another
Example: *She crowed over her rival's defeat.*

crowd /krˈaʊd/
to fill by pressing or thronging together
Example: *Fans crowded the concert hall.*
to urge on
Example: *The fans crowded their team toward victory.*

crumble /krˈʌmbəl/
to break into small pieces
Example: *The cookie crumbled in her hands.*

crumple /krˈʌmpəl/
to press, bend, or crush out of shape
Example: *The paper crumpled in his fist.*
to cause to collapse
Example: *The building crumpled after the explosion.*

crunch /krˈʌntʃ/
to chew or press with a crushing noise
Example: *He crunched on the fresh celery.*
to perform mathematical computations on
Example: *She crunched the numbers for the report.*
to make one's way with a crushing noise
Example: *He crunched through the snow.*

crush /krˈʌʃ/
to squeeze or force by pressure to alter or destroy structure
Example: *She crushed the can with her foot.*
to cause overwhelming emotional pain
Example: *The news of his betrayal crushed her.*
to experience an intense and usually passing infatuation
Example: *He crushed on his classmate throughout high school.*

cry /krˈaɪ/

to utter loudly
Example: *She cried for help.*
to proclaim publicly
Example: *He cried his merchandise in the market.*
to shed tears often noisily
Example: *The child cried over the lost toy.*
to require or strongly suggest a remedy or disposition
Example: *The situation cries out for a thorough investigation.*

cuddle /kˈʌdəl/
to hold close for warmth or comfort or in affection
Example: *The couple cuddled under the blanket.*

cue /kjˈuː/
to insert into a continuous performance
Example: *The actor was cued to enter the stage.*
to give a prompt to
Example: *The director cued the musicians to start.*

cuff /kˈʌf/
to furnish with a cuff
Example: *She cuffed her jeans to reveal her boots.*
to strike especially with or as if with the palm of the hand
Example: *He playfully cuffed his friend on the shoulder.*

cup /kˈʌp/
to treat by cupping
Example: *The therapist cupped her back to alleviate the pain.*
to curve into the shape of a cup
Example: *He cupped his hands to catch the water.*

curb /kˈɜːb/
to furnish with a curb

Example: *They curbed the sidewalk.*
to check or control with or as if with a curb
Example: *She curbed her impulse to yell.*
to lead a dog to a suitable place for defecation
Example: *He curbed his dog at the park.*

cure /kjˈɔː/
to restore to health, soundness, or normality
Example: *The medication cured her illness.*
to deal with in a way that eliminates or rectifies
Example: *He cured the dampness in the basement.*
to prepare or alter especially by chemical or physical processing for keeping or use
Example: *They cured the meat with salt.*

curl /kˈɜːl/
to form into coils or ringlets
Example: *Her hair curled perfectly.*
to form into a curved shape
Example: *He curled the ribbon with scissors.*
to furnish with curls
Example: *The stylist curled her hair for the wedding.*

curse /kˈɜːs/
to use profanely insolent language against
Example: *He cursed loudly when he stubbed his toe.*
to call upon divine or supernatural power to send injury upon
Example: *She cursed her enemy.*
to bring great evil upon
Example: *The witch cursed the land with sterility.*

curtsey /kˈɜːtsi/
to bend the knees and lower the body as a gesture of respect or submission

Example: *She curtseyed gracefully as the royals passed by.*
to bend quickly at the knees, with one foot in front of the other, especially to show respect
Example: *She curtsied to the queen.*

curve /kˈɜːv/
to have or take a turn, change, or deviation from a straight line or plane surface without sharp breaks or angularity
Example: *The road curves through the mountains.*

cuss /kˈʌs/
to say words that are not polite because you are angry
Example: *He cussed when he dropped the hammer on his foot.*

cut /kˈʌt/
to penetrate with or as if with an edged instrument
Example: *She cut the paper into shapes.*
to shorten by omissions
Example: *The editor cut the article for length.*
to go or pass around or about
Example: *He cut through the park to get to the meeting faster.*
to divide into segments
Example: *She cut the cake into eight pieces.*
to stop photographing motion pictures
Example: *The director cut the scene after the perfect take.*

Dd

dab /dˈab/
to strike or touch lightly
Example: *She dabbed her eyes with a tissue.*
to apply lightly or irregularly
Example: *He dabbed paint on the canvas.*
to inhale the vapours of a heated concentrate of cannabis
Example: *They dabbed at the party.*

dabble /dˈabəl/
to work or involve oneself superficially or intermittently especially in a secondary activity or interest
Example: *She dabbled in painting as a hobby.*
to reach with the bill to the bottom of shallow water to obtain food
Example: *The ducks dabbled in the pond.*
to wet by splashing or by little dips or strokes
Example: *Children dabbled their hands in the water fountain.*

dally /dˈali/
to act playfully
Example: *They dallied along the beach, enjoying the sunset.*
to deal lightly
Example: *He dallied with the idea of starting a new business.*
to waste time
Example: *Stop dallying and get to work!*

damage /dˈamɪdʒ/
to cause harm or loss
Example: *The storm damaged the roof severely.*

dampen /dˈampən/
to become deadened or depressed
Example: *The bad news dampened the mood at the party.*
to make slightly wet
Example: *She dampened the cloth before wiping the dust.*

dance /dˈɑːns/
to move one's body rhythmically usually to music
Example: *They danced all night at the wedding.*
to bring into a specified condition by dancing
Example: *The performance danced the audience into applause.*

dandle /dandl/
to move up and down in one's arms or on one's knee in affectionate play
Example: *He dandled the toddler on his knee.*

dangle /dˈaŋɡəl/
to hang loosely and usually so as to be able to swing freely
Example: *The pendant dangled from her necklace.*
to occur in a sentence without having a normally expected syntactic relation to the rest of the sentence
Example: *A preposition dangling at the end of the sentence.*
to be a hanger-on or a dependent
Example: *He was tired of the freeloaders dangling around.*

dare /dˈeə/
to challenge to perform an action especially as a proof of courage
Example: *She dared him to jump into the cold lake.*
to have the courage to contend against, venture, or try
Example: *He dared to speak out despite the risks.*

darken /dˈɑːkən/
become obscured
Example: *The skies darkened as the storm approached.*
to become gloomy
Example: *His mood darkened with the news.*

dart /dˈɑːt/
to throw with a sudden movement
Example: *She darted the ball towards the goal.*
to thrust or move with sudden speed
Example: *The squirrel darted across the road.*
to shoot with a dart containing a usually tranquilising drug
Example: *The veterinarian darted the wild animal before transport.*

dash /dˈaʃ/
to move with sudden speed
Example: *He dashed out the door to catch the bus.*
to break by striking or knocking
Example: *The waves dashed against the rocks.*
to make ashamed
Example: *His hopes were dashed after the rejection.*
to complete, execute, or finish off hastily
Example: *She dashed off an email before leaving.*
to knock, hurl, or thrust violently
Example: *He dashed the glass to the floor in anger.*
to affect by mixing in something different
Example: *She dashed a little salt into the soup.*

dawdle /dˈɔːdəl/
to spend time idly
Example: *Stop dawdling and get to work!*
to move lackadaisical
Example: *He dawdled back home, taking his time.*

daydream /dˈeɪdriːm/
to have a pleasant visionary or daydream
Example: *She daydreamed about her vacation while at work.*

dazzle /dˈazəl/
to lose clear vision especially from looking at bright light
Example: *She was dazzled by the headlights.*
to shine brilliantly
Example: *The performer's outfit dazzled under the stage lights.*
to impress deeply, overpower, or confound with brilliance
Example: *His performance dazzled the audience.*

deadpan /dˈɛdpan/
to express without emotion
Example: *She deadpanned the joke, keeping her face completely expressionless.*

deal /dˈiːl/
to concern oneself or itself
Example: *She deals with the problem efficiently.*
to take action with regard to someone or something
Example: *He dealt with the complaints personally.*
to distribute the cards to players
Example: *You deal the cards in the next game.*
to sell or distribute something as a business
Example: *He deals in rare books.*
to give as one's portion
Example: *Fate dealt him a difficult hand.*

debate /dɪbˈeɪt/
to discuss a question by considering opposed arguments
Example: *They debated the merits of the new policy.*
to turn over in one's mind
Example: *She debated whether to go out or stay home.*

to contend in words
Example: *The candidates will debate on live television.*

decay /dɪkˈeɪ/
to undergo decomposition
Example: *The fallen leaves decayed in the soil.*
to decline in health, strength, or vigour
Example: *His health slowly decayed.*
to decrease usually gradually in size, quantity, activity, or force
Example: *The town's population has decayed over the years.*

decide /dɪsˈaɪd/
to make a final choice or judgement about
Example: *She decided to accept the job offer.*
to fix the course or outcome
Example: *The last-minute goal decided the match.*
to induce to come to a choice
Example: *His argument finally made me decide to study abroad.*

decipher /dɪsˈaɪfɐ/
to make out the meaning of despite indistinctness or obscurity
Example: *He deciphered the faded letter.*

declaim /dɪklˈeɪm/
to speak rhetorically, specifically recite in elocution
Example: *The actor declaimed the lines with great passion.*
to speak pompously or bombastically
Example: *He often declaims about his achievements.*

declare /dɪklˈeə/
to make known formally, officially, or explicitly
Example: *The government declared a state of emergency.*
to state emphatically

Example: *She declared her intention to run for office.*

decline /dɪklˈaɪn/
to become less in amount
Example: *The company's profits declined last quarter.*
to tend toward an inferior state or weaker condition
Example: *His health declined after the diagnosis.*
to refuse especially courteously
Example: *She declined the invitation to the party.*
to slope downward
Example: *The path declines steeply here.*
to give in prescribed order the grammatical forms of a noun
Example: *In Latin class, we declined nouns as part of our exercises.*

decorate /dˈɛkəˌreɪt/
to add honour to
Example: *The veteran was decorated for his service.*
to furnish with something ornamental
Example: *They decorated the hall with flowers.*
to award a mark of honour to
Example: *She was decorated with the company's highest award.*

decrease /dɪˈkris/
to grow progressively less as in size, amount, number, or intensity
Example: *The noise decreased as the car drove away.*

decree /dɪkrˈiː/
to command or enjoin by or as if by an order or decision
Example: *The court decreed that the property must be shared.*
to determine or order judicially
Example: *The judge decreed the dissolution of the contract.*

decry /dɪkrˈaɪ/
to depreciate officially or publicly
Example: *Activists decried the government's inaction on environmental issues.*
to express strong disapproval of
Example: *Many decried the new policy as unfair.*

dedicate /dˈɛdɪkˌeɪt/
to devote to the worship of a divine being
Example: *The temple was dedicated to the goddess.*
to set apart to a definite use
Example: *They dedicated a portion of their earnings to charity.*
to commit to a goal or way of life
Example: *She dedicated her life to science.*
to inscribe or address by way of compliment
Example: *The book was dedicated to his mentor.*
to open to public use
Example: *The park was dedicated last weekend.*

deduce /dɪdjˈuːs/
to determine by reasoning or deduction
Example: *From the evidence, the detective deduced the identity of the culprit.*
to trace the course of
Example: *We deduced his route from the clues he left behind.*

deem /dˈiːm/
to come to think or judge
Example: *I deemed it necessary to intervene.*
to have an opinion
Example: *She is deemed to be the best candidate for the job.*

defend /dɪfˈɛnd/
to drive danger or attack away from

Example: *He defended his home from the intruders.*
to act as attorney for
Example: *She will defend the accused in court.*
to deny or oppose the right of a plaintiff
Example: *The company defended itself against the lawsuit.*
to retain or seek to retain against a challenge in a contest
Example: *The team defended their championship title successfully.*

defer /dɪfˈɜː/
to postpone induction of a person into military service
Example: *His entry into the military was deferred due to his studies.*
to delegate to another
Example: *She deferred the decision to her manager.*
to submit to another's wishes, opinion, or governance usually through deference or respect
Example: *He deferred to her judgement on the matter.*

defile /dɪˈfaɪl/
to make unclean or impure
Example: *The river was defiled by pollution.*
to march off in a line
Example: *The soldiers defiled out of the camp.*

define /dɪfˈaɪn/
to determine or identify the essential qualities or meaning of
Example: *Can you define the term "classical music"?*
to fix or mark the limits of
Example: *The treaty defines the boundaries between the two countries.*
to create with established rules or parameters
Example: *The game is defined by well-established rules.*

deflate /diːflˈeɪt/
to release air or gas from

Example: *He deflated the balloon slowly.*
to reduce in size, importance, or effectiveness
Example: *The critique deflated his ego.*

deflect /dɪflˈɛkt/
to turn aside especially from a straight course or fixed direction
Example: *The goalie deflected the soccer ball away from the net.*

defy /dɪfˈaɪ/
to confront with assured power of resistance
Example: *She defied the odds to win the race.*
to resist attempts at
Example: *The material defies easy classification.*
to challenge to do something considered impossible
Example: *He defied me to prove him wrong.*

delay /dɪlˈeɪ/
to stop, detain, or hinder for a time
Example: *Traffic was delayed during the festival.*
to cause to be slower or to occur more slowly than normal
Example: *The heavy snow delayed the launch of the shuttle.*

delegate /dɛləˌɡeɪt/
to assign responsibility or authority
Example: *The manager delegated the task to her team.*
to appoint as one's representative
Example: *She was delegated as the spokesperson for the group.*

delete /dɪlˈiːt/
to eliminate especially by blotting out, cutting out, or erasing
Example: *Please delete the unnecessary files from your computer.*

deliberate /dɪˈlɪbəˌreɪt/
to think about or discuss issues carefully, often with formal discussion before reaching a decision
Example: *The jury deliberated for hours before reaching a verdict.*

deliver /dɪlˈɪvɐ/
to set free
Example: *The court delivered the wrongfully convicted man.*
to take and hand over to or leave for another
Example: *The package was delivered this morning.*
to give birth or assist in the birth
Example: *The doctor delivered the baby successfully.*
to send to an intended target or destination
Example: *The missile was delivered to the target area.*
to produce the promised, desired, or expected results
Example: *The new software delivered exceptional performance.*

delve /dˈɛlv/
to dig or labour with or as if with a spade
Example: *Archaeologists delved the ancient site.*
to make a careful or detailed search for information
Example: *He delved into the history of the building.*

demand /dɪmˈɑːnd/
to call for something in an authoritative way
Example: *The situation demands immediate action.*
to call for urgently, imperiously, or insistently
Example: *She demanded an explanation.*
to require coming
Example: *The job demands a high level of commitment.*
to call for as useful or necessary
Example: *The project demands careful attention to detail.*

demonstrate /dˈɛmənstrˌeɪt/
to prove or make clear by reasoning or evidence
Example: *The scientist demonstrated the principle with an experiment.*
to show or prove the value or efficiency of to a prospective buyer
Example: *The salesperson demonstrated the car's advanced features during the test drive.*

demur /dɪmˈɜː/
to take exception
Example: *She demurred at the suggestion of working late.*
to file a demurrer
Example: *The defendant demurred to the charges in court.*

denounce /dɪnˈaʊns/
to pronounce especially publicly to be blameworthy or evil
Example: *Activists denounce the new law as unjust.*
to inform against
Example: *He was denounced to the authorities by his own colleague.*
to announce formally the termination of something
Example: *The treaty was denounced by both countries.*

deny /dɪnˈaɪ/
to declare something to be untrue
Example: *She denied all the accusations against her.*
to refuse to admit or acknowledge
Example: *He denied any involvement in the scandal.*
to report or note the absence of a symptom
Example: *The patient denied any pain during the examination.*

depend /dɪpˈɛnd/
to be determined, based, or contingent
Example: *Success in this job depends on your willingness to work hard.*

to be pending or undecided
Example: *The decision depends on the final report.*
to place reliance or trust
Example: *You can depend on me to keep your secret.*
to hang down
Example: *A cluster of ripe grapes depended on the vine.*

deplore /dɪpl'ɔː/
to feel or express grief for
Example: *She deplored the loss of the ancient tree.*
to consider unfortunate or deserving of deprecation
Example: *The council deplored the state of the abandoned buildings.*

deposit /dɪp'ɒsɪt/
to place especially for safekeeping or as a pledge
Example: *He deposited the money in a savings account.*
to lay down
Example: *The bird deposited twigs and leaves to build its nest.*

deprive /dɪpr'aɪv/
to take something away from
Example: *The storm deprived us of electricity for days.*
to withhold something from
Example: *The authoritarian regime deprived its citizens of basic freedoms.*

deride /dɪr'aɪd/
to laugh at or insult contemptuously
Example: *Critics deride the proposal as impractical.*
to subject to usually bitter or contemptuous ridicule or criticism
Example: *He was derided for his outdated beliefs.*

descend /dɪsˈɛnd/
to pass from a higher place or level to a lower one
Example: *The path descends steeply into the valley.*
to pass in discussion from what is logically prior or more comprehensive
Example: *The lecture descended from general concepts to specific cases.*
to originate or come from an ancestral stock or source
Example: *She descends from a long line of craftsmen.*
to incline, lead, or extend downward
Example: *The roof descends towards the rear of the house.*

describe /dɪskrˈaɪb/
to represent or give an account of in words
Example: *She described her vacation in vivid detail.*
to represent by a figure, model, or picture
Example: *The artist described the landscape in her painting.*
to trace or traverse the outline of
Example: *He described a circle in the air with his finger.*

desecrate /dˈɛsɪkrˌeɪt/
to treat disrespectfully, irreverently, or outrageously
Example: *Vandals desecrated the sacred site.*

design /dɪzˈaɪn/
to create, fashion, execute, or construct according to plan
Example: *She designed a beautiful new dress for the occasion.*
to make a drawing, pattern, or sketch of
Example: *He designed the new garden layout.*

despair /dɪspˈeə/
to lose all hope or confidence
Example: *She despaired at the news of the disaster.*

despoil /dɪspˈɔɪl/
to strip of belongings, possessions, or value
Example: *The invaders despoiled the village of its treasures.*

destroy /dɪstrˈɔɪ/
to ruin the structure, organic existence, or condition of
Example: *The fire destroyed the historic building.*
to put out of existence
Example: *The disease nearly destroyed the entire species.*

detach /dɪtˈɑtʃ/
to separate especially from a larger mass and usually without violence or damage
Example: *She detached the receipt from the invoice.*

detect /dɪtˈɛkt/
to discover or determine the existence, presence, or fact of
Example: *The sensor can detect small movements.*
to discover the true character of
Example: *The investigator detected the suspect's deceit.*

determine /dɪtˈɜːmɪn/
to settle or decide by choice of alternatives or possibilities
Example: *She was determined to leave early to avoid the traffic.*
to fix the form, position, or character of beforehand
Example: *Genetic factors determine much of one's personality.*
to limit in extent or scope
Example: *The terms of the contract determine the parties' obligations.*
to find out or come to a decision about by investigation, reasoning, or calculation
Example: *The study determined the cause of the outbreak.*

develop /dɪvˈɛləp/
to set forth or make clear by degrees or in detail
Example: *The writer developed the characters beautifully in the story.*
to create or produce especially by deliberate effort over time
Example: *The company developed a new innovative software.*
to become infected or affected by
Example: *He developed a cold after being out in the rain.*

devour /dɪvˈaʊə/
to eat up greedily or ravenously
Example: *She devoured the chocolate cake.*
to use up or destroy as if by eating
Example: *The fire devoured the entire forest.*
to prey upon
Example: *The sharks devoured their prey quickly.*
to enjoy avidly
Example: *He devoured every book on the subject.*

diagnose /ˌdaɪəgnˈəʊz/
to recognize a disease or condition by signs and symptoms
Example: *The doctor diagnosed the patient with diabetes.*
to analyse the cause or nature of a problem
Example: *The mechanic diagnosed the issue with the car as a faulty alternator.*

dictate /dɪkˈteɪt/
to speak or read for a person to transcribe or for a machine to record
Example: *The author dictated her novel to the secretary.*
to impose, pronounce, or specify authoritatively
Example: *The rules dictate that all entries must be submitted by tomorrow.*

die /dˈaɪ/
to pass from physical life
Example: *The old tree finally died after standing for centuries.*
to disappear or subside gradually
Example: *The storm died down by the evening.*
to long keenly or desperately
Example: *He was dying for a chance to prove himself.*
to cease functioning
Example: *The engine died just as we reached the driveway.*
to become indifferent
Example: *Interest in the fad quickly died.*

differ /dˈɪfɚ/
to be unlike or distinct in nature, form, or characteristics
Example: *The twins differ in personality but look almost identical.*

differentiate /dˌɪfɚˈɛnʃiˌeɪt/
to obtain the mathematical derivative
Example: *In calculus, we learned how to differentiate complex equations.*
to mark or show a difference in
Example: *Effective branding differentiates one product from another.*

dig /dˈɪg/
to break up, turn, or loosen earth with an implement
Example: *They dug a hole to plant the tree.*
to work hard or laboriously
Example: *She dug through archives for her research.*
to advance by or as if by removing or pushing aside material
Example: *The journalist dug deeper into the story.*

digest /ˈdaɪdʒɛst/
to distribute or arrange systematically

Example: *The professor digested the information into a clear outline.*
to convert food into absorbable form
Example: *The stomach digests the food we eat.*
to take into the mind or memory
Example: *The students digested the complex concepts during the lecture.*
to soften, decompose, or break down by heat and moisture or chemical action
Example: *The compost heap digests the organic matter over time.*
to compress into a short summary
Example: *The article was digested into a brief news clip.*

digress /daɪgrˈɛs/
to turn aside especially from the main subject of attention or course of argument
Example: *The speaker digressed from his topic to tell an anecdote.*

dilate /daɪlˈeɪt/
to enlarge, widen, or cause to expand
Example: *The doctor dilated the patient's pupils.*
to comment at length
Example: *He dilated on the subject for over an hour.*

dim /dˈɪm/
to reduce the light from
Example: *She dimmed the lights to create a romantic atmosphere.*

diminish /dɪmˈɪnɪʃ/
to make less or cause to appear less
Example: *Her confidence diminished as the meeting progressed.*
to lessen the authority, dignity, or reputation of
Example: *The scandal diminished his chances of being elected.*
to cause to taper
Example: *The road diminishes to a narrow path in the woods.*

dimple /dˈɪmpəl/
to mark with indentations on the surface
Example: *Her smile dimpled her cheeks.*

dine /dˈaɪn/
to take or give a dinner
Example: *We dined at a fancy restaurant last night.*

dip /dˈɪp/
to plunge or immerse momentarily or partially under the surface to moisten, cool, or coat
Example: *He dipped his toes into the cold lake.*
to lift a portion of by reaching below the surface with something shaped to hold liquid
Example: *She dipped water from the bucket with a cup.*
to suddenly drop down or out of sight
Example: *The sun dipped below the horizon.*

direct /daɪrˈɛkt/
to cause to turn, move, or point undeviating or to follow a straight course
Example: *She directed the car towards the highway.*
to point, extend, or project in a specified line or course
Example: *He directed the flashlight beam into the dark room.*
to regulate the activities or course of
Example: *The teacher directed the students' activities during the field trip.*
to impart orally
Example: *The manager directly informed us about the changes.*

disagree /dˌɪsəgrˈiː/
to fail to agree
Example: *The partners disagreed on the terms of the contract.*
to differ in opinion

Example: *We often disagree about where to go on vacation.*
to cause discomfort or distress
Example: *The rough sea disagreed with him, making him seasick.*

disappear /dˌɪsɐpˈiə/
to pass from view
Example: *The magician's bunny disappeared in front of our eyes.*
to cease to be
Example: *The pain disappeared after taking the medicine.*

disapprove /dˌɪsɐprˈuːv/
to pass unfavourable judgement on
Example: *His parents disapproved of his decision to drop out of college.*
to refuse approval to
Example: *The committee disapproved of the final draft of the report.*

disbelieve /dˌɪsbɪlˈiːv/
to withhold or reject belief
Example: *She disbelieved the rumours about the company merger.*

discern /dɪsˈɜːn/
to detect with the eyes
Example: *She could discern a figure in the mist.*
to recognize or identify as separate and distinct
Example: *He discerned the subtle differences between the two paintings.*
to come to know or recognize mentally
Example: *Through the discussion, I discerned his true intentions.*

discipline /dˈɪsɪplˌɪn/
to punish or penalise for the sake of enforcing obedience and perfecting moral character

Example: *The school disciplined the student for breaking the rules.*
to train or develop by instruction and exercise especially in self-control
Example: *She disciplined herself to wake up early every morning.*
to impose order upon
Example: *The coach disciplined the team to improve their performance.*

disclaim /dɪˈskleɪm/
to renounce a legal claim to
Example: *He disclaimed any ownership of the disputed property.*

disclose /dɪsklˈəʊz/
to make known or public
Example: *The company disclosed its sales figures for the quarter.*
to open
Example: *He disclosed his thoughts during the meeting.*

discombobulate /dɪskəmbˈɒbjʊlˌeɪt/
to cause to be in a state of confusion
Example: *The sudden changes in the schedule discombobulated the attendees.*

discourage /dɪsˈkʌrɪdʒ/
to deprive of courage or confidence
Example: *The constant criticism discouraged the young artist.*
to hinder by disfavouring
Example: *The bad weather discouraged us from going hiking.*

discover /dɪsˈkʌvɐ/
to make known or visible
Example: *The archaeologist discovered an ancient artefact.*
to obtain sight or knowledge of for the first time

Example: *He discovered a new talent in himself during the workshop.*

discriminate /dɪskrˈɪmɪnˌeɪt/
to make a difference in treatment or favour on a basis other than individual merit
Example: *The company discriminated against older workers.*
to distinguish by discerning or exposing differences
Example: *She could discriminate between the subtle flavours in the dish.*
to use good judgement
Example: *He discriminated between the good and bad offers.*

discuss /dɪskˈʌs/
to present in detail for examination or consideration
Example: *We discussed the proposal at length during the meeting.*

disentangle /dˌɪsɛntˈɑŋɡəl/
to free from entanglement
Example: *He disentangled the wires behind the television.*

disfavour /dɪsfˈeɪvɐ/
to withhold or withdraw favour from
Example: *The public disfavoured the actor after the scandal.*

disguise /dɪsɡˈaɪz/
to furnish with a false appearance or an assumed identity
Example: *He disguised himself with a wig and glasses.*
to obscure the existence or true state or character of
Example: *The company disguised its losses by manipulating the financial statements.*

dishevel /dɪˈʃɛvəl/
to throw into disorder or disarray
Example: *The wind dishevelled his neatly combed hair.*

dislodge /dɪslˈɒdʒ/
to drive from a position of hiding, defence, or advantage
Example: *The storm dislodged the tiles from the roof.*
to force out of a secure or settled position
Example: *The scandal dislodged him from his position.*

dismiss /dɪsmˈɪs/
to permit or cause someone to leave
Example: *The teacher dismissed the class early.*
to remove from position or service
Example: *The company dismissed several employees during the restructuring.*
to reject serious consideration of
Example: *He dismissed the idea as impractical.*
to put an action out of judicial consideration
Example: *The judge dismissed the case due to lack of evidence.*

dismount /dɪsmˈaʊnt/
to throw down or remove from a mount or an elevated position
Example: *The rider dismounted from the horse.*
to get out of an enclosed craft or vehicle
Example: *The passengers dismounted from the bus.*

disobey /ˌdɪsəʊbˈeɪ/
to fail to follow commands or guidance
Example: *The soldier disobeyed the direct order.*

disparage /dɪspˈarɪdʒ/
to belittle the importance or value

Example: *He disparaged her achievements.*
to lower in rank or reputation
Example: *The article disparaged the company's reputation.*

displace /dɪspl'eɪs/
to take the place of
Example: *Online shopping has displaced traditional retail in many areas.*
to remove from the usual or proper place
Example: *The earthquake displaced thousands of people.*

display /dɪspl'eɪ/
to place or spread for people to see
Example: *The museum displayed the artefacts in a new exhibit.*

disport /dɪsp'ɔːt/
to amuse oneself in light or lively fashion
Example: *The children disported themselves at the playground.*

dispute /dɪspj'uːt/
to engage in argument
Example: *They disputed over the correct answer to the problem.*

disregard /dˌɪsrɪg'ɑːd/
to pay no attention to
Example: *He disregarded the warning signs at his peril.*

disrespect /dˌɪsrɪsp'ɛkt/
to lack special regard or respect for
Example: *He disrespected authority through his actions.*

dissemble /dɪs'ɛmbəl/
to hide under a false appearance

Example: *She dissembled her intentions from her competitors.*
to put on the appearance of
Example: *He dissembled happiness despite being sad.*

dissolve /dɪsˈɒlv/
to cause to disperse or disappear
Example: *The company was dissolved after going bankrupt.*
to clear up
Example: *He dissolved the misunderstanding between them.*

distance /ˈdɪstəns/
to make or maintain a personal or emotional separation from
Example: *She distanced herself from the controversy.*
to leave far behind
Example: *The runner distanced his competitors in the marathon.*

distinguish /dɪstˈɪŋgwɪʃ/
to perceive a difference in
Example: *She could distinguish the rare bird from similar species.*
to single out
Example: *He was distinguished for his heroic actions.*

distort /dɪstˈɔːt/
to alter to give a false or unnatural picture or account
Example: *The report distorted the facts of the case.*
to twist out of a natural, normal, or original shape or condition
Example: *The funhouse mirror distorted her reflection.*

distract /dɪstrˈakt/
to draw or direct to a different object or in different directions at the same time
Example: *The loud noise distracted him from studying.*
to stir up or confuse with conflicting emotions or motives

Example: *She was distracted by her worries.*

distribute /dˈɪstrɪbjˌuːt/
to divide among several or many
Example: *The teacher distributed the tests to the class.*
to spread out to cover something
Example: *They distributed the flyers throughout the neighbourhood.*
to use in or as an operation to be mathematically distributive
Example: *We distributed properties in algebra class.*

distrust /dɪstrˈʌst/
to have no trust or confidence in
Example: *He distrusted the promises made by the politician.*

disturb /dɪstˈɜːb/
to interfere with
Example: *The children disturbed the sleeping baby.*

disuse /dɪsjˈuːs/
to discontinue the use or practice of
Example: *The old factory disused after the company relocated.*

dither /dˈɪðɐ/
to act nervously or indecisively
Example: *She dithered over which dress to wear.*

dive /dˈaɪv/
to plunge into something, such as water
Example: *He dove into the pool to cool off.*
to come or drop down precipitously
Example: *The stock prices dived after the announcement.*

divert /daɪvˈɜːt/

to turn from one course or use to another
Example: *They diverted the funds to more urgent projects.*
to give pleasure to especially by distracting the attention from what burdens or distresses
Example: *The comedy show diverted us from our worries.*

divide /dɪvˈaɪd/
to separate into two or more parts, areas, or groups
Example: *The river divides the city into two parts.*
to subject a number or quantity to the operation of finding how many times it contains another number or quantity
Example: *We divided large numbers in maths class.*

divulge /daɪvˈʌldʒ/
to make known something, such as a confidence or secret
Example: *She divulged the secrets of the plan to her friend.*

dodder /dˈɒdɐ/
to tremble or shake from weakness or age
Example: *The old man doddered down the street.*

dodge /dˈɒdʒ/
to move to and from or from place to place usually in an irregular course
Example: *He dodged through the crowd.*
to evade a responsibility or duty especially by trickery or deceit
Example: *She dodged the question by changing the subject.*

doff /dˈɒf/
to remove an article of wear from the body
Example: *He doffed his hat as he entered.*
to rid oneself of
Example: *After the race, he quickly doffed his sweaty clothes.*

donate /dəʊnˈeɪt/
to contribute to a public or charitable cause
Example: *She donated to the local food bank.*
to transfer a particle, such as an electron, to another atom or molecule
Example: *In the chemical reaction, the atom donates an electron to the other molecule.*

doodle /dˈuːdəl/
to make a casual scribble
Example: *During the meeting, he doodled on his notepad.*

dote /dˈəʊt/
to exhibit mental decline of or like that of old age
Example: *He doted as he aged.*
to be lavish or excessive in one's attention, fondness, or affection
Example: *She doted on her grandchildren, spoiling them with gifts.*

double-check /dˈʌbəl-tʃˈɛk/
to make a careful check of something already checked
Example: *He double-checked the figures to ensure accuracy.*

doubt /dˈaʊt/
to call into question the truth of
Example: *I doubt his alibi.*
to lack confidence in
Example: *She doubted her ability to complete the marathon.*

download /dˈaʊnləʊd/
to transfer data or files from one location to another
Example: *She downloaded the files to her computer.*

downplay /dˈaʊnpleɪ/
to make something seem less important or less bad than it really is

Example: *He downplayed the severity of the issue during the presentation.*

doze /dˈəʊz/
to fall into a light sleep
Example: *He dozed off during the boring lecture.*
to be in a dull or stupefied condition
Example: *She was dozing in the warm sun after lunch.*

draft /drˈɑːft/
to select for some purpose
Example: *They drafted her into the team because of her skills.*
to draw the preliminary sketch, version, or plan of
Example: *He drafted a blueprint for the new house.*

drag /drˈag/

to draw or pull slowly or heavily

Example: *They dragged the sofa to the other side of the room.*

to bring by or as if by force or compulsion
Example: *She was dragged into the project against her wishes.*
to hang or lag
Example: *The little boy dragged behind, tired from the walk.*

drain /drˈeɪn/
to make gradually dry or disappear
Example: *The hot sun drained the moisture from the soil.*

dramatise /drˈamɐtˌaɪz/
to adapt something, such as a novel, for theatrical presentation
Example: *The novel was dramatised into a successful stage play.*

to present or represent in a dramatic manner
Example: *The teacher dramatised the historical event to engage the students.*

drape /dr'eɪp/
to cover or adorn with or as if with folds of cloth
Example: *She draped the curtains over the new rods.*
to cause to hang or stretch out loosely or carelessly
Example: *The cloth was draped over the chair.*
to arrange in flowing lines or folds
Example: *He draped the fabric artistically around the display.*

draw /dr'ɔː/
to cause to move continuously toward or after a force applied in advance
Example: *She drew the curtain to let in more light.*
to extract the essence from
Example: *The machine drew water from the well.*
to cause to shrink, contract, or tighten
Example: *The cold weather drew the skin on his hands.*
to produce a likeness or representation of by making lines on a surface
Example: *He drew a beautiful landscape in his sketchbook.*
to give a portrayal of
Example: *The author drew a vivid picture of life in the countryside.*
to infer from evidence or premises
Example: *She drew a conclusion from the data presented.*

drawl /dr'ɔːl/
to utter in a slow lengthened tone
Example: *He drawled his words, making it hard to understand him.*

dream /dr'iːm/
to have a series of thoughts, images, or emotions while sleeping
Example: *She dreamt of flying over mountains.*

to pass time in reverie or inaction
Example: *He spent the afternoon dreaming about his future.*

drench /drˈɛntʃ/
to wet thoroughly
Example: *The rain drenched her clothes.*
to fill or cover completely as if by soaking or precipitation
Example: *The garden was drenched with water from the hose.*
to force to drink
Example: *The vet drenched the animal with medicine.*

dress /drˈɛs/
to make or set straight
Example: *The nurse dressed the patient's wound.*
to prepare for use or service
Example: *The chef dressed the salad with olive oil.*
to add decorative details or accessories to
Example: *They dressed the stage for the play.*
to put clothes on
Example: *She dressed her child in warm clothes.*
to apply dressings or medicaments to
Example: *He dressed the burn with ointment and bandages.*

dribble /drˈɪbəl/
to issue sporadically and in small bits
Example: *The water dribbled from the leaky faucet.*
to let or cause to fall in drops little by little
Example: *The juice dribbled down his chin.*
to propel by successive slight taps or bounces with hand, foot, or stick
Example: *He dribbled the basketball down the court.*

drift /drˈɪft/
to become driven or carried along
Example: *The boat drifted down the river.*

to accumulate in a mass or become piled up in heaps by wind or water
Example: *The snow drifted against the side of the house.*
to vary or deviate from a set course or adjustment
Example: *His thoughts drifted during the lecture.*

drill /drˈɪl/
to fix something in the mind or habit pattern of by repetitive instruction
Example: *The coach drilled the team on the new plays.*
to bore or drive a hole in
Example: *He drilled a hole in the wall to hang the picture.*

drink /drˈɪŋk/
to take in or suck up
Example: *The sponge drank up the spilled water.*
to join in a toast
Example: *They drank to the health of the newlyweds.*
to bring to a specified state by drinking alcoholic beverages
Example: *He drank himself into a stupor.*

drip /drˈɪp/
to let fall in drops
Example: *Water dripped from the leaky roof.*
to let out or seem to spill copiously
Example: *Her voice dripped with sarcasm.*

drive /drˈaɪv/
to frighten or prod into moving in a desired direction
Example: *The shepherd drove the sheep into the pen.*
to carry on or through energetically
Example: *She drove the project to completion.*
to operate the mechanism and controls and direct the course of a vehicle
Example: *He drives to work every day.*
to impart a forward motion to by physical force

Example: *The engine drives the car forward.*

drivel /drˈɪvəl/
to talk stupidly and carelessly
Example: *He drivelled on about trivial matters.*
to let saliva dribble from the mouth
Example: *The baby drivelled in its sleep.*

drone /drˈəʊn/
to make a sustained deep murmuring, humming, or buzzing sound
Example: *The air conditioner droned all night.*
to talk in a persistently dull or monotonous tone
Example: *The professor droned on during the lecture.*
to pass, proceed, or act in a dull, drowsy, or indifferent manner
Example: *He droned through the workday without much enthusiasm.*

drool /drˈuːl/
to secrete saliva in anticipation of food
Example: *The dog drooled at the sight of the steak.*
to make an effusive show of pleasure or often envious or covetous appreciation
Example: *The kids drooled over the new video game.*
to talk nonsense
Example: *He drooled out some incoherent stories.*

droop /drˈuːp/
to hang or incline downward
Example: *The flowers drooped in the heat.*
to become depressed or weakened
Example: *His spirits drooped after hearing the bad news.*

drop /drˈɒp/
to fall unexpectedly or suddenly

Example: *The glass dropped from her hand.*
to enter or pass as if without conscious effort of will into some state, condition, or activity
Example: *He dropped into a deep sleep.*
to utter or mention in a casual way
Example: *She dropped a hint about her birthday.*

drum /drˈʌm/
to make a succession of strokes or vibrations that produce sounds like beats
Example: *He drummed his fingers on the table.*
to stir up interest
Example: *They drummed up support for the campaign.*
to dismiss ignominiously
Example: *He was drummed out of the club.*
to drive or force by steady effort or reiteration
Example: *The manager drummed the importance of punctuality into the staff.*

dry /drˈaɪ/
to make relatively free from a liquid
Example: *He dried his hands with a towel.*

dub /dˈʌb/
to call by a distinctive title, epithet, or nickname
Example: *He was dubbed 'The King' by his fans.*
to trim or remove the comb and wattles of
Example: *They dubbed the rooster for the show.*
to execute poorly
Example: *He dubbed the shot and missed the goal.*
to provide a motion-picture film with a new soundtrack and especially dialogue in a different language
Example: *The movie was dubbed into English.*
to make a new recording of

Example: *They dubbed the music onto a new track.*

duck /dˈʌk/
to lower the head or body suddenly, such as in water
Example: *He ducked under the table to avoid being seen.*
to evade a duty, question, or responsibility
Example: *She ducked out of the meeting early.*

duel /djˈuːəl/
to encounter an opponent in a combat
Example: *The two rivals duelled at dawn.*

dump /dˈʌmp/
to let something fall in or as if in a heap or mass
Example: *She dumped the papers on the desk.*
to sell in quantity at a very low price
Example: *They dumped the old stock at a discount.*
to copy to an external storage or output device
Example: *He dumped the data onto a flash drive.*
to get rid of something or someone in an abrupt and often casual or careless way
Example: *He dumped his old phone for a new model.*

dunk /dˈʌŋk/
to dip or submerge temporarily in liquid
Example: *She dunked the cookie in her milk.*
to throw into the basket from above the rim
Example: *He dunked the basketball with ease.*

dust /dˈʌst/
to sprinkle with fine particles
Example: *She dusted the cake with powdered sugar.*
to defeat badly

Example: *They dusted the opposing team in the final match.*

dwell /dwˈɛl/
to remain for a time
Example: *He dwelled on the problem for days.*
to live as a resident
Example: *They dwell in a small cottage by the sea.*
to keep the attention directed
Example: *She dwelled on her memories of the past.*

dye /dˈaɪ/
to impart a new and often permanent colour to especially by impregnating with a dye
Example: *She dyed her hair bright red.*

Ee

ease /ˈiːz/
to free from something that pains, disquiets, or burdens
Example: *The medication eased his pain significantly.*
to move or pass slowly or easily
Example: *She eased into the day with a quiet morning.*

east /ˈiːst/
to go toward or in the direction of the sunrise
Example: *He easts towards the mountains every morning.*

eat /ˈiːt/
to take in through the mouth as food
Example: *They ate the meal with great enjoyment.*
to affect something by gradual destruction or consumption
Example: *The rust ate away at the metal.*
to enjoy eagerly or avidly
Example: *She ate up the celebrity gossip.*

eavesdrop /ˈiːvzdrɒp/
to listen secretly to what is said in private
Example: *He eavesdropped on the private meeting and got caught.*

echo /ˈɛkəʊ/
to restate in support or agreement
Example: *His sentiments echoed those of the president.*
to send back a sound by the reflection of sound waves
Example: *The sound of laughter echoed through the hallways.*

edge /ˈɛdʒ/
to move or force gradually

Example: *She edged closer to get a better view.*
to defeat by a small margin
Example: *He edged out the competition in a close race.*
to be on the narrow part adjacent to a border
Example: *The path edged the river beautifully.*

educate /ˈɛdʒuːkˌeɪt/
to train by formal instruction and supervised practice especially in a skill, trade, or profession
Example: *The program educates future leaders.*
to develop mentally, morally, or aesthetically especially by instruction
Example: *His travels educated him about the world's cultures.*
to persuade or condition to feel, believe, or act in a desired way
Example: *The campaign is designed to educate the public about the health risks.*

effuse /ɪˈfju/
to pour or flow out
Example: *The volcano effused lava.*
to make a great or excessive display of enthusiasm
Example: *He effused gratitude towards his supporters.*

elaborate /ɪˈlabərət/
to expand something in detail
Example: *She elaborated on her plan to improve the business.*
to produce by labour
Example: *The team elaborated a detailed model for the project.*
to build up from simple ingredients
Example: *The chef elaborated a spectacular meal from basic ingredients.*

elbow /ˈɛlbəʊ/
to shove aside by pushing with or as if with the elbow
Example: *He elbowed his way through the crowd.*

to make an angle
Example: *The pipe elbows at the junction.*

elect /ɪl'ɛkt/
to select by vote for an office, position, or membership
Example: *She was elected as the new chairperson.*
to choose especially by preference
Example: *They elected to travel by train instead of flying.*

elevate /'ɛlɪv‚eɪt/
to lift or make higher
Example: *The crane elevated the beams to the top of the building.*
to improve morally, intellectually, or culturally
Example: *The discourse in the class elevated our understanding of the subject.*

elucidate /ɪl'uːsɪd‚eɪt/
to make lucid especially by explanation or analysis
Example: *The professor elucidated the complex topic with clear examples.*

elude /ɪl'uːd/
to escape the perception, understanding, or grasp of
Example: *The fugitive eluded capture for months.*

embellish /ɛmb'ɛlɪʃ/
to heighten the attractiveness of by adding decorative or fanciful details
Example: *She embellished her narrative with colourful descriptions.*

emboss /ɛmb'ɒs/
to raise the surface of into bosses specially to ornament with raised work
Example: *The artisan embossed the leather with intricate patterns.*

to raise in relief from a surface
Example: *The image was embossed on the paper.*

embrace /ɛmbrˈeɪs/
to clasp in the arms
Example: *They embraced warmly at the reunion.*
to take up especially readily or gladly
Example: *She embraced the opportunity to study abroad.*
to take in or include as a part, item, or element of a more inclusive whole
Example: *The museum embraced the new art movement in its latest exhibition.*

embroider /ɛmbrˈɔɪdə/
to ornament with needlework
Example: *She embroidered the quilt by hand.*
to elaborate on
Example: *He embroidered the tale with his own embellishments.*

emerge /ɪmˈɜːdʒ/
to become manifest
Example: *The full moon emerged from behind the clouds.*
to rise from or as if from an enveloping fluid
Example: *The submarine emerged from the depths of the ocean.*
to rise from an obscure or inferior position or condition
Example: *He emerged as a key player on the team.*
to come into being through evolution
Example: *New technologies emerge every day.*

empathise /ˈɛmpəθˌaɪz/
to experience empathy
Example: *She empathised with their struggle, having faced similar challenges herself.*

emphasise /ˈɛmfəsˌaɪz/
to place emphasis on
Example: *The speaker emphasised the importance of patience in achieving success.*

employ /ɛmplˈɔɪ/
to make use of
Example: *The company employs the latest technology.*
to use advantageously, such as time
Example: *She employed her time in studying for the exam.*
to devote to or direct toward a particular activity or person
Example: *They employed a specialist to oversee the project.*

empower /ɛmpˈaʊɐ/
to give official authority or legal power to
Example: *The documents empower the agent to act on behalf of the principal.*
to promote the self-actualization or influence of
Example: *The program empowers youth through education.*

empty /ˈɛmpti/
to remove from what holds or encloses
Example: *He emptied the box of its contents.*

emulate /ˈɛmjʊlˌeɪt/
to strive to equal or excel
Example: *She emulated her older sister's academic success.*

encase /ɛnkˈeɪs/
to enclose in or as if in a case
Example: *The artefact was encased in glass for protection.*

encircle /ɛnsˈɜːkəl/

to form a circle around
Example: *The spectators encircled the performers.*
to pass completely around
Example: *The trail encircles the lake.*

enclose /ɛnklˈəʊz/
to close or hold in
Example: *The fence encloses the backyard.*
to include along with something else in a parcel or envelope
Example: *She enclosed a check with the letter.*

encompass /ɛnkˈʌmpəs/
to go completely around
Example: *The new park will encompass over 50 acres.*

encounter /ɛnkˈaʊntɚ/
to meet as an adversary or enemy
Example: *The explorers encountered fierce resistance from the locals.*
to come upon face-to-face
Example: *She encountered a deer on the trail.*
to come upon or experience especially unexpectedly
Example: *They encountered numerous difficulties during the project.*

encourage /ɛnkˈʌrɪdʒ/
to inspire with courage, spirit, or hope
Example: *His coach encouraged him before the big game.*
to spur on
Example: *The crowd encouraged the runners to finish strong.*
to give help or patronage to
Example: *The program encourages small businesses through grants.*

encroach /ɛnkrˈəʊtʃ/
to enter by gradual steps or by stealth into the possessions or rights of another
Example: *The weeds encroached on the garden.*
to advance beyond the usual or proper limits
Example: *The city is encroaching upon the rural areas.*

end /ˈɛnd/
to bring to the point that marks the extent of something
Example: *The meeting ended at noon.*
to reach a specified ultimate rank, situation, or place
Example: *He ended his career as a respected scientist.*

endanger /ɛndˈeɪndʒɐ/
to create a dangerous situation
Example: *The extreme weather endangered the lives of the hikers.*

endorse /ɛndˈɔːs/
to write on the back of
Example: *She endorsed the check before depositing it.*
to approve openly
Example: *The company endorsed the new environmental standards.*
to report or note the presence of a symptom
Example: *The doctor endorsed the symptoms in the medical record.*

endure /ɛndjˈɔː/
to continue in the same state
Example: *The monument has endured through centuries.*

energise /ˈɛnədʒˌaɪz/
to make energetic, vigorous, or active
Example: *The lively discussion energised the participants.*

enfold /ɛnfˈəʊld/
to surround with a covering
Example: *The darkness enfolded the city as the storm approached.*
to clasp within the arms
Example: *She enfolded her child in a warm hug.*

enforce /ɛnfˈɔːs/
to effect or gain by force
Example: *The police enforce the law to maintain order.*
to carry out effectively
Example: *The teacher enforced the rules to keep the classroom orderly.*

engage /ɛngˈeɪdʒ/
to offer as backing to a cause or aim
Example: *The charity engaged local businesses to support their cause.*
to entangle or entrap in
Example: *He was engaged in a complex legal battle.*
to begin and carry on an enterprise or activity
Example: *They engaged in a project to renovate the building.*
to do or take part in something
Example: *She engaged in volunteer work on the weekends.*
to enter into conflict or battle
Example: *The armies engaged at dawn.*

engrave /ɛngrˈeɪv/
to impress deeply as if with a graver
Example: *The artist engraved the intricate design into the metal.*
to cut figures, letters, or designs on for printing
Example: *He engraved the book cover with elaborate patterns.*

engulf /ɛngˈʌlf/
to flow over and enclose

Example: *The rising floodwaters quickly engulfed the low-lying village.*

enhance /ɛnhˈɑːns/
to increase or improve in value, quality, desirability, or attractiveness
Example: *Proper lighting significantly enhanced the ambiance of the room.*

enjoy /ɛndʒˈɔɪ/
to take pleasure or satisfaction in
Example: *She enjoys reading historical novels.*
to have for one's use, benefit, or lot
Example: *He enjoyed the privileges of an elite membership.*

enlarge /ɛnlˈɑːdʒ/
to make larger
Example: *We enlarged the kitchen for more space.*
to give greater scope to
Example: *The seminar enlarged participants' understanding of the subject.*
to set free
Example: *The act of writing can enlarge the imagination.*

enlighten /ɛnlˈaɪtən/
to furnish knowledge to
Example: *The documentary enlightened viewers about the complexities of climate change.*

enquire /ɛnkwˈaɪə/
to ask about
Example: *She enquired about the schedule to plan her day.*
to search into

Example: *The investigation enquired into the undisclosed matters of the case.*

enshroud /ɪnʃˈraʊd/
to cover or enclose with or as if with a shroud
Example: *Mist enshrouded the mountains, making them appear mystical.*

ensnare /ɛnsnˈeə/
to take in or as if in a snare
Example: *The hunter ensnared the wild animal in a trap.*

entangle /ɛntˈɑŋɡəl/
to wrap or twist together
Example: *The kitten entangled itself in the yarn.*
to involve in a perplexing or troublesome situation
Example: *He found himself entangled in a web of deceit.*

enter /ˈɛntɐ/
to go or come in
Example: *She entered the room quietly.*
to make a beginning
Example: *The company entered the Asian market this year.*
to play a part
Example: *He entered the discussions with enthusiasm.*

entertain /ˌɛntətˈeɪn/
to show hospitality to
Example: *They entertained their guests with great care and affection.*
to keep, hold, or maintain in the mind
Example: *She entertained the idea of moving abroad for her studies.*

enthuse /ɛnθjˈuːs/
to show enthusiasm
Example: *He was enthused about his recent trip to Japan.*

entice /ɛntˈaɪs/
to attract artfully or adroitly or by arousing hope or desire
Example: *The advertisement enticed customers with promises of great savings.*

entreat /ɛntrˈiːt/
to plead with specially to persuade
Example: *She entreated her friend to stay longer.*

entwine /ɛntwˈaɪn/
to twine together or around
Example: *The vines entwined around the fence.*

enumerate /ɪnjˈuːmərˌeɪt/
to ascertain the number of
Example: *She enumerated the items in the inventory.*
to specify one after another
Example: *He enumerated his reasons for disagreeing with the plan.*

enunciate /ɪnˈʌnsɪˌeɪt/
to make a definite or systematic statement of
Example: *The speaker enunciated her points clearly during the presentation.*
to utter articulate sounds
Example: *He enunciated his words clearly despite the struggle.*

envelop /ɪnˈvɛləp/
to enclose or enfold completely with or as if with a covering
Example: *The fog enveloped the bridge, obscuring it from view.*

to mount an attack on
Example: *The military forces enveloped the enemy position.*

envision /ɛnvˈɪʒən/
to picture to oneself
Example: *She envisioned a future where renewable energy would be predominant.*

envy /ˈɛnvi/
to feel jealousy toward or on account of
Example: *He envied his colleague's success.*

equivocate /ɪkwˈɪvəkˌeɪt/
to use equivocal language especially with intent to deceive
Example: *He often equivocates during interviews to avoid giving direct answers.*
to avoid committing oneself in what one says
Example: *Politicians usually equivocate when faced with controversial questions.*

erase /ɪrˈeɪz/
to remove written or drawn marks from
Example: *She erased the error from her notebook.*
to remove from existence or memory
Example: *Time relentlessly erased the memories of his home.*

escape /ɛskˈeɪp/
to avoid a threatening evil
Example: *The family escaped the fire without any injuries.*
to get free of
Example: *The rabbit escaped from the garden.*
to fail to be noticed or recallable by
Example: *The mistake escaped the teacher's notice.*

escort /ɛˈskɔrt/
to accompany as a companion
Example: *The security team escorted the celebrity through the crowd.*

espy /ɛspˈaɪ/
to catch sight of
Example: *From the lookout, she espied a ship approaching the harbour.*

establish /ɪstˈæblɪʃ/
to institute permanently by enactment or agreement
Example: *The new law was established by the government.*
to make firm or stable
Example: *The company has established a strong reputation in the industry.*
to bring into existence
Example: *They established a new charity to help the homeless.*

estimate /ɛstəˌmeɪt/
to judge tentatively or approximately the value, worth, or significance of
Example: *He estimated the cost of repairs to be around $1,000.*

etch /ˈɛtʃ/
to produce on a hard material by eating into the material's surface
Example: *The artist etched fine lines into the metal plate.*
to delineate or impress clearly
Example: *The experience was etched into his memory forever.*

evade /ɪvˈeɪd/
to take refuge in escape or avoidance
Example: *She evaded the question by changing the topic.*

to slip away
Example: *The cat evaded capture by squeezing under the fence.*

evaluate /ɪvˈɑljuːˌeɪt/
to determine the significance, worth, or condition of usually by careful appraisal and study
Example: *The manager evaluated the team's performance for the year.*

evaporate /ɪvˈɑpərˌeɪt/
to diminish quickly
Example: *His enthusiasm evaporated once he saw the amount of work involved.*
to expel moisture from
Example: *The heat from the sun evaporated the moisture on the ground.*

evoke /ɪvˈoʊk/
to call forth or up
Example: *The photograph evoked memories of her childhood.*
to re-create imaginatively
Example: *The novel evokes a vivid picture of medieval times.*

exaggerate /ɛgzˈædʒərˌeɪt/
to enlarge beyond bounds or the truth
Example: *He frequently exaggerates the difficulties he faces.*

examine /ɛgzˈæmɪn/
to inspect closely
Example: *The mechanic examined the car for any defects.*
to test by questioning to determine progress, fitness, or knowledge
Example: *The teacher examined the students at the end of the semester.*

excavate /ˈɛkskəvˌeɪt/
to expose to view by or as if by digging away a covering
Example: *Archaeologists excavated the ancient ruins.*
to dig out and remove
Example: *They excavated the old foundations to make way for the new building.*

exchange /ɛkstʃˈeɪndʒ/
to part with, give, or transfer in consideration of something received as an equivalent
Example: *They exchanged gifts during the holiday season.*

exclaim /ɛksklˈeɪm/
to cry out or speak in strong or sudden emotion
Example: *She exclaimed in surprise when she won the prize.*

exclude /ɛksklˈuːd/
to expel or bar especially from a place or position previously occupied
Example: *He was excluded from the club for not following the rules.*

excuse /ɪkˈskjuz/
to make apology for
Example: *She excused her tardiness by explaining the traffic jam.*
to forgive entirely or disregard as of trivial import
Example: *The manager excused the error as it was minor.*
to grant exemption or release to
Example: *The student was excused from the final exam due to illness.*
to serve as excuse for
Example: *His youth cannot excuse his misconduct.*

exhale /ɛkshˈeɪl/
to rise or be given off as vapour
Example: *He exhaled a cloud of smoke.*

to breathe out
Example: *She exhaled deeply to calm her nerves.*

exhibit /ɛgzˈɪbɪt/
to present to view
Example: *The museum exhibits artifacts from ancient Greece.*

exhort /ɛgzˈɔːt/
to incite by argument or advice
Example: *The leader exhorted his followers to remain calm.*

exist /ɛgzˈɪst/
to have real being whether material or spiritual
Example: *Do ghosts really exist?*
to continue to be
Example: *The old laws still exist in some countries.*
to have life or the functions of vitality
Example: *Thousands of tiny organisms exist in the pond.*

exits /ˈɛgzɪts/
to go out or away
Example: *He exits the room quickly after the meeting.*

expand /ɛkspˈænd/
to open
Example: *The company expanded its operations overseas.*
to express at length or in greater detail
Example: *He expanded on his ideas during the presentation.*
to increase in extent, number, volume, or scope
Example: *The city's population has expanded rapidly.*
to feel generous or optimistic
Example: *During the holiday season, she expanded with a sense of generosity, giving more than ever before.*
to consider probable or certain

Example: *I expect he will arrive by noon.*
to anticipate or look forward to the coming or occurrence of
Example: *They eagerly expect the release of the new film.*
to be pregnant
Example: *She is expecting her first child next month.*

experience /ɛksp'iərɪəns/
to learn by something personally encountered
Example: *She experienced great joy when she visited the Grand Canyon for the first time.*

explain /ɛkspl'eɪn/
to make plain or understandable
Example: *He explained how the machine works.*
to give the reason for or cause of
Example: *The scientist explained the phenomenon as a natural occurrence.*
to show the logical development or relationships of
Example: *The teacher explained the steps leading up to the Civil War.*

exploit /ˌɛks'plɔɪt/
to make productive use of
Example: *He exploits every opportunity to improve his skills.*
to make use of meanly or unfairly for one's own advantage
Example: *She felt exploited by the company, as they paid her very little for her work.*

explore /ɛkspl'ɔː/
to investigate, study, or analyse
Example: *Scientists continue to explore the nature of the universe.*
to travel over for adventure or discovery
Example: *They explored the remote island for rare plants.*
to examine especially for diagnostic purposes

Example: *The doctor explored the area to understand the extent of the injury.*

expose /ɪkˈspoʊz/
to deprive of shelter, protection, or care
Example: *The storm exposed the village to severe damage.*
to make known
Example: *The journalist exposed the scandal.*
to cause to be visible or open to view
Example: *The excavation exposed an ancient settlement.*

expound /ɛkspˈaʊnd/
to explain by setting forth in careful and often elaborate detail
Example: *He expounded his theory in a detailed lecture.*

express /ɛksprˈɛs/
to represent in words, signs, or symbols
Example: *He expressed his feelings through music.*
to send by express
Example: *She expressed the package overnight to ensure it arrived on time.*
to subject to pressure so as to extract something
Example: *The machine expresses juice from the oranges.*

extend /ɛkstˈɛnd/
to spread or stretch forth
Example: *He extended his hand in greeting.*
to make the offer of
Example: *The company extended an offer of employment to the candidate.*
to reach in scope or application
Example: *The law extends to all citizens.*
to cause to be of greater area or volume
Example: *They extended the kitchen by breaking down the wall.*

extinguish /ɛkstˈɪŋgwɪʃ/
to end
Example: *The rain extinguished the barbecue.*
to cause to be void
Example: *The court order extinguished his claim to the property.*

extract /ˈɛkˌstrɑkt/
to draw forth
Example: *She extracted a promise from him.*

extrapolate /ɛkstrˈɑpəlˌeɪt/
to predict by projecting past experience or known data
Example: *We extrapolate future trends from the current data.*

extricate /ˈɛkstrɪkˌeɪt/
to free or remove from an entanglement or difficulty
Example: *He managed extricated himself from the complicated situation.*
to distinguish from a related thing
Example: *He extricated the truth from the myths.*

exult /ɛgzˈʌlt/
to be extremely joyful
Example: *They exulted in their unexpected victory.*

eye /ˈaɪ/
to watch or study closely
Example: *The detective eyed the suspect carefully.*

eyeball /ˈaɪbɔːl/
to look at intently especially in making an evaluation or choice
Example: *He eyeballed the distance before making the jump.*

Ff

fabricate /fˈabrɪkˌeɪt/
to make up for the purpose of deception
Example: *He fabricated a story about why he was late.*
to construct from diverse and usually standardised parts
Example: *They fabricate aircraft components in the new facility.*

face /fˈeɪs/
to confront impudently
Example: *She faced her critics with remarkable composure.*
to line near the edge especially with a different material
Example: *The tailor faced the jacket with silk to enhance its appearance.*
to meet face-to-face or in competition
Example: *The two teams will face each other in tomorrow's final.*

fail /fˈeɪl/
to lose strength
Example: *After the marathon, his legs failed him.*
to fall short
Example: *He failed to meet the project's original objectives.*

faint /fˈeɪnt/
to lose consciousness because of a temporary decrease in the blood supply to the brain
Example: *She fainted from exhaustion during the hike.*
to lose courage or spirit
Example: *He fainted before reaching his goal*

fake /fˈeɪk/
to alter, manipulate, or treat to give a spuriously genuine appearance to

Example: *He faked the signature on the document.*

fall /fɔːl/
to descend freely by the force of gravity
Example: *Leaves usually fall from the trees as a sign of Autumn.*
to become born
Example: *Calves usually fall in the spring.*
to become lower in degree or level
Example: *Temperatures fall dramatically at night in the desert.*
to leave an erect position suddenly and involuntarily
Example: *She slipped on the ice and fell.*
to commit an immoral act
Example: *He fell into temptation despite his better judgement.*
to occur at a certain time
Example: *The festival falls in July this year.*
to come within the limits, scope, or jurisdiction of something
Example: *This matter falls under the jurisdiction of the federal courts.*
to pass suddenly and passively into a state of body or mind or a new state or condition
Example: *He fell into a deep sleep.*
to set about heartily or actively
Example: *They fell to work as soon as they arrived.*

falter /fɒltɐ/
to walk unsteadily
Example: *He faltered as he walked across the icy sidewalk.*
to speak brokenly or weakly
Example: *Overcome with emotion, her voice faltered.*
to lose drive or effectiveness
Example: *The campaign faltered due to a lack of funds.*

familiarise /fəmˈɪliərˌaɪz/
to make known or familiar

Example: *She familiarised herself with the new software quickly.*
to make well acquainted
Example: *The teacher familiarised the students with the lab equipment.*

fan /fˈan/
to drive away the chaff of grain by means of a current of air
Example: *The farmer fanned the wheat with a machine.*
to move or impel air with a fan
Example: *The system fanned cool air through the building.*
to blow or breathe upon
Example: *She fanned her face with her hand to cool herself.*
to spread like a fan
Example: *The river fanned out into multiple streams.*

fancy /fˈansi/
to have a liking
Example: *I fancy going for a walk in the park.*
to form a conception of
Example: *He fancied himself a great artist.*
to believe mistakenly or without evidence
Example: *She fancied that she could win the lottery.*
to visualise or interpret as
Example: *He fancied the clouds as fantastical creatures.*

fib /fˈɪb/
to tell a trivial lie
Example: *He fibbed about having done his homework.*

fiddle /fˈɪdəl/
to play on a fiddle
Example: *She fiddled a joyful tune at the campfire.*
to move the hands or fingers restlessly
Example: *Nervous, he fiddled with his keys during the interview.*

to alter or manipulate deceptively for fraudulent gain
Example: *The accountant fiddled the accounts to hide the losses.*

fidget /fˈɪdʒɪt/
to move or act restlessly or nervously
Example: The child fidgeted in his seat during the long lecture.

fight /fˈaɪt/
to contend in battle or physical combat
Example: The warriors fought bravely to defend their village.
to put forth a determined effort
Example: She fought to overcome her fear of public speaking.

file /ˈfaɪl/
to rub, smooth, or cut away with or as if with a file
Example: The jeweller filed the rough edges of the metal.
to arrange for preservation and reference
Example: He filed the documents in the cabinet for easy retrieval.

fill /fˈɪl/
to put into as much as can be held or conveniently contained
Example: She filled the glass with water to the brim.
to possess and perform the duties of
Example: He filled the role of director during the project.

finalise /fˈaɪnəlˌaɪz/
to put in final or finished form
Example: The team finalised the report before the deadline.
to give final approval to
Example: The manager finalised the plans for the marketing campaign.

find /fˈaɪnd/

to come upon often accidentally
Example: *She found a rare coin in the attic.*
to come upon by searching or effort
Example: *After hours of research, he finally found the information he needed.*
to discover by the intellect or the feelings
Example: *He found comfort in his friend's advice.*
to determine and make a statement about
Example: *The jury found the defendant guilty.*

finger /fˈɪŋgɐ/
to touch or feel with the fingers
Example: *She fingered the fabric to test its texture.*
to point out
Example: *The witness fingered the suspect in the line-up.*
to extend in the shape or manner of a finger
Example: *The road fingers into the valley.*

finish /ˈfɪnɪʃ/
to come to an end
Example: *The concert finished with a standing ovation.*
to defeat or ruin utterly and finally
Example: *The scandal finished his career in politics.*

fish /fˈɪʃ/
to attempt to catch fish
Example: *They fished in the lake all afternoon.* to seek something by roundabout means
Example: *He fished for compliments by mentioning his achievements.*
to engage in a search by groping or feeling
Example: *She fished in her bag for her keys.*

fit /fˈɪt/

to conform correctly to the shape or size of
Example: *The dress fits her perfectly.*
to be suitable for or to
Example: *This task fits his skills.*
to experience or be affected with a seizure and especially an epileptic seizure
Example: *The patient fitted due to high fever.*

fix /fˈɪks/
to make firm, stable, or stationary
Example: *They fixed the shelf to the wall.*
to hold or direct steadily
Example: *He fixed his gaze on the horizon.*
to set in order
Example: *She fixed her hair before the interview.*
to get even with
Example: *He fixed the person who betrayed him.*

flail /flˈeɪl/
to strike with or as if with a flail
Example: *He flailed his arms to get their attention.*

flank /flˈaŋk/
to be situated at the side of
Example: *The guards flanked the entrance, standing vigilant.*

flap /flˈap/
to sway loosely usually with a noise of striking and especially when moved by wind
Example: *The curtains flapped in the evening breeze.*
to talk foolishly and persistently
Example: *He flapped about his adventures, much to everyone's annoyance.*

flare /flˈeə/
to burn with an unsteady flame
Example: *The candle flared in the drafty room.*
to shine with a sudden light
Example: *The headlights flared as the car approached.*
to open or spread outward
Example: *The skirt of her dress flared as she twirled.*
to express strong emotion
Example: *His temper flared during the argument.*
to display conspicuously
Example: *The team flared their banners proudly.*

flash /flˈaʃ/
to appear suddenly
Example: *A deer flashed in front of the car.*
to give off light suddenly or in transient bursts
Example: *Lightning flashed across the sky.*
to have sudden insight
Example: *An idea flashed in her mind.*

flatten /flˈatən/
to make flat or dull
Example: *They flattened the dough with a rolling pin.*

flatter /flˈatɐ/
to praise excessively especially from motives of self-interest
Example: *He flattered his boss hoping for a promotion.*
to display to advantage
Example: *The lighting flattered the artwork, making the colours pop.*

flaunt /flˈɔːnt/
to display or obtrude oneself to public notice
Example: *He flaunted his wealth at every opportunity.*
to wave or flutter showily

Example: *She flaunted her new scarf as she walked.*

flee /fl'iː/
to run away often from danger or evil
Example: *The townspeople fled the approaching storm.*
to pass away swiftly
Example: *The weekend fled by.*

flex /fl'ɛks/
to bend especially repeatedly
Example: *The gymnast flexed her muscles during the routine.*
to talk in a boastful or aggressive way
Example: *He flexed about his achievements at the meeting.*
to move muscles to cause flexion of a joint
Example: *She flexed her knees before starting the race.*

flick /fl'ɪk/
to move or propel with a light quick movement
Example: *She flicked the switch to turn on the light.*
to strike lightly with a quick sharp motion
Example: *He flicked the paper aeroplane, sending it across the room.*

flinch /fl'ɪntʃ/
to withdraw or shrink from or as if from pain
Example: *She flinched when the doctor gave her an injection.*

fling /fl'ɪŋ/
to throw forcefully, impetuously, or casually
Example: *He flung the ball across the yard.*

flip /fl'ɪp/
to toss so as to cause to turn over in the air

Example: *She flipped the pancake skilfully.*
to change from one state, position, or subject to another
Example: *He flipped from joyous to sad in a moment.*
to buy and usually renovate so as to quickly resell at a higher price
Example: *They flipped the old house for a profit.*

flirt /flˈɜːt/
to move erratically
Example: *Leaves flirted down from the trees.*
to behave amorously without serious intent
Example: *She flirted with him during the party.*
to come close to reaching or experiencing something
Example: *The temperature flirted with record highs.*

flit /flˈɪt/
to pass quickly or abruptly from one place or condition to another
Example: *The hummingbird flitted from flower to flower.*
to move in an erratic fluttering manner
Example: *Thoughts flitted through his mind.*

float /flˈəʊt/
to rest on the surface of or be suspended in a fluid
Example: *The boat floated on the calm lake.*
to drift on or through or as if on or through a fluid
Example: *They floated down the river on rafts.*
to put forth for acceptance
Example: *The company floated the idea of a merger.*

flop /flˈɒp/
to swing or move loosely
Example: *The fish flopped on the deck of the boat.*
to throw or move oneself in a heavy, clumsy, or relaxed manner
Example: *He flopped into the chair exhausted.*
to change or turn suddenly

Example: *The play flopped after just three performances.*
to go to bed
Example: *After the party, they all flopped down to sleep.*
to fail completely
Example: *The new TV show flopped and was soon cancelled.*

flounce /flˈaʊns/
to move with exaggerated jerky or bouncy motions
Example: *She flounced out of the room in anger.*
to trim with flounces
Example: *The dress was flounced at the hem.*

flounder /flˈaʊndɚ/
to struggle to move or obtain footing
Example: *The hikers floundered in the muddy terrain.*
to proceed or act clumsily or ineffectually
Example: *He floundered during his presentation.*

flourish /flˈʌrɪʃ/
to grow luxuriantly
Example: *The garden flourished under her care.*
to be in a state of activity or production
Example: *Business flourished with the new market expansion.*
to make bold and sweeping gestures
Example: *He flourished his hand as he spoke.*

flout /flˈaʊt/
to treat with contemptuous disregard
Example: *They flouted the rules and faced the consequences.*

flow /flˈəʊ/
to move with a continual change of place among the constituent particles

Example: *The river flowed gently to the sea.*
to proceed smoothly and readily
Example: *Conversation flowed at the dinner party.*
to hang loose and billowing
Example: *The curtains flowed in the breeze.*
to derive from a source
Example: *Much of their happiness flows from their family.*
to deform under stress without cracking or rupturing
Example: *The metal flowed under pressure.*

flub /fl'ʌb/
to make a mess of
Example: *He flubbed his lines during the play.*

fluff /fl'ʌf/
to make fluffy
Example: *She fluffed the pillows before the guests arrived.*
to spoil by a mistake
Example: He fluffed his chance at the job interview.

flush /fl'ʌʃ/
to fly away suddenly
Example: *The birds flushed from the bushes as we approached.*
to expose or chase from a place of concealment
Example: *The hunters flushed the rabbit from its burrow.*

flute /fl'u:t/
to play a flute
Example: *She fluted beautifully at the concert.*
to produce a flute-like sound
Example: *The wind fluted through the trees.*

flutter /fl'ʌtɐ/

to flap the wings rapidly
Example: *The bird fluttered its wings as it hovered.*
to move with quick wavering or flapping motions
Example: *Flags fluttered in the wind.*
to move about or behave in an agitated aimless manner
Example: *His thoughts fluttered anxiously before the exam.*

fly /flˈaɪ/
to move in or pass through the air
Example: *The plane flew across the sky.*
to fade and disappear
Example: *Her enthusiasm quickly flew away.*
to move, pass, or spread quickly
Example: *Rumours fly faster than the truth.*
to work successfully
Example: *Their new business idea really flew.*

foam /fˈəʊm/
to cause air bubbles to form in
Example: *He foamed the milk for the cappuccino.*
to become covered with or as if with foam
Example: *The sea foamed as the waves broke.*

focus /fˈəʊkəs/
to cause to be concentrated
Example: *She focused her efforts on finishing the project.*
to adjust one's eye or a camera to a particular range
Example: *He focused the camera on the distant bird.*

fold /fˈəʊld/
to lay one part over another part of
Example: *She folded the letter and put it in the envelope.*
to fail completely
Example: *His business folded within a year.*

follow /fˈɒləʊ/
to go or come after a person or thing in place, time, or sequence
Example: *She followed him out the door.*
to engage in as a calling or way of life
Example: *He follows the profession of a lawyer.*
to be or act in accordance with
Example: *She follows the rules strictly.*
to result or occur as a consequence, effect, or inference
Example: *Night follows day.*

fondle /fˈɒndəl/
to handle tenderly, lovingly, or lingeringly
Example: *He fondled the delicate fabric of the dress.*
to touch sexually
Example: *She fondled him suggestively.*

forbid /fəbˈɪd/
to proscribe from or as if from the position of one in authority
Example: *The law forbids texting while driving.*
to hinder or prevent as if by an effectual command
Example: *His condition forbids strenuous exercise.*

force /fˈɔːs/
to do violence to
Example: *The storm forced the old tree to break.*
to compel by physical, moral, or intellectual means
Example: *She was forced to admit the truth.*
to press, drive, pass, or effect against resistance or inertia
Example: *He forced his way through the crowd.*
to achieve or win by strength in struggle or violence
Example: *They forced the enemy to retreat.*

forecast /fˈɔːkɑːst/

to calculate or predict usually as a result of study and analysis of available pertinent data
Example: *The weather station forecasted heavy rain for the weekend.*
to serve as a forecast of
Example: *Dark clouds forecast a storm.*

foretell /fɔːtˈɛl/
to tell beforehand
Example: *The prophet foretold great calamity.*

forewarn /fɔːwˈɔːn/
to warn in advance
Example: *Visitors were forewarned of the dangers of hiking in the area during stormy weather.*

forge /fˈɔːdʒ/
to form by heating and hammering
Example: *The blacksmith forged the iron into a beautiful gate.*
to make or imitate falsely especially with intent to defraud
Example: *He forged the signature on the document.*
to form or bring into being especially by an expenditure of effort
Example: *She forged a new career in the arts.*

forget /fəgˈɛt/
to lose the remembrance of
Example: *He forgot his keys at home.*
to treat with inattention or disregard
Example: *She forgot the insult and moved on.*
to give up hope for or expectation of
Example: *They had almost forgotten the chance of rescue.*

forgive /fəgˈɪv/
to cease to feel resentment against

Example: *She decided to forgive her brother after he apologised sincerely.*

to give up resentment of or claim to requital

Example: *He decided to forgive his friend's mistake and move on from the incident.*

form /fˈɔːm/
to give a particular shape to
Example: *The artist used clay to form a beautiful sculpture.*
to serve to make up or constitute
Example: *Water and cement form the basis of concrete.*

forsake /fɔːsˈeɪk/
to renounce or turn away from entirely
Example: *He chose to forsake his corporate job for a life in the wilderness.*

fortify /fˈɔːtɪfˌaɪ/
to make strong
Example: *The city fortified the levees to prevent future flooding.*

formulate /fˈɔːmjʊlˌeɪt/
to reduce to or express in a formula
Example: *The scientist worked to formulate a new theory on particle physics.*
to put into a systematised statement or expression
Example: *The policy was formulated to ensure fairness in hiring practices.*

found /fˈaʊnd/
to take the first steps in building
Example: *They founded a start-up that focuses on renewable energy solutions.*

to set or ground on something solid
Example: *The philosophy is founded on principles of social justice.*
to melt a material and pour into a mould
Example: *The foundry workers found the metal to create engine parts.*

frame /frˈeɪm/
to enclose as if in a frame
Example: *The artist framed the landscape perfectly in her canvas.*
to give expression to
Example: *The politician framed his argument around the importance of education.*
to contrive the evidence against so that a verdict of guilty is assured
Example: *He was wrongly framed for a crime he did not commit.*
to fit or adjust especially to something or for an end
Example: *The tailor framed the suit to fit perfectly.*

free /frˈiː/
to relieve or rid of what restrains, confines, restricts, or embarrasses
Example: *The court freed the journalist from the lawsuit.*

freeze /frˈiːz/the to solidify because of abstraction of heat
Example: *Water will freeze into ice at 0 degrees Celsius.*
to cause to become fixed, immovable, unavailable, or unalterable
Example: *The computer system froze, making the data inaccessible.*

fret /frˈɛt/
to eat or gnaw into
Example: *The acid fretted the metal surface.*
to cause to suffer emotional strain
Example: *She fretted about her upcoming job interview.*

frighten /frˈaɪtən/

to make afraid
Example: *The loud noise frightened the small child.*

frisk /frˈɪsk/
to search for something by running the hand rapidly over the clothing and through the pockets
Example: *The security guard frisked the attendees at the entrance.*
to leap, skip, or dance in a lively or playful way
Example: *The lambs frisked in the field.*

frolic /frˈɒlɪk/
to amuse oneself
Example: *The children frolicked in the park on the sunny day.*
to play and run about happily
Example: *The puppies frolicked in the backyard.*

froth /frˈɒθ/
to cause to foam
Example: *He frothed the milk for the cappuccino.*
to become covered with or as if with froth
Example: *The river frothed as it rushed over the rocks.*

frown /frˈaʊn/
to contract the brow in displeasure or concentration
Example: *She frowned when she could not solve the puzzle.*
to give evidence of displeasure or disapproval by or as if by facial expression
Example: *He frowned upon the idea of skipping the meeting.*

fry /frˈaɪ/
to cook in a pan or on a griddle overheat especially with the use of fat
Example: *She fried the eggs for breakfast.*
to get very hot or burn as if being fried

Example: *The desert sun fried the landscape, leaving it barren.*

fulfil /fʊlfˈɪl/
to meet the requirements of
Example: *He fulfilled all the criteria for the scholarship.*
to convert into reality
Example: *She fulfilled her dream of becoming a doctor.*

fumble /fˈʌmbəl/
to grope for or handle something clumsily or aimlessly
Example: *He fumbled for his keys in the dark.*

fume /fjˈuːm/
to expose to or treat with fumes
Example: *The metals were fumed to create a patina.*
to utter while in a state of excited irritation or anger
Example: *He fumed about the traffic jam.*

furl /fˈɜːl/
to wrap or roll close to or around something
Example: *The sailors furled the sails as the storm approached.*

furrow /fˈʌrəʊ/
to make or form furrows, grooves, wrinkles, or lines
Example: *The farmer furrowed the field for planting.*

fuss /fˈʌs/
to create or be in a state of restless activity
Example: *The baby fussed all night, unable to sleep.*

Gg

gabble /gˈɑbəl/
to talk fast or foolishly
Example: *They gabble on without noticing the audience's confusion.*
to utter inarticulate or animal sounds
Example: *The turkey gabbled loudly in the yard.*

gag /gˈɑg/
to restrict use of the mouth of by inserting something into it to prevent speech or outcry
Example: *The kidnappers gagged their hostages.*
to provide or write quips or pranks for
Example: *He was hired to gag for the new comedy show.*
to choke or cause to retch
Example: *The smoke from the fire gagged her.*

gallivant /gˈɑlɪvˌɑnt/
to travel, roam, or move about for pleasure
Example: *They gallivanted around Europe for the summer.*

gallop /gˈɑləp/
to progress or ride at a gallop
Example: *The horse galloped across the field.*
to run fast
Example: *He galloped to catch the bus.*

gamble /gˈɑmbəl/
to bet on an uncertain outcome
Example: *He gambled away his savings at the casino.*

gambol /gˈɑmbɒl/

to skip about in play
Example: *The children gambolled through the meadows.*

gape /gˈeɪp/
to open or part widely
Example: *The canyon gaped before them.*
to gaze stupidly or in open-mouthed surprise or wonder
Example: *They gaped at the spectacular fireworks display.*

gargle /gˈɑːɡəl/
to hold a liquid in the mouth or throat and agitate with air from the lungs
Example: *He gargled with salt water to soothe his sore throat.*
to speak or sing as if gargling
Example: *The actor gargled his lines in a comedic voice.*

gash /gˈæʃ/
to make a cut in
Example: *The knife slipped and gashed his finger.*

gasp /gˈɑːsp/
to catch the breath convulsively and audibly
Example: *She gasped in horror at the news.*
to breathe laboriously
Example: *He gasped for air after the long sprint.*

gather /gˈæðɐ/
to bring together
Example: *They gathered their belongings and left.*
to serve as an attraction for
Example: *The festival gathered a large crowd.*

gauge /gˈeɪdʒ/

to precisely measure the size, dimensions, or other measurable quantity of
Example: *He gauged the length of the room accurately.*

gawk /gˈɔːk/
to gape or stare stupidly
Example: *Tourists gawked at the street performers.*

gaze /gˈeɪz/
to fix the eyes in a steady intent look often with eagerness or studious attention
Example: *She gazed at the stars, lost in thought.*

generalise /dʒˈɛnərəlˌaɪz/
to draw a general conclusion from
Example: *It is risky to generalise from a single incident.*
to spread or extend throughout the body
Example: *The infection generalised rapidly, becoming serious.*

genuflect /dʒˈɛnəflˌɛkt/
to bend the knee
Example: *They genuflect before entering the chapel.*
to be humbly obedient or respectful
Example: *He genuflected often before his superior.*

gesticulate /dʒɛstˈɪkjʊlˌeɪt/
to make gestures especially when speaking
Example: *The teacher gesticulated wildly to emphasise her point.*

gesture /dʒˈɛstʃʊ/
to express or direct by a motion
Example: *He gestured for them to sit down.*

get /gˈɛt/
to gain possession of
Example: *He finally got the car he always wanted.*
to have an emotional effect on
Example: *The sad movie really got to her.*
to leave immediately
Example: *It is late; we should get going.*

gibber /dʒˈɪbɐ/
to speak rapidly, inarticulately, and often foolishly
Example: *Nervous, he began to gibber unintelligibly during the interview.*

giggle /gˈɪgəl/
to laugh with repeated short catches of the breath
Example: *The children giggled at the clown's antics.*

give /gˈɪv/
to make gifts or presents
Example: *She gives a lot during the holidays.*
to yield as a product, consequence, or effect
Example: *The experiment gave some unexpected results.*
to present to view or observation
Example: *The guide gave us a clear view of the historical landmarks.*
to care to the extent of
Example: *Who really gives a damn about the rumours?*

glance /glˈɑːns/
to take a quick look at something
Example: *She glanced at her watch and hurried off.*
to strike a surface obliquely to go off at an angle
Example: *The stone glanced off the window, missing it narrowly.*
to make sudden quick movements
Example: *His eyes glanced around the room nervously.*
to touch on a subject or refer to it briefly or indirectly
Example: *The speaker only glanced at the main issues.*

glare /gl'eə/
to shine with a harsh uncomfortably brilliant light
Example: *The sun glared down on the desert landscape.*
to stare angrily or fiercely
Example: *He glared at the person who interrupted him.*

glide /gl'aɪd/
to move smoothly, continuously, and effortlessly
Example: *The skaters glided across the ice with grace.*

glimpse /gl'ɪmps/
to get a brief look at
Example: *As the car sped by, she glimpsed at the celebrity.*

gloat /gl'əʊt/
to observe or think about something with triumphant and often malicious satisfaction, gratification, or delight
Example: *He gloated over his rival's misfortune.*

glow /gl'əʊ/
to shine with or as if with an intense heat
Example: *The coals in the fireplace glowed in the dark room.*
to have a rich warm typically ruddy colour
Example: *The children's cheeks glowed from playing outside in the cold.*
to show exuberance or elation
Example: *She glowed with pride at her accomplishments.*

glower /'glaʊɚ/
to look or stare with sullen annoyance or anger
Example: *The cat glowered at the intrusive dog.*

gnash /n'aʃ/

to strike or grind together
Example: *He gnashed his teeth in frustration.*

gnaw /nˈɔː/
to bite or chew on with the teeth
Example: *The puppy gnawed at the furniture.*
to be a source of vexation to
Example: *The problem gnawed at her all week.*

go /gˈəʊ/
to move on a course
Example: *She will be going home early.*
to move out of or away from a place expressed or implied
Example*:*   *He went from the room in silence.*
to be habitually in a certain state or condition
Example*:*   *They go barefoot in the summer.*
to become lost, consumed, or spent
Example*:*   *All his money went on unexpected bills.*
to move along in a specified manner
Example*:*   *The project is going smoothly.*
to be compatible, suitable, or becoming
Example*:*   *Bright colours don't go well with his complexion.*

goad /gˈəʊd/
to incite or rouse
Example*:*   *He was goaded into running the marathon by his friends.*

gobble /gˈɒbəl/
to swallow or eat greedily
Example*:*   *He gobbled up his lunch in just a few minutes.*
to take eagerly
Example: *She gobbled up the opportunity to study abroad.*
to make the natural guttural noise of a male turkey
Example*:*   *The turkey gobbled loudly as we approached.*

to read rapidly or greedily
Example: *He gobbled down the pages of the mystery novel.*

goggle /ɡˈɒɡəl/
to stare with wide or protuberant eyes
Example: *She goggled at the extravagant costumes at the parade.*

goose /ɡˈuːs/
to poke between the buttocks with an upward thrust
Example: *Someone goosed him in the crowd, causing him to jump.*
to increase the activity, speed, power, intensity, or amount of
Example: *The coach goosed the pace during training.*

gossip /ɡˈɒsɪp/
to relate a rumour or report
Example: *They gossiped about the new neighbours' supposed wealth.*

gouge /ɡˈaʊdʒ/
to scoop out with or as if with a gouge
Example: *He gouged a hole in the wood to fit the hinge.*
to thrust the thumb into the eye of
Example: *In the fight, he gouged his opponent's eye.*
to make someone pay too much for something
Example: *The tourists were gouged for simple souvenirs at the market.*

govern /ɡˈʌvən/
to exercise continuous sovereign authority over
Example: *The president governs the nation with the aid of a chosen cabinet.*
to control, direct, or strongly influence the actions and conduct of
Example: *The rules govern how members are expected to behave.*

to serve as a precedent or deciding principle for
Example: *The court's decision will govern future cases of this nature.*

grab /gr'ab/
to take or seize by or as if by a sudden motion or grasp
Example: *She grabbed the last piece of cake before anyone else could.*
to obtain without consideration of what is right or wrong
Example: *He grabbed the opportunity to travel, regardless of the consequences.*

grade /gr'eɪd/
to assign to a grade or assign a grade to
Example: *The teacher graded the essays over the weekend.*
to level off to a smooth horizontal or sloping surface
Example: *They graded the dirt road to prevent water pooling.*

grant /gr'ɑːnt/
to consent to carry out for a person
Example: *The king granted his request for an audience.*
to bestow or transfer formally
Example: *The university granted him an honorary degree.*
to be willing to concede
Example: *I grant that the task is difficult, but it is not impossible.*

grapple /gr'apəl/
to seize with or as if with a grapple
Example: *The wrestlers grappled with each other for the championship belt.*
to grasp with the hands
Example: *He grappled the railing as the ship rocked.*
to bind closely
Example: *The documentary grapples with complex social issues.*
to begin to understand or deal with something in a direct or effective

way
Example: *She grappled with her emotions during the intense meeting.*

grasp /grˈɑːsp/
to take or seize eagerly
Example: *She grasped the opportunity to travel abroad.*
to clasp or embrace especially with the fingers or arms
Example: *He grasped her hand reassuringly.*
to lay hold of with the mind
Example: *He quickly grasped the complex concepts during the lecture.*

grate /grˈeɪt/
to reduce to small particles by rubbing on something rough
Example: *She grated the cheese for the pasta.*
to cause to make a rasping sound
Example: *The old door grated on its hinges as it opened.*
to cause irritation
Example: *His constant complaining grated on her nerves.*

gravitate /grˈavɪtˌeɪt/
to move under the influence of gravitation
Example: *The apple gravitated towards the ground.*
to move toward something
Example: *People gravitate towards him because of his charismatic personality.*

graze /grˈeɪz/
to feed on growing herbage, attached algae, or phytoplankton
Example: *The cows grazed peacefully in the field.*
to eat small portions of food throughout the day
Example: *She grazes on small snacks rather than having large meals.*

greet /ɡrˈiːt/
to address with expression of kind wishes upon meeting or arrival
Example: *He greeted each guest at the door with a smile.*
to meet or react to in a specified manner
Example: *She was greeted with applause as she walked onto the stage.*
to appear to the perception of
Example: *The morning greeted him with a beautiful sunrise.*

grieve /ɡrˈiːv/
to cause to suffer
Example: *The news of the accident grieved the entire community.*
to feel or show grief over
Example: *She grieved over the loss of her beloved pet for months.*
to submit a formal grievance concerning
Example: *He grieved the unfair treatment he received at work.*

grill /ɡrˈɪl/
to broil on a grill
Example: *He grilled steaks for the family barbecue.*
to question intensely
Example: *The lawyer grilled the witness during the cross-examination.*

grimace /ɡrˈɪmɪs/
to distort one's face in an expression usually of pain, disgust, or disapproval
Example: *He grimaced at the bitter taste of the medicine.*

grin /ɡrˈɪn/
to draw back the lips so as to show the teeth especially in amusement or laughter
Example: *She grinned at the clever joke.*

grind /ɡrˈaɪnd/

to reduce to powder or small fragments by friction
Example: *She ground the coffee beans into a fine powder.*
to wear down, polish, or sharpen by friction
Example: *He ground the knife to a sharp edge.*
to weaken or destroy gradually
Example: *The daily grind slowly wore down his enthusiasm.*
to rub or press harshly
Example: *The shoes ground into her heels painfully.*
to operate or produce by turning a crank
Example: *He ground the old organ as the children danced.*

grip /grˈɪp/
to seize or hold firmly
Example: *The climber gripped the rock tightly.*
to hold the interest of strongly
Example: *The mystery novel gripped her from the first page.*

gripe /grˈaɪp/
to complain with grumbling
Example: *He always gripes about the weather.*
to cause pinching and spasmodic pain in the bowels of
Example: *Something in the meal gripped his stomach.*

grit /grˈɪt/
to give forth a grating sound
Example: *The old gate grits when it swings.*
to cover or spread with grit
Example: *The icy roads were gritted to prevent accidents.*

groan /grˈəʊn/
to utter a deep moan indicative of pain, grief, or annoyance
Example: *He groaned under the weight of the heavy boxes.*
to make a harsh sound under sudden or prolonged strain
Example: *The old floorboards groaned as she walked across them.*

groom /ɡrˈuːm/
to clean and maintain the appearance of
Example: *She groomed her horse before the show.*
to make neat or attractive
Example: *He groomed himself carefully for the interview.*
to make someone ready for a specific objective
Example: *The coach groomed the team for the national championships.*

grope /ɡrˈəʊp/
to feel or look for something blindly
Example: *He groped for his glasses in the dark.*

grouch /ɡrˈaʊtʃ/
to complain in an angry way
Example: *He groused about having to work overtime.*

ground /ɡrˈaʊnd/
to provide a reason or justification for
Example: *The decision was well-grounded in legal precedent.*
to bring to or place on the ground
Example: *The pilot grounded the plane safely during the storm.*
to prohibit from taking part in some usual activities
Example: *She was grounded for breaking curfew.*

grovel /ɡrˈɒvəl/
to creep with the face to the ground
Example: *He grovelled at their feet, begging for forgiveness.*
to lie or creep with the body prostrate in token of subservience or abasement
Example: *The subject grovelled before the king.*
to give oneself over to what is base or unworthy
Example: *He grovelled for their approval.*

grow /ɡrˈəʊ/
to spring up and develop to maturity
Example: *The planted seeds soon began to grow.*
to develop from a parent source
Example: *The article grew from a short paragraph into a comprehensive feature.*
to pass into a condition
Example: *The sky grew dark as the storm approached.*

growl /ɡrˈaʊl/
to utter a growl
Example: *The dog growled when the stranger approached.*
to complain angrily
Example: *He growled about the unfair decision.*

grumble /ɡrˈʌmbəl/
to mutter in discontent
Example: *She grumbled about the cold weather.*

grump /ɡrˈʌmp/
to utter in a grumpy manner
Example: *He grumped about having to wake up early.*

grunt /ɡrˈʌnt/
to utter a deep short sound
Example: *The pig grunted as it searched for food.*

guarantee /ɡˌɑrɑːntˈiː/
to undertake to answer for the debt, default, or miscarriage of
Example: *The company guaranteed the loan for its subsidiary.*
to engage for the existence, permanence, or nature of
Example: *The manufacturer guarantees the durability of its products.*

to give security to
Example: *She guaranteed her brother's safety during his stay.*
to assert confidently
Example: *He guaranteed that the project would be completed on time.*

guard /gˈɑːd/
to protect an edge of with an ornamental border
Example: *They guarded the manuscript with a decorative leather border.*
to watch over to prevent escape, disclosure, or indiscretion
Example: *The security guard watched the entrance carefully.*

guess /gˈɛs/
to form an opinion of from little or no evidence
Example: *I guess he must be around 30 years old.*
to arrive at a correct conclusion about by conjecture, chance, or intuition
Example: *She guessed the answer to the riddle.*

guffaw /gˈʌfɔː/
to laugh loudly or boisterously
Example: *He guffawed at the comedian's joke.*

guide /gˈaɪd/
to direct, supervise, or influence usually to a particular end
Example: *The tour guide guided us through the ancient ruins.*

gulp /gˈʌlp/
to swallow hurriedly or greedily or in one swallow
Example: *He gulped down his coffee before rushing out the door.*
to take in readily as if by swallowing
Example: *She gulped the fresh air after exiting the stuffy room.*

gurgle /gˈɜːgəl/
to flow in a broken irregular current
Example: *The brook gurgled over the rocks.*
to make a sound like that of a gurgling liquid
Example: *The baby gurgled happily in her crib.*

gush /gˈʌʃ/
to issue copiously or violently
Example: *Water gushed from the broken pipe.*
to make an effusive display of affection or enthusiasm
Example: *She gushed over the gorgeous wedding dress.*

guzzle /gˈʌzəl/
to drink especially liquor greedily, continually, or habitually
Example: *He guzzled the beer as if he had not drunk for days.*

gyrate /dʒˈaɪreɪt/
to revolve around a point or axis
Example: *The dancer gyrated to the beat of the music.*
to oscillate with or as if with a circular or spiral motion
Example: *The leaves gyrated in the wind*

Hh

hack /hˈak/
to cut or sever with repeated irregular or unskilful blows
Example: *He hacked at the branches with the dull blade.*
to gain illegal access to
Example: *Someone hacked into the company's secure network.*
to cough in a short dry manner
Example: *He hacks all morning because of the dry air.*

haggle /hˈagəl/
to cut roughly or clumsily
Example: *He haggled the wood into rough shapes.*

hail /hˈeɪl/
to precipitate hail
Example: *It hailed heavily during the picnic.*
to pour down or strike like hail
Example: *Questions hailed down on the speaker.*
to greet with enthusiastic approval
Example: *The crowd hailed the returning hero.*
to greet or summon by calling
Example: *She hailed a cab from the curb.*

hallucinate /hælˈuːsɪnˌeɪt/
to affect with visions or imaginary perceptions
Example: *The patient hallucinated due to the high fever.*

halt /hˈɒlt/
to cease marching or journeying
Example: *The parade halted at the city square.*
to cause the discontinuance of

Example: *The judge halted the proceedings until order was restored.*

hammer /hˈamɐ/
to strike blows especially repeatedly with or as if with a hammer
Example: *He hammered the nail into the wall.*
to make repeated efforts, especially reiterating an opinion or attitude
Example: *She hammered her point home during the debate.*

hand /hˈand/
to give, pass, or transmit with the hand
Example: *She handed him the documents.*
to lead, guide, or assist with the hand
Example: *He handed the elderly man across the street.*

handle /hˈandəl/
to try or examine with the hand
Example: *She handled the fabric to test its quality.*
to put up with
Example: *He could not handle the stress of the job.*
to act on or perform a required function
Example: *She handled the complaints efficiently.*

hang /hˈaŋ/
to hover or remain stationary in the air
Example: *The helicopter hung in the air above the crowd.*
to apply to a wall
Example: *We hung the painting in the living room.*
to die by being suspended by the neck
Example: *The traitor was hanged at dawn.*

harass /hərˈas/
to create an unpleasant or hostile situation for especially by uninvited and unwelcome verbal or physical conduct
Example: *She was harassed by constant calls and messages.*
to worry and impede by repeated raids

Example: *The village was harassed by the marauding invaders.*

harden /hˈɑːdən/
to make hard or harder
Example: *Repeated challenges hardened his resolve.*
to confirm in disposition, feelings, or action
Example: *His heart hardened after the betrayal.*
to inure to unfavourable environmental conditions
Example: *Plants in the desert are hardened to survive extreme heat.*
to protect from blast, heat, or radiation
Example: *The bunker was hardened against radiation.*

hark /hˈɑːk/
to pay close attention
Example: *She harked to the sound of the distant drums.*

harm /hˈɑːm/
to damage or injure physically or mentally
Example: *The scandal harmed his reputation.*

harmonise /hˈɑːmənˌaɪz/
to bring into consonance or accord
Example: *The new regulations were harmonised with existing laws.*
to provide or accompany with harmony
Example: *She harmonised the melody on her guitar.*

harvest /hˈɑːvɪst/
to gather, catch, hunt, or kill for human use, sport, or population control
Example: *Farmers harvest the wheat in early autumn.*

hassle /hˈasəl/
to annoy persistently or acutely
Example: *He felt hassled by the many minor requirements.*

hasten /hˈeɪstən/
to move or act quickly
Example: *She hastened to finish the report before the deadline.*

hatch /hˈætʃ/
to produce young by incubation
Example: *The eggs hatched into tiny chicks.*
to bring into being
Example: *They hatched a plan to travel the world.*

hate /hˈeɪt/
to feel extreme enmity toward
Example: *He hated the idea of going back.*
to have a strong aversion to
Example: *I hate being lied to.*

haul /hˈɔːl/
to cause something to move by pulling or drawing
Example: *They hauled the boat onto the beach.*
to bring before an authority for interrogation or judgement
Example: *The suspect was hauled into court.*

head /hˈɛd/
to put the striking part of a weapon, tool, or implement on
Example: *He headed the nail with a single strike.*
to act as leader or director of
Example: *She headed the new project team.*
to get in front of to hinder, stop, or turn back
Example: *The police headed off the suspects at the pass.*

head-butt /hˈɛd- bˈʌt/
to hit someone deliberately on the head or face using the front of your head

Example: *The soccer player head-butts an opponent.*

heal /hˈiːl/
to make free from injury or disease
Example: *He healed her wound at the hospital.*
to patch up or correct
Example: *Time can heal many disagreements.*
to restore to original purity or integrity
Example: *They tried to heal the divisions within the community.*

hear /hˈiə/
to perceive or become aware of by the ear
Example: *Did you hear that noise?*
to listen to with attention
Example: *She heard his explanation but remained unconvinced.*

hearten /hˈɑːtən/
to give heart to
Example: *His kind words heartened her in her time of grief.*

heat /hˈiːt/
to become warm or hot
Example: *The room heated up quickly with the fire blazing.*
to start to spoil from heat
Example: *The food will heat and spoil if left out too long.*

heave /hˈiːv/
to utter with obvious effort or with a deep breath
Example: *He heaved a sigh of relief.*
to cause to swell or rise
Example: *The sea heaved beneath the boat.*
to draw, pull, or haul on
Example: *The crew heaved the anchor aboard.*

heckle /hˈɛkəl/
to harass and try to disconcert with questions, challenges, or gibes
Example: *The speaker was heckled by an angry crowd.*

hector /hˈɛktɐ/
to behave in an arrogant or intimidating way
Example: *He often hectored his subordinates.*

hedge /hˈɛdʒ/
to enclose or protect with or as if with a dense row of shrubs or low trees
Example: *They hedged the garden to provide privacy.*
to confine to prevent freedom of movement or action
Example: *The contract was hedged with numerous conditions.*
to protect oneself from losing or failing by a counterbalancing action
Example: *He hedged his investments to reduce risk.*

heed /hˈiːd/
to give consideration or attention to
Example: *They heeded the warnings before proceeding.*

heft /hˈɛft/
to heave up
Example: *He hefted the sack onto his shoulder.*
to test the weight of by lifting
Example: *She hefted the box to gauge its weight.*

help /hˈɛlp/
to give assistance or support to
Example: *Can you help me move this table?*
to make more pleasant or bearable
Example: *Music helped her get through the tough times.*

hem /hˈɛm/

to finish with a hem
Example: *She hemmed the new curtains perfectly.*
to surround in a restrictive manner
Example: *The troops were hemmed in by enemy forces.*
to utter the sound represented by hem
Example: *He hemmed and hawed over the decision.*

herald /hˈɛrəld/
to give notice of
Example: *The early flowers herald the coming of spring.*
to greet especially with enthusiasm
Example: *The crowd heralded the heroes with cheers.*
to signal the approach of
Example: *Dark clouds heralded the storm.*

hesitate /hˈɛsɪtˌeɪt/
to hold back in doubt or indecision
Example: *She hesitated before entering the abandoned house.*
to delay momentarily
Example: *He hesitated at the door, unsure whether to knock.*

hew /hjˈuː/
to cut with blows of a heavy cutting instrument
Example: *They hewed logs to build the cabin.*

hiccup /hˈɪkʌp/
to make a hiccup
Example: *He could not stop hiccupping after the spicy meal.*

hide /hˈaɪd/
to put out of sight
Example: *She hid the gifts in the closet.*
to keep secret

Example: *He could no longer hide the truth from his friends.*
to screen from or as if from view
Example: *The curtains hid the construction site.*
to turn away in shame or anger
Example: *She hid her face with her hands in embarrassment.*

hike /hˈaɪk/
to travel by any means
Example: *They hiked across the island on foot.*
to move, pull, or raise with a sudden motion
Example: *He hiked his backpack higher on his shoulders as he climbed.*

hinder /ˈhɪndɚ/
to make slow or difficult the progress of
Example: *The heavy snow hindered our travel plans.*
to hold back
Example: *She hindered his foolish actions.*

hint /hˈɪnt/
to convey indirectly and by allusion rather than explicitly
Example: *He hinted that there might be a surprise at the party.*

hiss /hˈɪs/
to make a sharp sibilant sound
Example: *The snake hissed at us from its hiding spot.*
to utter or whisper angrily or threateningly and with a hiss
Example: *She hissed a warning to her brother during the meeting.*

hit /hˈɪt/
to reach with or as if with a sudden blow
Example: *The baseball player hit the ball out of the park.*
to cause to come into contact

Example: *The car hit a tree during the storm.*
to affect especially detrimentally
Example: *The economic downturn hit the community hard.*
to make a request of
Example: *She hit her friend up for a loan.*
to discover or meet especially by chance
Example: *He hit on a brilliant idea while taking a shower.*
to indulge in excessively
Example: *She hit the snooze button one too many times.*

hitch /hˈɪtʃ/
to move by jerks or with a tug
Example: *He hitched the trailer to his truck with some difficulty.*
to catch or fasten by or as if by a hook or knot
Example: *She hitched her dress on a nail.*
to join in marriage
Example: *They got hitched in a small ceremony last weekend.*

hoard /hˈɔːd/
to collect and often hide away a supply of
Example: *He hoarded old newspapers in his attic.*
to keep to oneself
Example: *She hoarded her thoughts during the meeting.*

hobble /hˈɒbəl/
to move along unsteadily or with difficulty, especially limping along
Example: *The injured player hobbled off the field.*

hog /hˈɒg/
to cut short
Example: *He hogged the conversation, not letting anyone else speak.*
to cause to arch
Example: *The heavy books hogged the shelf downward.*
to take more than one's due

Example: *She hogged the blankets all night.*
to tear up or shred into bits by machine
Example: *The machine efficiently hogged the recycled materials.*

hoist /hˈɔɪst/
to raise into position by or as if by means of tackle
Example: *They hoisted the flag at dawn.*

hold /hˈəʊld/
to have possession or ownership of or have at one's disposal
Example: *She holds the title of the youngest champion.*
to keep under restraint
Example: *The police held the suspect at the scene.*
to make liable or accountable or bound to an obligation
Example: *The contract holds them to complete the work by next month.*
to prevent from leaving or getting away
Example: *The snowstorm held us captive in the cabin.*

holler /hˈɒlɐ/
to call or cry out
Example: *He hollered for help when he saw the rising waters.*

hone /hˈəʊn/
to sharpen or smooth with a whetstone
Example: *She honed her culinary skills over the years.*
to make more acute, intense, or effective
Example: *He honed his argument before the debate.*

honk /hˈɒŋk/
to make a sound resembling the cry of a goose
Example: *The car honked loudly at the pedestrians.*

hook /hˈʊk/
to form into a hook
Example: *He hooked his arm through hers as they walked.*
to seize or make fast by or as if by a hook
Example: *She hooked the fish with ease.*
to make by drawing loops of yarn, thread, or cloth through a coarse fabric with a hook
Example: *She hooked a beautiful rug for the living room.*
to work as a prostitute
Example: *She hooked to pay her bills after losing her job.*

hoot /hˈuːt/
to shout or laugh usually derisively
Example: *The audience hooted in disapproval.*
to make the natural throat noise of an owl or a similar cry
Example: *The owl hooted in the dark forest.*
to make a loud clamorous mechanical sound
Example: *The old engine hooted as it started up.*

hop /hˈɒp/
to move by a quick springy leap or in a series of leaps
Example: *The rabbit hopped across the lawn.*
to make a quick trip especially by air
Example: *We hopped a flight to Paris for the weekend.*
to set about doing something
Example: *He hopped right to work without delay.*

hope /hˈəʊp/
to desire with expectation of obtainment or fulfilment
Example: *She hopes to travel the world one day.*
to expect with confidence
Example: *He hopes that the weather will be good for the picnic.*

horrify /hˈɒrɪfˌaɪ/

to cause to feel horror
Example: *The scene of the accident horrified the onlookers.*
to fill with distaste
Example: *She was horrified by the lack of manners at the table.*

hound /hˈaʊnd/
to pursue with or as if with hounds
Example: *Reporters hounded the celebrity for comments.*
to drive or affect by persistent harassing
Example: *He was hounded by his past mistakes.*

hover /hˈɒvɐ/
to position over something without selecting it
Example: *The helicopter hovered above the crowded event.*
to be in a state of uncertainty, irresolution, or suspense
Example: *He hovered between accepting the job offer or starting his own business.*

howl /hˈaʊl/
to emit a loud sustained doleful sound characteristic of members of the dog family
Example: *The wolves howled at the moon.*
to cry out loudly and without restraint under strong impulse
Example: *The fans howled with excitement.*
to go on a spree or rampage
Example: *They howled through the night, celebrating their team's victory.*

huddle /hˈʌdəl/
to arrange carelessly or hurriedly
Example: *They huddled the documents in a pile on the desk.*
to crowd together
Example: *The team huddled together for warmth.*
to wrap oneself closely in

Example: *She huddled herself in a blanket as the night grew colder.*

huff /hˈʌf/
to emit puffs
Example: *He huffed in frustration as he struggled with the jar lid.*
to react or behave indignantly
Example: *She huffed at the accusation, denying any wrongdoing.*
to make angry
Example: *His dismissive remarks huffed her greatly.*

hug /hˈʌg/
to press tightly in one's arms especially as a sign of affection
Example: *They hugged each other tightly after the long journey.*
to stay close to
Example: *The path hugs the riverbank for miles.*
to hold fast
Example: *He hugged the belief that things would improve.*

hum /hˈʌm/
to utter a sound like that of the speech sound \m\ prolonged
Example: *She hummed a tune while cooking.*
to be busily active
Example: *The marketplace was humming with activity.*

humiliate /hjuːmˈɪlɪˌeɪt/
to reduce someone to a lower position in one's own eyes or others' eyes
Example: *He felt humiliated by the public criticism.*

humour /hjˈuːmɐ/
to soothe or content someone by indulgence
Example: *He humoured her whims without complaint.*
to adapt oneself to
Example: *She humoured the peculiarities of her reclusive uncle.*

hunch /hˈʌntʃ/
to push or put in a rough, careless, or hasty manner
Example: *He hunched the old furniture into the storeroom.*
to thrust or bend over into a humped or crooked position
Example: *She hunched over the desk, absorbed in her work.*

hunt /hˈʌnt/
to pursue for food or in sport
Example: *They hunt deer in these woods.*
to pursue with intent to capture
Example: *Detectives hunt the suspect across several states.*
to drive or chase especially by harrying
Example: *The hounds hunted the fox across the fields.*

hurl /hˈɜːl/
to send or thrust with great vigour
Example: *She hurled the ball towards the basket.*
to throw down with violence
Example: *The storm hurled branches and debris all over the streets.*
to utter with vehemence
Example: *He hurled insults at the opposing team.*

hurrah /hərˈɑː/
to express excitement, pleasure, or approval
Example: *The crowd hurrahed as the fireworks began.*

hurry /hˈʌri/
to carry or cause to go with haste
Example: *She hurried the children into the car.*
to impel to greater speed
Example: *He hurried to finish the project before the deadline.*

hurt /hˈɜːt/

to inflict with physical pain
Example: *The fall hurt his knee.*
to cause emotional pain or anguish to
Example: *His harsh words hurt her feelings.*

hurtle /hˈɜːtəl/
to move rapidly or forcefully
Example: *The car hurtled down the highway.*

hush /hˈʌʃ/
to put at rest
Example: *She hushed the baby with a gentle rocking.*
to keep from public knowledge
Example: *They hushed up the scandal to avoid embarrassment.*

hustle /hˈʌsəl/
to crowd or push roughly
Example: *He hustled through the crowded market.*
to obtain by energetic activity
Example: *She hustled to get referrals for her business.*

hypnotise /hˈɪpnətˌaɪz/
to induce hypnosis in
Example: *The therapist hypnotised him to help recover his lost memories.*
to influence by or as if by suggestion
Example: *She was easily hypnotised by his charismatic demeanour.*

Ii

idealise /aɪdˈiəlaɪz/
to attribute ideal characteristics to
Example: *She idealised her childhood, focusing only on the good parts.*
to treat idealistically
Example: *The author idealises rural life in his novels.*

identify /aɪdˈɛntɪfˌaɪ/
to perceive or state the identity of
Example: *The detective quickly identified the suspect in the line-up.*
to conceive as united
Example: *He identifies his personal success with hard work.*

idolise /ˈaɪdəlˌaɪz/
to love or admire to excess
Example: *Young fans often idolise celebrities, mimicking their styles and habits.*

ignite /ɪgnˈaɪt/
to set afire
Example: *The campers ignited the bonfire at dusk.*
to subject to fire or intense heat
Example: *The blacksmith ignites the iron before forging it.*
to set in motion
Example: *Her inspiring speech ignited a movement among the youth.*

ignore /ɪgnˈɔː/
to refuse to take notice of
Example: *He ignored the insulting remarks.*
to reject as ungrounded

Example: *She ignored the rumours, knowing they were false.*

illuminate /ɪlˈuːmɪnˌeɪt/
to supply or brighten with light
Example: *The new streetlights illuminate the previously dark neighbourhood.*
to make clear
Example: *The teacher illuminated complex topics with simple explanations.*
to decorate with gold or silver or brilliant colours or with often elaborate designs or miniature pictures
Example: *Medieval manuscripts were often illuminated by skilled artisans.*

illustrate /ˈɪləstrˌeɪt/
to provide with visual features intended to explain or decorate
Example: *The children's book was illustrated with colourful drawings.*
to make clear by giving or by serving as an example or instance
Example: *She illustrated her point with a well-chosen anecdote.*
to light up
Example: *His smile illustrated his face when he saw her.*

imagine /ɪmˈædʒɪn/
to form a mental image of
Example: *She imagined herself flying above the clouds.*
to form a notion of without sufficient basis
Example: *He imagined the worst possible outcome for his test results.*

imbibe /ɪmbˈaɪb/
to take in or up
Example: *He imbibed the beautiful scenery on his hike.*
to receive into the mind and retain

Example: *She imbibed the knowledge from the lecture eagerly.*

imitate /ˈɪmɪtˌeɪt/
to follow as a pattern, model, or example
Example: *Young artists often imitate the styles of their predecessors.*
to be or appear like
Example: *He imitates his favourite rock stars by dressing like them.*
to produce a copy of
Example: *The factory imitates popular brand designs at lower prices.*

immerse /ɪmˈɜːs/
to plunge into something that surrounds or covers
Example: *He immersed himself in the warm bath after a long day.*
to baptise by immersion
Example: *The priest immersed the man in holy water.*

immolate /ˈɪməˌleɪt/
to kill or destroy especially by fire
Example: *The ancient city was tragically immolated during the war, as vividly depicted in the historical novel.*
to offer in sacrifice
Example: *Ancient cultures would immolate offerings to appease their gods.*

impair /ɪmpˈeə/
to diminish in function, ability, or quality
Example: *Excessive gaming impairs his ability to focus on studies.*

impale /ɪmpˈeɪl/
to pierce with or as if with something pointed
Example: *The knight impaled the dragon with his spear.*
to fix in an inescapable or helpless position

Example: *The scandal impaled his career, leaving him no escape from public scrutiny.*
to join on a heraldic shield divided vertically by a pale
Example: *The family crest was impaled to signify the union of two noble houses.*

impart /ɪmpˈɑːt/
to give, convey, or grant from or as if from a store
Example: *The teacher imparted wisdom and knowledge to her students.*
to communicate the knowledge of
Example: *He imparted his plans to the team with clarity.*

impede /ɪmpˈiːd/
to interfere with or slow the progress of
Example: *Heavy snow impeded the morning commute.*

implant /ˈɪmˌplɑnt/
to fix or set securely or deeply
Example: *The surgeon implanted the medical device into her heart.*
to insert in living tissue
Example: *The new technique involves implanting electrodes in the brain.*

implore /ɪmplˈɔː/
to ask or beg earnestly
Example: *She implored him to reconsider his decision to leave.*

imply /ɪmplˈaɪ/
to involve or indicate by inference, association, or necessary consequence rather than by direct statement
Example: *His silence implies agreement.*
to contain potentially

Example: *The document implies certain conditions that are not explicitly stated.*

import /ɪmˈpɔːt/
to bring from a foreign or external source
Example: *The company imports most of its raw materials from abroad.*
to bear or convey as meaning or portent
Example: *Her actions import a significant change in attitude.*

impose /ɪmpˈəʊz/
to establish or apply by authority
Example: *The government imposed new taxes.*
to force into the company or on the attention of another
Example: *He imposed his presence on the gathering, despite being uninvited.*
to arrange in the proper order for printing
Example: *The printer imposed the pages of the brochure to streamline the production process.*

impress /ˈɪmˌprɛs/
to affect especially forcibly or deeply
Example: *Her speech impressed the audience with its sincerity.*
to apply with pressure to imprint
Example: *The artist impressed his signature into the clay.*

imprint /ˈɪmprɪnt/
to mark by or as if by pressure
Example: *The experience imprinted itself deeply on his mind.*
to fix indelibly or permanently
Example: *The trauma imprinted itself on her memory.*

imprison /ɪmprˈɪzən/

to put in or as if in prison
Example: *The unjust law imprisoned thousands of innocents.*

improve /ɪmprˈuːv/
to enhance in value or quality
Example: *She improved her skills by taking online sources.*
to use for good purpose
Example: *He improved his time by learning a new language.*

improvise /ˈɪmprəvˌaɪz/
to compose, recite, play, or sing extemporaneously
Example: *The musician improvised a solo on stage.*
to make, invent, or arrange offhand
Example: *He improvised a meal from the few ingredients he had left.*

inaugurate /ɪnˈɔːgjʊrˌeɪt/
to induct into an office with suitable ceremonies
Example: *The president was inaugurated on a cold January morning.*

inch /ˈɪntʃ/
to move by small degrees
Example: *He inched closer to the stage to get a better view.*

incline /ˈɪnklaɪn/
to lean, tend, or become drawn toward an opinion or course of conduct
Example: *She is inclined to agree with you.*
to bend the head or body forward
Example: *He inclined his head in respect.*

include /ɪnklˈuːd/
to take in or comprise as a part of a whole or group

Example: *The conference includes participants from over fifty countries.*
to contain between or within
Example: *The book includes many photographs.* to shut up
Example: *The shelter includes the animals to keep them safe during the storm.*

increase /'ɪnˌkrɪs/
to become progressively greater
Example: *Her interest in the subject increased as she studied more.*
to multiply by the production of young
Example: *The rabbit population in the area has increased rapidly.*

incriminate /ɪnkr'ɪmɪnˌeɪt/
to charge with or show evidence or proof of involvement in a crime or fault
Example: *The evidence incriminated several high-profile individuals in the scandal.*

indent /ˌɪn'dɛnt/
to set something, such as a line of a paragraph, in from the margin
Example: *The first line of each paragraph was indented.*
to notch the edge of
Example: *The craftsman indented the soft metal to create a decorative pattern.*
to draw up in two or more exactly corresponding copies
Example: *The contract was indented in triplicate.*

indicate /'ɪndɪkˌeɪt/
to point out or point to
Example: *The signs indicate the exit routes.*
to state or express briefly
Example: *The report indicated the need for more research.*

induce /ɪndjˈuːs/
to move by persuasion or influence
Example: *The advertisement induced many customers to try the new product.*
to cause the formation of
Example: *Certain conditions induce the formation of crystals.*
to infer from particulars
Example: *From the symptoms, the doctor induced that the patient was suffering from an allergic reaction.*

indulge /ɪndˈʌldʒ/
to yield to the desire of
Example: *He indulged his craving for sweets.*
to give free rein to
Example: *She indulged her imagination, dreaming of travelling the world.*

infect /ɪnfˈɛkt/
to contaminate with a disease-producing substance or agent
Example: *The patient was infected with a rare virus.*
to work upon or seize upon to induce sympathy, belief, or support
Example: *Her enthusiasm infected the whole team.*

infer /ɪnfˈɜː/
to derive as a conclusion from facts or premises
Example: *From the evidence, the jury inferred the defendant's guilt.*

infest /ɪnfˈɛst/
to spread or swarm in or over in a troublesome manner
Example: *The kitchen was infested with ants.*
to live in or on as a parasite
Example: *The fish are infested with a type of worm that can be harmful to humans.*

inflame /ɪnfl'eɪm/
to cause to redden or grow hot from anger or excitement
Example: *The unfair accusation inflamed his temper.*
to excite to excessive or uncontrollable action or feeling
Example: *The speech inflamed the crowd.*
to set on fire
Example: *The dry brush was quickly inflamed by the sparks.*
to cause inflammation in
Example: *The infection inflamed her throat, making it difficult to swallow.*

inflame /ɪnfl'eɪm/
to cause to redden or grow hot from anger or excitement
Example: *The unfair accusation inflamed his temper.*
to excite to excessive or uncontrollable action or feeling
Example: *The speech inflamed the crowd.*
to set on fire
Example: *The dry brush was quickly inflamed by the sparks.*
to cause inflammation in
Example: *The infection inflamed her throat, making it difficult to swallow.*

inflate /ɪnfl'eɪt/
to swell or distend with air or gas
Example: *The balloon inflated rapidly when filled with helium.*
to expand or increase abnormally or imprudently
Example: *The stock market inflated so it worried the economists.*
to puff up
Example: *His ego inflated after receiving the prestigious award.*

inflect /ɪnfl'ɛkt/
to change or vary the pitch of
Example: *She inflected her voice to express different emotions.*
to affect or alter noticeably

Example: *His mood inflected the tone of the entire meeting.*
to turn from a direct line or course
Example: *The path inflected sharply to the right.*
to vary a word by inflection
Example: *In some schools, inflecting verbs correctly is very essential for the learning process.*

influence /ˈɪnfluːəns/
to affect or alter by indirect or intangible means
Example: *His childhood experiences influenced his outlook on life.*
to have an effect on the condition or development of
Example: *Nutrition influences a child's cognitive development.*

inform /ɪnfˈɔːm/
to communicate knowledge to
Example: *The teacher informed the students about the test.*
to give character or essence to
Example: *Historical events inform the novelist's books.*

infuse /ɪnfjˈuːz/
to cause to be permeated with something that alters usually for the better
Example: *The chef infused the sauce with fresh herbs for better flavour.*
to steep in liquid without boiling to extract the soluble constituents or principles
Example: *She infused the water with lavender to make a relaxing tea.*
to administer or inject by infusion
Example: *The patient was infused with antibiotics over several hours.*

ingest /ɪndʒˈɛst/
to take in for or as if for digestion
Example: *The baby bird ingests worms fed by its mother.*

inhale /ɪnhˈeɪl/
to draw in by breathing
Example: *She took a deep breath and inhaled the fresh morning air.*
to take in eagerly or greedily
Example: *He inhaled his dinner after a long day of work.*

initiate /ˌɪˈnɪʃiˌeɪt/
to cause or facilitate the beginning of
Example: *The program was initiated to improve literacy among children.*
to induct into membership by or as if by special rites
Example: *The fraternity initiates its new members with a series of challenges.*
to instruct in the rudiments or principles of something
Example: *The workshop initiates beginners into the basics of woodworking.*

inject /ɪndʒˈɛkt/
to introduce into something forcefully
Example: *The doctor injected the medication into the patient's bloodstream.*
to introduce as an element or factor in or into some situation or subject
Example: *The author injects a sense of humour into the otherwise sombre narrative.*

injure /ˈɪndʒɐ/
to inflict bodily hurt on
Example: *The player was injured during the football match.*
to harm, impair, or tarnish the standing of
Example: *The scandal seriously injured his reputation.*

ink /ˈɪŋk/
to draw or write in ink
Example: *She inked her thoughts in her diary every night.*

to affix one's signature to
Example: *The CEO inked the contract after months of negotiations.*

inquire /ɪnkwˈaɪə/
to put a question
Example: *He inquired about the application process.*
to make investigation or inquiry
Example: *The detective inquired into the details of the case.*

inscribe /ɪnskrˈaɪb/
to write, engrave, or print as a lasting record
Example: *His name was inscribed on the trophy.*
to dedicate to someone
Example: *The book was inscribed to his mentor.*
to draw within a figure so as to touch in as many places as possible
Example: *The artist inscribed a circle within the square.*
to register the name of the holder of
Example: *They inscribed her name on the list of club members.*

insert /ˈɪnˌsɜt/
to put or thrust in
Example: *She inserted the key into the lock.*
to be in attachment to the part to be moved
Example: *The engineer inserted the bolt through the hole to secure the beam.*

insinuate /ɪnsˈɪnjuːˌeɪt/
to impart or suggest in an artful or indirect way
Example: *His comments insinuated that there was an undisclosed reason for the policy change.*

insist /ɪnsˈɪst/

to be emphatic, firm, or resolute about something intended, demanded, or required
Example: *She insisted that everyone be treated with respect.*

inspect /ɪnspˈɛkt/
to view closely in critical appraisal
Example: *The inspector inspected the construction site for safety violations.*

inspire /ɪnspˈaɪə/
to spur on
Example: *His courage inspired his team to push forward despite the challenges.*
to draw forth or bring out
Example: *The teacher's method inspired creativity in her students.*
to spread rumour by indirect means or through the agency of another
Example: *Social media inspired people's interest in the event.*

install /ɪnstˈɔːl/
to set up for use or service
Example: *The technician installed the new software on our computers.*
to establish in an indicated place, condition, or status
Example: *They installed him as the new chairman of the board.*

instigate /ˈɪnstɪɡˌeɪt/
to goad or urge forward
Example: *He instigated the protesters to violence.*

instruct /ɪnstrˈʌkt/
to provide with authoritative information or advice
Example: *The coach instructed the players on how to improve their technique.*

insult /ˈɪnˌsəlt/
to treat with insolence, indignity, or contempt
Example: *His rude remarks insulted his competitor.*

interact /ˌɪntərˈækt/
to act upon one another
Example: *The chemicals interact to produce a dramatic reaction.*

intercept /ˌɪntɚˈsɛpt/
to stop, seize, or interrupt in progress or course or before arrival
Example: *The police intercepted the stolen goods before they left the city.*
to include between two points, curves, or surfaces
Example: *The road intercepts the stream at several points.*

interfere /ˌɪntəfˈiə/
to enter or take a part in the concerns of others
Example: *He interfered in his friend's marital disputes.*
to strike one foot against the opposite foot or ankle in walking or running
Example: *His feet interfered, causing him to stumble.*

interject /ˌɪntədʒˈɛkt/
to throw in between or among other things
Example: *She interjected witty comments throughout the conversation.*

interlace /ˌɪntəlˈeɪs/
to unite by or as if by lacing together
Example: *The storylines of the film were cleverly interlaced.*
to vary by alternation or intermixture
Example: *The novel interlaces humour with tragedy, creating a rich narrative texture.*

interlock /ˌɪntəlˈɒk/
to become locked together or interconnected
Example: *The gears interlock perfectly, ensuring smooth operation of the machine.*

interpret /ɪntˈɜːprɪt/
to explain or tell the meaning of
Example: *The professor interpreted the ancient text for his students.*

interrogate /ɪntˈɛrəɡˌeɪt/
to question formally and systematically
Example: *The detective interrogated the suspect for several hours.*
to give or send out a signal to trigger an appropriate response
Example: *The software interrogates the system to ensure all components function properly.*

interrupt /ˈɪntərˌʌpt/
to stop or hinder by breaking in
Example: *The sudden storm interrupted the outdoor concert.*

intertwine /ˌɪntətwˈaɪn/
to unite by twining one with another
Example: *The vines intertwined around the old fence.*

intervene /ˌɪntəvˈiːn/
to occur, fall, or come between points of time or events
Example: *The government intervened to stabilise the economic crisis.*

interview /ˈɪntəvjˌuː/
a meeting at which information is obtained from a person
Example: *She was interviewed by the manager for the position.*

intone /ɪntˈəʊn/
to utter in musical or prolonged tones
Example: *The priest intoned the prayers during the ceremony.*

introduce /ˌɪntrədjˈuːs/
to lead to or make known by a formal act, announcement, or recommendation
Example: *He introduced me to his colleague, Dr. Smith.*

invent /ɪnvˈɛnt/
to produce for the first time using the imagination or of ingenious thinking and experiment
Example: *He invented a new way to store renewable energy.*

inventory /ˈɪnvəntrˌi/
to make an inventory of
Example: *We need to inventory the warehouse items by next week.*

invert /ˌɪnˈvɜːt/
to reverse in position, order, or relationship
Example: *The software inverts colours to enhance accessibility.*

investigate /ɪnvˈɛstɪɡˌeɪt/
to observe or study by close examination and systematic inquiry
Example: *Scientists are investigating the causes of the mysterious disease.*

invite /ˌɪnˈvaɪt/
to request the presence or participation of
Example: *We invited several experts to the conference.*

invoke /ɪnvˈəʊk/
to petition for help or support

Example: *The villagers invoked the deity during the drought.*

irritate /ˈɪrɪtˌeɪt/
to provoke impatience, anger, or displeasure in
Example: *The constant noise from the construction site irritated the office workers.*

iterate /ˈɪtərˌeɪt/
to say or do again or again and again
Example: *The teacher iterated the importance of homework to the students.*

Jj

jab /dʒˈab/
to push or drive quickly, abruptly, or forcefully
Example: *She jabbed the needle into the fabric.*

jabber /dʒˈabɐ/
to talk rapidly, indistinctly, or unintelligibly
Example: *The children jabbered excitedly about their day.*

jam /dʒˈam/
to become blocked, wedged, or stuck fast
Example: *The paper jammed in the printer again.*
to improvise on a musical instrument with a group
Example: *They jammed together on Friday nights.*

jangle /dʒˈaŋɡəl/
to make a harsh or discordant often ringing sound
Example: *The keys jangled in her pocket.*
to quarrel verbally
Example: *They jangled over the smallest issues.*
to talk idly
Example: *He jangled on about nothing in particular.*

jeer /dʒˈiə/
to speak or cry out with derision or mockery
Example: *The crowd jeered at the speaker.*

jerk /dʒˈɜːk/
to give a quick, suddenly arrested push, pull, or twist to
Example: *He jerked the door open.*
to mix and serve behind a soda fountain

Example: *He jerks sodas at the local diner.*
to preserve in long sun-dried slices
Example: *His family usually jerked meat for preservation.*

jest /dʒˈɛst/
to say things intended to be humorous
Example: *He loved to jest with his friends.*

jibe /dʒˈaɪb/
to be in accord
Example: *Their stories jibe perfectly.*
to utter taunting words
Example: *He jibed at his opponent during the debate.*

jiggle /dʒˈɪɡəl/
to cause to move with quick little jerks or oscillating motions
Example: *She jiggled the handle to open the door.*

jingle /dʒˈɪŋɡəl/
to make a light clinking or tinkling sound
Example: *The bells jingled as she walked.*
to rhyme or sound in a catchy repetitive manner
Example: *The commercial's jingle was stuck in my head.*

jog /dʒˈɒɡ/
to run or ride at a slow trot
Example: *They jogged through the park every morning.*
to rouse to alertness
Example: *The loud noise jogged his memory.*
to give a slight shake or push to
Example: *She jogged his arm to get his attention.*
to align the edges by hitting or shaking against a flat surface
Example: *He jogged the papers into a neat stack.*

join /dʒˈɔɪn/
to put or bring together to form a unit
Example: *They joined hands and sang together.*

joke /dʒˈoʊk/
to say something to provoke laughter
Example: *He joked about the situation to lighten the mood.*

jolt /dʒˈoʊlt/
to interfere with roughly, abruptly, and disconcertingly
Example: *The sudden stop jolted the passengers.*

jostle /dʒˈɒsəl/
to come in contact or into collision
Example: *The shoppers jostled each other during the sale.*

judge /dʒˈʌdʒ/
to form an opinion about through careful weighing of evidence and testing of premises
Example: *She judged the national dancing competition.*

juggle /dʒˈʌgəl/
to handle or deal with usually several things at one time to satisfy often competing requirements
Example: *She juggled work, school, and family responsibilities.*

jumble /dʒˈʌmbəl/
to move in a confused or disordered manner
Example: *The letters were jumbled together in the box.*

jump /dʒˈʌmp/
to spring into the air
Example: *The cat jumped onto the table.*

to move haphazardly or irregularly
Example: *The stock prices jumped all over the place.*
to make a sudden physical or verbal attack
Example: *He jumped at the chance to prove himself.*

justify /dʒˈʌstɪfˌaɪ/
to prove or show to be just, right, or reasonable
Example: *She justified her actions to her boss.*
to make even by spacing lines of text
Example: *The text was justified to align with both margins.*

jut /dʒˈʌt/
to extend out, up, or forward
Example: *The rocks jutted out over the water.*

Kk

keen /kˈiːn/
to lament, mourn, or complain loudly
Example: *The mourners keened over the loss.*

keep /kˈiːp/
to retain in one's possession or power
Example: *She kept all her old letters.*
to take notice of by appropriate conduct
Example: *They keep the tradition alive.*
to maintain in a good, fitting, or orderly condition
Example: *He keeps his room very tidy.*
to restrain from departure or removal
Example: *They were kept indoors due to the storm.*

kick /kˈɪk/
to strike out with the foot or feet
Example: *The child kicked the ball across the field.*
to show opposition
Example: *He kicked against the decision.*
to function with vitality and energy
Example: *The new policy really kicked things into gear.*

kid /kˈɪd/
to gently criticise or tease in a friendly or good-humoured way
Example: *They kid him about his new haircut.*

kill /kˈɪl/
to cause the death of a person, animal, or plant
Example: *The hunter killed the deer.*
to make a markedly favourable impression

Example: *She really killed it at the audition.*

kiss /kˈɪs/
to touch with the lips especially as a mark of affection or greeting
Example: *She kissed her mother on the cheek before leaving.*

knead /nˈiːd/
to work and press into a mass with or as if with the hands
Example: *She kneaded the dough until it was smooth.*

knee /nˈiː/
to strike with the knee
Example: *He accidentally kneed the table while getting up.*

kneel /nˈiːl/
to position the body so that one or both knees rest on the floor
Example: *They knelt in prayer during the service.*

knit /nˈɪt/
to form by interlacing yarn or thread in a series of connected loops with needles
Example: *She knitted a scarf for her friend.*
to link firmly or closely
Example: *Their shared experiences knitted them together as friends.*

knock /nˈɒk/
to strike something with a sharp blow
Example: *He knocked on the door before entering.*
to make a pounding noise
Example: *The pipes knocked loudly in the cold weather.*
to find fault
Example: *She always knocks his ideas without considering them fully.*

knot /nˈɒt/
to tie in or with a knot
Example: *He knotted the rope securely.*
to unite closely or intricately
Example: *Their lives were knotted together in unexpected ways.*

know /nˈəʊ/
to be or become cognizant
Example: *She knows the answer to the question.*
to have knowledge
Example: *He knows a lot about ancient history.*

kowtow /kˈaʊtaʊ/
to show obsequious deference
Example: *He refused to kowtow to the unreasonable demands.*
to kneel and touch the forehead to the ground in token of homage, worship, or deep respect
Example: *They kowtowed before the altar.*

Ll

label /lˈeɪbəl/
to describe or designate with or as if with a label
Example: *She labelled all the boxes for the move.*

lace /lˈeɪs/
to draw together the edges of by or as if by a lace passed through eyelets
Example: *She laced up her shoes tightly.*
to mark with streaks of colour
Example: *The sky was laced with pink and orange hues.*
to add something to impart pungency, savour, or zest to
Example: *He laced the punch with a bit of lemon juice.*
to make a verbal attack
Example: *She laced into him for being late.*

lament /lɐmˈɛnt/
to express sorrow, mourning, or regret for often demonstratively
Example: *They lamented the loss of their beloved pet.*

land /lˈɑnd/
to set or put on shore from a ship
Example: *The ship landed its passengers safely.*
to cause to reach or come to rest in a particular place
Example: *He landed the plane smoothly.*
to catch and bring in
Example: *She landed a big fish during the trip.*

languish /lˈɑŋgwɪʃ/
to be or become feeble, weak, or enervated
Example: *The plants languished in the drought.*

to assume an expression of grief or emotion appealing for sympathy
Example: *He languished in the hope of receiving a reply.*

lap /lˈap/
to fold over or around something
Example: *She lapped the blanket around the baby.*
to hold protectively in or as if in the lap
Example: *He lapped the puppy in his arms.*
to shape or fit by working two surfaces together with or without abrasives until a very close fit is produced
Example: *The craftsman lapped the metal pieces precisely.*
to traverse a course
Example: *The runner lapped his competitors.*

lash /lˈaʃ/
to move violently or suddenly
Example: *The wind lashed at the trees.*
to make a verbal attack or retort
Example: *He lashed out at his critics.*
to bind with or as if with a line
Example: *They lashed the poles together with rope.*

latch /lˈatʃ/
to lay hold with or as if with the hands or arms
Example: *The child latched onto his mother's leg.*
to associate oneself intimately and often artfully
Example: *She latched onto the idea immediately.*
to make fast with or as if with a latch
Example: *He latched the gate securely.*

lather /ˈlaðɚ/
to form a lather or a froth like lather
Example: *The soap quickly lathered in the water.*
to beat severely

Example: *He lathered the carpet to remove the stain.*

laud /lˈɔːd/
to praise someone or something
Example: *The critics lauded her performance.*

laugh /lˈɑːf/
to show emotion with a chuckle or explosive vocal sound
Example: *They laughed at the joke.*
to utter with a laugh
Example: *She laughed out her response.*

launch /lˈɔːntʃ/
to release, catapult, or send off
Example: *They launched the rocket into space.*
to enter energetically
Example: *He launched into his speech with enthusiasm.*

lavish /lˈavɪʃ/
to expend or bestow with profusion
Example: *She lavished attention on her guests.*

lay /lˈeɪ/
to beat or strike down with force
Example: *The storm laid the trees flat.*
to put or set down
Example: *He laid the book on the table.*
to bring forth and deposit
Example: *The hen laid an egg.*
to press down giving a smooth and even surface
Example: *The workers laid the concrete smoothly.*
to dispose or spread over or on a surface
Example: *She laid the cloth over the table.*

to impose as a duty, burden, or punishment
Example: *They laid the responsibility on him.*

lead /ˈlid/
to guide on a way especially by going in advance
Example: *She led the group through the forest.*
to direct the operations, activity, or performance of
Example: *He led the team to victory.*
to be first
Example: *She led in the polls.*

leaf /ˈliːf/
to shoot out or produce leaves
Example: *The trees leafed in spring.*
to turn over pages specially to browse or skim
Example: *She leafed through the magazine.*

lean /ˈliːn/
to incline, deviate, or bend from a vertical position
Example: *He leaned against the wall.*
to rely for support or inspiration
Example: *She leaned on her friends for support.*
to incline in opinion, taste, or desire
Example: *He leans towards classical music.*
to make lean
Example: *They lean the meat before cooking.*

leap /ˈliːp/
to spring free from or as if from the ground
Example: *The frog leaped into the pond.*
to pass abruptly from one state or topic to another
Example: *She leaped from one idea to another.*

leave /lˈiːv/
to cause to remain as a trace or aftereffect
Example: *The storm left a path of destruction.*
to cause or allow to be or remain in a specified condition
Example: *He left the door open.*
to go away from
Example: *She left the house early.*
to put, deposit, or deliver before or in the process of departing
Example: *He left the package at the door.*

lecture /lˈɛktʃɐ/
to deliver a lecture or a course of lectures
Example: *She lectured on ancient history.*
to reprove formally
Example: *He lectured the students on the importance of punctuality.*

leer /lˈiə/
to cast a sidelong glance
Example: *He leered at her from across the room.*

lend /lˈɛnd/
to give for temporary use on condition that the same or its equivalent be returned
Example: *She lent him her book.*
to give the assistance or support of
Example: *He lent his support to the project.*

lengthen /lˈɛŋθən/
to make longer
Example: *She lengthened the skirt by adding more fabric.*

let /lˈɛt/
to cause to

Example: *Let me know if you need any help.*
to permit to enter, pass, or leave
Example: *He let the dog out.*
to make an adjustment to
Example: *She let out the hem of the dress.*

level /lˈɛvəl/
to make a line or surface horizontal
Example: *He levelled the picture frame.*
to knock down
Example: *The storm levelled the small shack.*
to make even or uniform
Example: *They levelled the playing field.*
to deal frankly and openly
Example: *It is time to level with you about the situation.*

license /lˈaɪsəns/
to give permission or consent to
Example: *The state licensed her to practise medicine.*

lick /lˈɪk/
to lap with or as if with the tongue
Example: *The dog licked his hand.*
to strike repeatedly
Example: *The flames licked the walls of the building.*

lie /lˈaɪ/
to be or to stay at rest in a horizontal position
Example: *She lies on the couch every afternoon.*
to be in a helpless or defenceless state
Example: *The town lay in ruins.*
to make an untrue statement with intent to deceive
Example: *He lied about his whereabouts.*
to create a false or misleading impression

Example: *The photo lies about the true size of the house.*

lift /lˈɪft/
to raise from a lower to a higher position
Example: *She lifted the box onto the table.*

light /lˈaɪt/
to become light
Example: *The sky began to light as dawn approached.*
to take fire
Example: *The kindling lighted quickly.*
to ignite something
Example: *He lights candles during his romantic dinners with his wife.*

lighten /lˈaɪtən/
to make light or clear
Example: *The paint will lighten the room.*
to become lighter or less burdensome
Example: *The load lightened as they used up supplies.*
to become more cheerful
Example: *Her mood lightened when she heard the good news.*

like /lˈaɪk/
to feel attraction toward or take pleasure in
Example: *I like chocolate.*
to wish to have
Example: *She would like a cup of tea.*

lilt /lˈɪlt/
to sing or play in a lively cheerful manner
Example: *He lilted a merry tune.*

limp /lˈɪmp/
to walk with an uneven and usually slow movement or gait
Example: *He limped after twisting his ankle.*
to proceed slowly or with difficulty
Example: *The project limped along due to lack of funding.*

linger /lˈɪŋgɚ/
to be slow in parting or in quitting something
Example: *They lingered over coffee after dinner.*
to remain existent although often waning in strength, importance, or influence
Example: *The scent of her perfume lingered in the room.*

lisp /lˈɪsp/
to pronounce the sibilants \s\ and \z\ imperfectly especially by turning them into \th\ and \th̲\
Example: *The child lisped adorably.*
to speak falteringly, childishly, or with a lisp
Example: *He lisped his words nervously.*

list /lˈɪst/
to have or show a list of
Example: *The book lists all the ingredients.*
to become entered in a catalogue with a selling price
Example: *The house is listed for sale.*
to tilt to one side
Example: *The ship listed to port.*
to cut away a narrow strip from the edge of
Example: *He listed the board to make it smooth.*
to place in a specified category
Example: *They listed the symptoms for diagnosis.*

listen /lˈɪsən/
to pay attention to sound

Example: *She listened to the music intently.*

live /ˈlɪv/
to be alive
Example: *He lived a long life.*
to maintain oneself
Example: *They live on a small income.*
to occupy a home
Example: *They live in a beautiful house.*
to remain in human memory or record
Example: *His name will live on in history.*
to have a life rich in experience
Example: *She knows how to live.*

load /ˈləʊd/
to put a load in or on
Example: *They loaded the truck with supplies.*
to place as a burden or obligation
Example: *The task loaded him with responsibilities.*
to place or be a material weight or physical stress on
Example: *The roof was loaded with snow.*
to become copied or transferred into memory for use or display on a digital device
Example: *The program is loading on my computer.*

loaf /ˈləʊf/
to spend time in idleness
Example: *They loafed around the house all day.*

lob /ˈlɒb/
to let hang heavily
Example: *The branch lobbed over the fence.*
to throw, hit, or propel easily or in a high arc
Example: *He lobbed the ball over the net.*

to direct to elicit a response
Example: *She lobbed a question at the speaker.*

locate /ləʊkˈeɪt/
to determine or indicate the place, site, or limits of
Example: *They located the source of the leak.*

lock /lˈɒk/
to fasten in or out or to make secure or inaccessible by or as if by means of locks
Example: *He locked the door behind him.*
to make fast, motionless, or inflexible especially by the interlacing or interlocking of parts
Example: *The gears locked into place.*

log /lˈɒg/
to cut trees for lumber
Example: *They logged the forest for timber.*
to make a note or record of
Example: *She logged her hours in the journal.*
to move an indicated distance or attain an indicated speed as noted in a
log
Example: *The ship logged 500 miles in one day.*

loiter /lˈɔɪtɐ/
to delay an activity with idle stops and pauses
Example: *They loitered in the park after school.*
to remain in an area for no obvious reason
Example: *The teenagers loitered outside the store.*

loll /lˈɒl/
to hang loosely or laxly

Example: *His tongue lolled out of his mouth.*
to act or move in a lax, lazy, or indolent manner
Example: *They lolled on the couch all afternoon.*

long /lˈɒŋ/
to feel a strong desire or craving especially for something not likely to be attained
Example: *She longed for a vacation.*

look /lˈʊk/
to make sure or take care
Example: *The child looked both ways before crossing the street.*
to ascertain using one's eyes
Example: *She looked out the window.*
to have an appearance that befits or accords with
Example: *He looks happy.*

loom /lˈuːm/
to come into sight in enlarged or distorted and indistinct form often because of atmospheric conditions
Example: *The mountains loomed in the distance through the fog.*
to appear in an impressively great or exaggerated form
Example: *The deadline loomed large in her mind.*

loop /lˈuːp/
to make or form a loop
Example: *He looped the rope around the post.*
to cause to move in an arc
Example: *The plane looped in the sky.*

loosen /lˈuːsən/
to release from restraint
Example: *She loosened the dog's leash.*

to make looser
Example: *He loosened his tie after the meeting.*
to relieve the bowels of constipation
Example: *The medicine helped to loosen his bowels.*
to cause or permit to become less strict
Example: *They loosened the rules for the event.*

lope /lˈəʊp/
to move or ride at a lope
Example: *The horse loped across the field.*

lose /lˈuːz/
to bring to destruction
Example: *He lost everything in the fire.*
to miss from one's possession or from a customary or supposed place
Example: *She lost her keys again.*
to suffer deprivation of
Example: *They lost their home in the flood.*
to fail to keep, sustain, or maintain
Example: *He lost his job due to downsizing.*

lounge /lˈaʊndʒ/
to act or move idly or lazily
Example: *They lounged by the pool all afternoon.*

love /lˈʌv/
to hold dear
Example: *She loves her family deeply.*
to feel a lover's passion, devotion, or tenderness for
Example: *He loves his partner with all his heart.*
to like or desire actively
Example: *I love pizza!*
to thrive in
Example: *These plants love the sun.*

lower /ˈloʊɚ/
to look sullen
Example: *He lowered his gaze in anger.*
to be or become dark, gloomy, and threatening
Example: *The sky lowered as the storm approached.*
to reduce in value, number, or amount
Example: *They lowered the prices for the sale.*
to depress as to direction
Example: *She lowered the blinds.*

lug /lˈʌg/
to carry laboriously
Example: *He lugged the heavy suitcase up the stairs.*
to introduce in a forced manner
Example: *She lugged the unrelated topic into the conversation.*

lull /lˈʌl/
to cause to sleep or rest
Example: *The gentle rocking of the boat lulls her to sleep.*
to cause to relax vigilance
Example: *The calm before the storm lulled them into a false sense of security.*

lumber /lˈʌmbɚ/
to move ponderously
Example: *The bear lumbered through the forest.*
to clutter with or as if with lumber
Example: *The garage was lumbered with old furniture.*
to heap together in disorder
Example: *They lumbered all the items into one corner.*
to log and saw the timber of
Example: *They lumbered the forest for wood.*

lunge /lˈʌndʒ/

to move with or as if with a lunge
Example: *The fencer lunged at his opponent.*
to perform a lunge exercise
Example: *She lunged forward in her workout routine.*

lurch /lˈɜːtʃ/
to move with a lurch
Example: *The car lurched forward unexpectedly.*
to roll or tip abruptly
Example: *The ship lurched in the rough seas.*
to defeat by a lurch
Example: *They were lurched out of the competition at the last moment.*

lure /lˈɔː/
to recall or exercise by means of a lure
Example: *The falconer lured the bird back with food.*
to draw with a hint of pleasure or gain
Example: *The ad lured customers into the store.*

lurk /lˈɜːk/
to lie in wait in a place of concealment especially for an evil purpose
Example: *The thief lurked in the shadows.*
to read messages without contributing on an Internet discussion forum or social media platform
Example: *He lurked on the forum, reading but never posting.*

Mm

made /mˈeɪd/
create or produce
Example: *She made a beautiful painting.*
cause to exist or happen
Example: *The announcement made everyone excited.*
formulated or constructed
Example: *They made a plan for the project.*
achieved or attained
Example: *He made his goals for the year.*
prepared or assembled
Example: *She made a delicious dinner.*
earned or gained
Example: *He made a lot of money from his investments.*
constituted or amounted to
Example: *Her efforts made a big difference.*

maintain /meɪntˈeɪn/
to keep something in good condition or preserve it
Example: *He maintains his car well to ensure it runs smoothly.*
to support or uphold a belief, opinion, or argument
Example: *She maintains that exercise is essential for health.*
to continue to have or hold onto something
Example: *They maintain a close friendship despite the distance.*
to provide for the sustenance or livelihood of someone or something
Example: *He works hard to maintain his family.*
to affirm or assert something strongly
Example: *She maintains her innocence in the matter.*

manage /mˈanɪdʒ/
to handle or control

Example: *She managed the situation with great skill.*
to direct or supervise
Example: *He manages a team of engineers.*
to succeed in accomplishing
Example: *She managed to finish the project on time.*
cope with or handle successfully
Example: *He managed his stress through meditation.*
to be in charge of or responsible for
Example: *She manages the daily operations of the store.*
to achieve one's aims
Example: *He managed to get the promotion he wanted.*
to administer or run
Example: *She manages the finances for the organisation.*

manoeuvre /mənˈuːvɐ/
to move or glide skilfully
Example: *Sarah manoeuvred the car through heavy traffic.*
to perform a planned movement
Example: *The military unit manoeuvred into position.*
to manipulate or handle in a skilful manner
Example: *Sam manoeuvred the negotiations to his advantage.*
to scheme or plan carefully
Example: *They manoeuvred to gain control of the company.*
to execute tactical movements, especially in warfare or competition
Example: *The team manoeuvred to outwit their opponents.*

mangle /mˈaŋgəl/
to severely damage or mutilate by crushing or twisting
Example: *The machine mangled the fabric.*
to ruin or spoil, especially through clumsiness or incompetence
Example: *He mangled the presentation with his poor delivery.*

manhandle /mˈanhandəl/
to handle roughly or aggressively

Example: *The security guard manhandled the protester out of the building.*

manipulate /mənˈɪpjʊlˌeɪt/
to control or influence skilfully, especially in an unfair or deceptive manner
Example: *He manipulated the situation to his advantage.*
to handle or operate with skill
Example: *She manipulated the controls with precision.*
to alter or change, often in a skilful or subtle manner
Example: *He manipulated the data to show a favourable result.*
to arrange in a skilful way
Example: *She manipulated the pieces to fit perfectly.*

manufacture /mˌanjuːfˈaktʃɐ/
to produce goods or products, typically in large quantities, especially by using machinery or industrial processes
Example: *The factory manufactures thousands of cars each year.*

manoeuvre /mənˈuːvɐ/
to move or glide skilfully
Example: *Sarah manoeuvred the car through heavy traffic.*
to perform a planned movement
Example: *The military unit manoeuvred into position.*
to manipulate or handle in a skilful manner
Example: *Sam manoeuvred the negotiations to his disadvantage.*
to scheme or plan carefully
Example: *They manoeuvred to gain control of the company.*
to execute tactical movements, especially in warfare or competition
Example: *The team manoeuvred to outwit their opponents.*

mangle /mˈaŋɡəl/
to severely damage or mutilate by crushing or twisting

Example: *The car was mangled in the accident, leaving it almost unrecognisable.*

to ruin or spoil, especially through clumsiness or incompetence

Example: *The priest mangled the speech by mispronouncing several keywords.*

to cut or tear something, often fabric or flesh, with jagged or irregular edges

Example: *The machine mangled the cloth, leaving it unusable.*

manipulate /mən'ɪpjʊlˌeɪt/

to control or influence skilfully, especially in an unfair or deceptive manner

Example: *Surgeons must learn to manipulate their instruments with great precision.*

to handle or operate with skill

Example: *Sara tried to manipulate the outcome of the meeting to benefit her own interests.*

to alter or change, often in a skilful or subtle manner

Example: *The company was accused of manipulating the financial records to hide losses.*

manufacture /mˌanjuːˈfaktʃɐ/

to produce goods or products, typically in large quantities, especially by using machinery or industrial processes

Example: *The factory manufactures thousands of cars every month.*

map /mˈap/

to create a visual representation or diagram of an area, showing its geographical features, such as roads, rivers, and landmarks

Example: *The cadets mapped the route to Lethem two weeks before their patrol.*

to plan or outline something systematically

Example: *D'Nae will map the program for the 2024 Girls Guide Summer Camp.*

to associate or relate one set of information or concepts to another

Example: *I like how the presenter mapped hospitality services and tourism in her presentation.*

march /mˈɑːtʃ/

to walk with regular and measured steps, especially in a military formation or procession

Example: *The troops marched across the field with precision.*

advancing steadily and purposefully

Example: *The workers marched toward the factory to demand better wages.*

walking in a forceful manner

Example: *The angry protesters marched through the streets chanting slogans.*

causing movement in a direction

Example: *The strong wind marched the leaves across the yard.*

mark /mˈɑːk/

to make a visible impression or indication

Example: *The painter marked where the new door frame would go with a pencil.*

to signify or identify

Example: *The red flag marks the location of the buried treasure.*

to grade or evaluate

Example: *The teacher marked the students' essays over the weekend.*

to note or acknowledge

Example: *His achievements mark him as one of the best athletes in the country.*

to leave a trace or evidence

Example: *The scratches on the floor mark where the furniture used to be.*

market /mˈɑːkɪt/
to promote or sell goods or services
Example: *Your product will not sell itself; you must market it effectively.*
to engage in commercial activity
Example: *The car dealership markets its cars using a new strategy quarterly.*
to analyse and target a specific audience or demographic
Example: *Walking vendors in Guyana, market their goods to housewives and the elderly, who seldom leave their homes to shop.*

marry /mˈɑri/
to join in marriage
Example: *John and Jane decided to marry in a small ceremony by the beach.*
to unite or combine two things
Example: *The flavours of chocolate and peanut butter marry perfectly in this dessert.*
to perform a marriage ceremony
Example: *The minister will marry the couple at the church next Sunday.*

marvel /mˈɑːvəl/
to be astonished or amazed
Example: *I always marvel at the beauty of the sunset.*
to admire or wonder at something
Example: *Children often marvel at the magic tricks performed by magicians.*
to be surprised or impressed by something
Example: *Jason marvelled at her intelligence and wit.*

mash /mˈɑʃ/
to crush or smash something into a soft mass

Example: *Sarah mashed the potatoes with a fork until they were creamy.*

to mix or stir ingredients together until smooth

Example: *We need to mash the butter and sugar together before adding the flour.*

mask /mˈɑːsk/

to cover or conceal something

Example: *Shanice masked her pregnancy under loose clothing and bulky sweaters for seven months.*

to disguise or hide one's identity

Example: *Anil masks his identity as a Trinidadian by speaking French only amongst his colleagues.*

to alter or change the appearance or sound of something

Example: *The kidnapper masked his voice when he called her parents.*

massage /mˈɑsɑːʒ/

to manipulate the muscle and soft tissues of the body for therapeutic purposes or relaxation

Example: *Kaitlin gently massaged the nape of her neck to ease the tension she felt.*

match /mˈatʃ/

to correspond or be identical to something

Example: *John matched his stride to Susan's as they took their morning walk for the first time after her accident.*

to pair or combine items that complement each other

Example: *The girls will match their turquoise shoes with turquoise and pink purses.*

to compete against someone or something in a contest or game

Example: *Battalion 6 cadets are matched against Battalion 4 cadets for the triathlon games.*

to compare or evaluate two things for similarity or compatibility

Example: *The two explorers matched their findings and were in awe at the similarities they had discovered in such diverse locations.*

mate /ˈmeɪt/
to pair animals for breeding
Example: *The zookeepers mated the tigers in hopes of increasing the population.*
to join as a pair or couple
Example: *The puzzle pieces mate perfectly.*
to match or complement each other
Example: *These colours mate well together in the painting.*

matter /mˈatɐ/
to be of importance or significance
Example: *You matter to this family, Dad.*
to be relevant or have relevance
Example: *As the lone survivor of the crash, what he must report matters.*
to be of consequence or have an effect
Example: *Does it matter whether I speak up or not?*

maul /mˈɔːl/
to handle or treat roughly or violently
Example: *She was mauled by the angry bear*

maunder /mˈɔːndɐ/
to talk or move in a rambling, aimless manner
Example: *Kristen continued to maunder on about her trip to Alaska.*
to wander or stroll idly
Example: *Still in shock from the news, he maundered aimlessly along the shores of the river.*
to speak or write in a confused or meaningless way

Example: *Jermaine maundered on about his mother's untimely death in a strange land.*

mean /mˈiːn/
to intend to convey or signify
Example: *What do you mean by that?*
to have a purpose or goal
Example: *Studying hard means you will do well on the exam.*
to indicate or denote something
Example: *The red light means stop.*
to have a particular significance or importance
Example: *The results of the experiment mean a breakthrough in cancer research.*
to result in or bring about
Example: *Missing the bus means I will be late for work.*

meander /miːˈandɐ/
to follow a winding or indirect course
Example: *The river meanders through the valley.*
to wander aimlessly or casually
Example: *We meandered through the streets of the old town, enjoying the architecture.*
to move slowly or idly
Example: *The hiker meandered along the forest trail, taking in the scenery.*

measure /mˈɛʒɐ/
to ascertain the dimensions, quantity, or capacity of something
Example: *The students each measured their desk using handspans.*
to gauge or determine the amount, extent, or degree of something
Example: *The field behind my school measures 4 kilometres by 6 kilometres.*
to be a standard unit of measurement

Example: *I will measure three cups of peas; you measure out the flour.*

to act based on a particular standard or criteria

Example: *The guard took measures to ensure that the lock could not be broken.*

to compare or evaluate something against a standard or benchmark

Example: *Dave measured his accomplishments against those of his brothers.*

meddle /mˈɛdəl/
to interfere or involve oneself in someone else's business or affairs without being asked or invited

Example: *Adrian constantly meddles in Jeremiah's affairs.*

mediate /mˈiːdɪˌeɪt/
to intervene or reconcile in a dispute between two or more parties

Example: *The headteacher mediated the discord between the science and maths teachers.*

to bring about a settlement or agreement through negotiation or arbitration

Example: *This counsellor is known for mediating satisfactorily on behalf of both parties.*

meditate /mˈɛdɪtˌeɪt/
to focus one's mind for a period, often for relaxation or spiritual purposes

Example: *Amy meditates every morning before starting her day.*

to ponder or reflect deeply on a particular subject

Example: *Aaron meditated on the meaning of life while sitting by the lake.*

to engage in mindfulness or breathing exercises to achieve a state of calmness and clarity

Example: *The yoga class ended with a session of meditating.*

meet /mˈiːt/
to come into the presence or company of someone or something
Example: *I meet Joe on my way home from school every day.*
to fulfil or satisfy a requirement or condition
Example: *The reality of the job did not meet the hype of the advertisement.*
to have a confrontation or encounter, often in a formal setting
Example: *We meet at crossroads every time we have a budget presentation at my company.*
to experience or undergo
Example: *I meet my best self when working under pressure.*

melt /mˈɛlt/
to change from a solid to a liquid state due to heat
Example: *As the temperature steadily rose, the butter melted before our eyes.*
to disappear or vanish gradually
Example: *The weird truck had melted into thin air.*

memorise /mˈɛmɔːrˌaɪz/
to learn and remember something by heart or through repetition
Example: *The group of five-year olds had memorised the planets of the Solar System.*

menace /mˈɛnɪs/
to threaten or pose a danger to someone or something
Example: *The class prefect was menaced by the grade 7 students.*
to behave in a threatening or aggressive manner
Example: *The commander menaced the ranks with threats of dismissal.*

mend /mˈɛnd/
to repair or fix something that is broken or damaged
Example: *How can you mend a broken heart?*

to improve or make better
Example: *Tyrell mended his relationship with his mother after eleven years.*
to heal or recover from an injury or illness
Example: *Saskia is mending nicely after her nasty fall while biking.*
to amend or correct a mistake or fault
Example: *Todd mended his attitude and the band welcomed him back with open arms.*

mention /mˈɛnʃən/
to refer to or bring up something briefly in speech or writing
Example: *Please, do not mention my name in that meeting.*

mentor /mˈɛntɔː/
to advise, guide, or train someone, especially someone younger or less experienced, over a period
Example: *Sarah mentored Jules throughout the ninth grade.*

meow /mɪˈaʊ/
the sound a cat makes
Example: *The tabby meowed insistently as the key turned in the lock of the front door.*

mesh /mˈɛʃ/
to fit or interlock together closely
Example: *The gears meshed perfectly, allowing the machinery to function smoothly.*
to coordinate or harmonise well with something else
Example: *Her ideas and mine meshed seamlessly, leading to a successful collaboration.*
to become entangled or caught up in something
Example: *The fishing net meshed with the propeller, causing it to jam.*

to connect or integrate different systems or components
Example: *The software meshes with our existing infrastructure, simplifying our workflow.*

mew /mjˈuː/
to make a high-pitched, plaintive cry, often characteristic of a cat or kitten
Example: *The kittens mew when they are hungry.*
to confine or enclose, especially in a small or restricted space
Example: *The prisoners were mewed in tiny cells.*
to moult or shed feathers, as in the case of birds
Example: *The hawk mewed as it moulted its old feathers.*

migrate /maɪgrˈeɪt/
to move from one place to another, often for breeding, feeding, or environmental reasons
Example: *The birds will migrate soon.*

milk /mˈɪlk/
to draw or extract milk from an animal
Example: *The farmer milks the cows twice a day.*
to exploit or take advantage of something for benefit or profit
Example: *The company tried to milk the situation for all it was worth.*
to express or squeeze out liquid from something
Example: *Dawn milked the lemon to get juice for the recipe.*
to nurture or encourage a situation or feeling to continue for one's own advantage
Example: *The politician tried to milk sympathy from the audience during the speech.*

mime /ˈmaɪm/
to perform a dramatic or comedic act without speaking, using only gestures, facial expressions, and body movements to convey meaning

Example: *She mimed her distress and the observant officer rescued her.*

mimic /mˈɪmɪk/
to imitate or copy the actions, speech, or appearance of someone or something
Example: *Toddlers mimic the gestures of their parents.*

mince /mˈɪns/
to cut or chop into small pieces
Example: *Kimmy minced the garlic finely for the sauce.*
to walk with short, quick steps in an affectedly dainty manner
Example: *Laura minces along in her high heels.*
to express oneself delicately or euphemistically, often to avoid causing offence
Example: *He minces his words when giving criticism.*

mind /mˈaɪnd/
to be concerned or pay attention to something
Example: *Please mind your manners at the dinner table.*
to take care of or attend to something
Example: *Can you mind the store while I run an errand?*
to object or feel offended by something
Example: *Do you mind if I open the window?*
to remember or bear in mind
Example: *Mind your keys; you do not want to forget them.*
to obey or follow instructions
Example: *The dog minds its owner's commands.*

mine /mˈaɪn/
to dig or extract minerals or resources from the earth
Example: *The workers mine coal from the underground shafts.*
to search carefully or systematically to obtain information
Example: *Journalists often mine social media for new stories.*

to exploit or utilise something for gain or advantage
Example: *Jim mined his personal experiences for material in his novel.*
to extract valuable information or data from a large dataset
Example: *The analyst mined the company's sales data for insights.*

mingle /mˈɪŋgəl/
to mix or blend
Example: *Eve mingled the ingredients for the cake batter.*
to socialise or interact with others in a casual or relaxed manner
Example: *Guests mingled at the cocktail party, chatting, and enjoying appetisers.*
to move or go among people or things
Example: *Harry mingled through the crowd, trying to find his friends.*
to combine or merge into a single entity
Example: *The aromas of the different spices mingled together in the kitchen.*

misdirect /mɪsdaɪrˈɛkt/
to give someone incorrect or misleading information or instruction
Example: *The mischievous students misdirected the teacher who was looking for the library.*
to aim or send something in the wrong direction.
Example: *The archer misdirected the arrow and it shattered Mr. Paul's window.*

mishear /mɪsˈhˈiə/
to hear something incorrectly or inaccurately
Example: *The sniper misheard the instruction and opened fire causing the suspect to escape.*

misjudge /mɪsdʒˈʌdʒ/

to form an incorrect or inaccurate opinion or assessment about someone or something
Example: *The officer misjudged the situation and was about to arrest the teen who was helping the elderly lady.*

mislead /mɪsl'iːd/
to give someone the wrong idea or impression, typically by giving false or incomplete information
Example: *Savitree was misleading them about her interest in studying Theology all alone.*

mispronounce /mɪsprən'aʊns/
to pronounce a word incorrectly
Example: *Everyone finds it funny when my baby brother mispronounces my name.*

miss /m'ɪs/
to fail to hit, reach, or catch something
Example: *The great Rohan Kanhai missed the ball completely.*
to fail to attend, participate in, or experience something
Example: *I missed the bus and had to walk to school.*
to feel the absence or loss of something or someone
Example: *I miss my family when I am away from home.*
to fail to notice or perceive something
Example: *I missed the fine print at the bottom of the contract.*
to fail to achieve or reach a target or goal
Example: *Hanna missed the deadline for submitting her assignment.*

misspell /mɪssp'ɛl/
to spell a word incorrectly
Example: *Brandon missed the word by one letter.*

mistake /mɪstˈeɪk/
to identify or interpret something incorrectly
Example: *I mistook her for someone else because of the similar hairstyle.*
to confuse or misinterpret one thing as something else
Example: *Do not mistake his silence for agreement; he might just be thinking.*
to make an error or blunder
Example: *I mistook the time of the meeting and arrived an hour early.*
to misunderstand or misinterpret someone's words or actions
Example: *Jenna mistook his kindness for romantic interest.*

misunderstand /mɪsˌʌndəstˈand/
to fail to understand or interpret something correctly
Example: *If Wilburg misunderstands basic maths, how is it he plans to pursue studies in Physics?*

mix /mˈɪks/
to combine or blend different substances or ingredients together
Example: *"Mix the dry and wet ingredients thoroughly." Mum said, sternly.*
to interact socially with others in a casual or informal manner
Example: *I can hardly wait to see how the pre-schoolers from the two schools will mix on the playground.*

moan /mˈəʊn/
to make a low, mournful sound, indicating pain, discomfort, or dissatisfaction
Example: *The injured dog moaned softly.*
to express one's unhappiness or discontent audibly
Example: *June moaned about the long hours she had to work.*
to express a strong desire or longing for something
Example: *The child moaned for ice cream.*

mock /mˈɒk/
to ridicule or make fun of someone or something in a contemptuous or derisive manner
Example: *The bullies mocked him for his torn clothes.*
to mimic or imitate someone or something in a mocking or sarcastic way
Example: *Denny mocked Drew's accent, which hurt her feelings.*
to treat something with scorn or contempt
Example: *They mocked the idea of cooperation, preferring to work alone.*
to simulate or pretend something for practice or demonstration purposes
Example: *The students mocked a debate to prepare for the competition.*

model /mˈɒdəl/
to serve as an example or pattern to be imitated or followed
Example: *Model the new high schools after the old multilateral schools.*
to pose for an artist or photographer to be depicted in a work of art
Example: *Naomi modelled Cleopatra with poise and ease.*
to create a representation or simulation of something to study or analyse it
Example: *Have the design for the new car modelled so it can be properly analysed.*
to demonstrate or showcase something as an example of excellence or best practice
Example: *Model the replica of Stabroek Market built by your company, at the Berbice Expo today.*

modify /mˈɒdɪfˌaɪ/
to make changes or alterations to something to improve or adjust it
Example: *The exam was modified to suit the shortened school term.*

moisten /mˈɔɪstən/
to make something slightly wet or damp
Example: *She nervously moistened her lips as she prepared to speak.*

molest /məlˈɛst/
to harass, abuse, or harm someone
Example: *He was arrested for molesting children in the neighbourhood.*
to bother, annoy, or disturb someone persistently
Example: *The mosquitoes molested us all night, preventing us from sleeping.*
to interfere with or disturb something in a harmful or unwanted way
Example: *The construction noise molested the peace and quiet of the neighbourhood.*

mollify /mˈɒlɪfˌaɪ/
to soothe, calm, or pacify someone's anger, agitation, or distress
Example: *The passage of time did nothing to mollify his resentment towards his parents.*

mollycoddle /mˈɒlɪkˌɒdəl/
to treat someone with excessive indulgence or care, often to the point of being overprotective
Example: *The constant mollycoddling he was accustomed to left him with a stinking attitude.*

monitor /mˈɒnɪtɐ/
to observe, watch, or keep track of something over time
Example: *She monitors her heart rate while exercising.*
to check or oversee the progress, performance, or condition of something
Example: *The teacher monitors the students' progress throughout the semester.*
to listen to or intercept communications for specific purposes

Example: *The government monitors phone calls for potential threats.*
to display or show information continuously for reference or control
Example: *The computer monitors the temperature of the room.*

moo /mˈuː/
the sound made by a cow
Example: *The cow mooed frightenedly as the scorching brand was placed on her rump.*

moor /mˈɔː/
to secure a boat or ship in place by anchoring or tying it to a fixed object, such as a dock or buoy
Example: *It was a struggle in the lashing rain, but the sailor moored the boat successfully.*

mope /mˈəʊp/
to be gloomy, dejected, or listless, especially while sulking or feeling sorry for oneself
Example: *It has been two weeks since her cat died, and she is still moping.*

mosey /mˈəʊsi/
to move or walk in a leisurely or relaxed manner, with no particular destination in mind
Example: *I mosey along among the orchids on lazy days.*

motion /mˈəʊʃən/
to make a gesture or movement with one's head, hand, or body to convey a message or signal
Example: *Chad motioned excitedly to his friends, pointing out to sea.*
to suggest or propose something formally during a meeting or discussion

Example: *The chairman motioned for the minutes of the previous meeting to be made accessible to the board.*

motivate /mˈəʊtɪvˌeɪt/
to provide someone with a reason or incentive to do something, typically by arousing their interest, enthusiasm, or desire
Example: *I am motivated to start swimming lessons this summer, because it is to be held at the Pegasus poolside.*

mould /mˈəʊld/
to shape or form something
Example: *She moulded the clay into a vase.*
to influence or shape someone's character, behaviour, or opinions over time
Example: *Parents play a significant role in moulding their children's values.*
to deteriorate or decay over time, often due to being exposed to moisture
Example: *The bread began to mould after being left out in the humid air.*

mount /mˈaʊnt/
to climb or ascend onto something
Example: *Kaleigh mounted the horse with ease.*
to fix or attach something securely in place
Example: *Dad mounted clocks in every room of the house.*
to increase in intensity, magnitude, or importance
Example: *Excitement steadily mounted as the horses thundered around the corner and into sight.*

mourn /mˈɔːn/
to feel or express deep sorrow or grief over the loss of someone or something

Example: *The family still mourns the tragic loss of Jason by drowning.*

mouth /ˈmaʊθ/
to articulate or pronounce words with one's mouth
Example: *She mouthed the words silently to avoid being overheard.*

move /mˈuːv/
to change position or location
Example: *Move the shelves from over counter to the beside the microwave.*
to stir or be emotionally affected
Example: *Jack's speech moved us to tears.*

mow /ˈmoʊ/
to cut down grass or other vegetation with a mower
Example: *Randy mows grass in his neighbourhood to earn money for school.*
to make a sweeping or cutting motion with a weapon or tool
Example: *In one thoughtless act, the tree that had stood for centuries was mowed down.*

muffle /mˈʌfəl/
to wrap or cover something to reduce or deaden sound
Example: *Ellen muffled her sobs with her fist.*

mug /mˈʌg/
to attack someone in a public place, typically to rob them
Example: *They had already mugged her before we could warn her.*
to make exaggerated facial expressions, especially for comedic effect or to mimic someone

Example: *Yearbook photos were a disaster this year as the students mugged weird faces every time their photos were taken.*

mull /mˈʌl/
to think deeply and at length about something
Example: *We mulled over solutions for the unfair dismissal of our colleague, into the early hours of the morning.*
to heat, sweeten, and flavour wine or cider with spices
Example: *My grandma tried mulling her jamon wine with cloves, but it did not taste as expected.*

multiply /ˈməltəˌplaɪ/
to increase in number or quantity
Example: *If you multiply six by three, you get eighteen.*
to reproduce or generate offspring
Example: *Rabbits multiply quickly, so they can become a nuisance in gardens.*
to duplicate or replicate something
Example: *Martha plans to multiply her savings by investing in the stock market.*
to become more numerous or widespread
Example: *As rumours spread, they can multiply and cause panic.*

mumble /mˈʌmbəl/
to speak indistinctly or in a low voice, making it difficult for others to understand
Example: *The bullet riddled man mumbled the word pinecone, several times before he died.*

munch /ˈməntʃ/
to eat something steadily and often audibly
Example: *Bugs Bunny is often seen munching on a carrot.*

murder /mˈɜːdɐ/
to unlawfully kill someone with premeditation or malice
Example: *My friend was brutally murdered several years ago.*

murmur /mˈɜːmɐ/
to speak softly or indistinctly
Example: *We watched helplessly as the charlatan murmured into the ear of the unsuspecting elderly patient.*

muse /mjˈuːs/
to ponder or meditate on something deeply
Example: *We mused over the findings of the judge in the case of the missing teens.*
to be absorbed in one's thoughts, often to the point of distraction
Example: *I mused over the loss of my finances and determined never to be duped again.*

muss /mˈʌs/
to make something messy or untidy
Example: *Brian affectionately mussed up his little brother's hair.*

mutilate /mjˈuːtɪlˌeɪt/
to severely damage or disfigure something by cutting off or removing a part of it
Example: *The enraged man mutilated the body of the man he found his wife with.*

mutter /mˈʌtɐ/
to speak or utter something in a low, indistinct, or barely audible manner, often expressing discontent, annoyance, or disapproval
Example: *Jessie muttered under her breath in annoyance at Kyle's imposition.*

Nn

nag /nˈɑg/
to repeatedly complain or criticise someone about small, unimportant things
Example: *Wives, do not nag at your husbands.*

nail /nˈeɪl/
to fasten or attach something with nails
Example: *They nailed her to the cross because of her insensitive comment.*
to accomplish or achieve something successfully
Example: *Ashanti nailed the triple jump on her first attempt.*
to identify or catch someone in the act of doing something wrong
Example: *The hidden camera helped police nail the kidnapper before she escaped.*

name /nˈeɪm/
to give a title or label to someone or something
Example: *They named their baby daughter Lily.*
to identify or designate someone or something
Example: *Can you name all the counties in Guyana?*
to mention or specify someone or something
Example: *Heather named the ingredients needed for the recipe.*
to appoint or nominate someone for a particular role or position
Example: *The president named him as the ambassador to India.*

nap /nˈɑp/
to sleep for a short period of time
Example: *Children under 6 years old should nap after lunch every day.*

narrate /nɐrˈeɪt/
to tell or describe a story or event
Example: *Max Ehrmann narrates a powerful poem called the 'Desiderata'.*

narrow /nˈɑrəʊ/
to become less in width or to make something less wide
Example: *The driveway narrowed to a strip that could not be traversed by vehicle.*
to limit or restrict
Example: *Failing the last exam narrowed my chances of being chosen for the scholarship.*
to reduce the scope or range of something
Example: *Constant disappointments have narrowed my expectations of people.*

navigate /nˈɑvɪgˌeɪt/
to plan and follow a route, typically for travel
Example: *He navigates the seas expertly.*

neaten /nˈiːtən/
to make something tidy or orderly
Example: *Be sure to neaten your braids before leaving for school.*

need /nˈiːd/
signifies a requirement or necessity for something
Example: *I need peace and quiet after a long day at school.*

neglect /nɪglˈɛkt/
to fail to care for or pay attention to something properly
Example: *Their neglect of the property resulted in its rapid deterioration.*

negotiate /nɪgˈoʊʃiˌeɪt/
to discuss or bargain to reach an agreement
Example: *The union will negotiate for better working conditions for its members.*

neigh /nˈeɪ/
the sound made by a horse
Example: *Chestnut neighed frightenedly when he spotted the rattlesnake.*

nest /nˈɛst/
to build or settle into a nest
Example: *The birds nested in the tree outside our window.*
to arrange or place things in a nested or layered manner
Example: *Gail nested the smaller bowls inside the larger ones for storage.*
to find or create a comfortable or cosy space
Example: *Paul nested into the corner of the couch with a good book.*
to embed one set of data or code within another
Example: *The HTML tags are properly nested to ensure the webpage displays correctly.*

nestle /nˈɛsəl/
to settle or snuggle comfortably or closely in a place or against someone or something
Example: *We found the kitten nestled against C'mas in her kennel.*

nibble /nˈɪbəl/
to take small bites or gentle bites, usually of food
Example: *Adrian nibbled sleepily at his sandwich.*

nick /nˈɪk/

to make a small cut or notch in something
Example:	*The car's bumper was nicked in a minor accident.*
to steal or take something, often in a small or surreptitious manner
Example:	*Someone nicked my pen from my desk.*
to catch or snag on something
Example:	*Her sweater got nicked on a nail as she walked by.*
to arrest or apprehend someone
Example:	*The police nicked the suspect as he tried to flee the scene.*
to make a mistake or error
Example:	*Justina nicked the recipe and forgot to add sugar.*

nicker /nˈɪkɐ/
the soft, low sound made by a horse, often as a sign of contentment or greeting
Example:	*Champion nickered and tossed his head when he saw Chelsey approaching the stall.*

nip /nˈɪp/
to bite or pinch something lightly with the teeth or beak
Example:	*The puppy nipped at my fingers while playing.*
to cause a sharp, stinging sensation
Example:	*The cold wind nipped at my cheeks as I walked outside.*
to cut or trim something quickly and lightly
Example:	*The tailor nipped the loose threads off the edge of the fabric.*
to move or act quickly and briefly
Example:	*She nipped into the room t grab her coat.*
to seize or catch something quickly
Example:	*The goalkeeper nipped the ball before it crossed the goal line.*

nod /nˈɒd/

to move the head up and down as a gesture of agreement or acknowledgement
Example: *The traumatised child could only nod in response to the questions the counsellor asked.*
to move the head forward and downward, usually as a sign of drowsiness or sleepiness
Example: *Kent nodded off on the bus while on his way home from work.*

nominate /nˈɒmɪnˌeɪt/
to propose or officially suggest someone for a position, role, or honour
Example: *Mrs. Ross is the best person to nominate for the job.*

normalise /nˈɔːməlˌaɪz/
to make something conform to a standard or norm, or to make something usual or typical
Example: *Normalise allowing your children to express their views on matters of importance to them.*

notch /nˈɒtʃ/
to cut a V-shaped groove or indentation into something
Example: *The hunter notched his arrow before taking aim.*
to achieve or reach a particular level or position, often by gradual progress
Example: *The company notched record profits last quarter.*
to distinguish or mark something as significant
Example: *His performance notched him as a rising star in the music industry.*

note /nˈəʊt/
to observe or pay attention to something
Example: *Doreen noted the changes in her son's behaviour.*
to make a brief written record of something
Example: *The secretary noted the meeting time in her calendar.*

to acknowledge or recognize something
Example: *The club noted his contribution to the project.*
to mention or point out something for consideration
Example: *The teacher noted the errors in the students' homework.*

notice /nˈəʊtɪs/
to become aware of something or to observe something
Example: *Have you noticed how dark the clouds are this morning?*

notify /nˈəʊtɪfˌaɪ/
to inform someone about something officially or formally
Example: *The principal notified the parents of the amendment of the school's rules.*

nudge /nˈʌdʒ/
to push or poke someone gently, often to draw their attention or encourage them to act
Example: *She nudged her way through the crowd to see the dancers in the ring.*

number /ˈnəmbɚ/
to assign a number to something to identify or classify
Example: *The librarian numbered each book in the library for easy organisation.*
to be a certain quantity or amount
Example: *The books in the series number five in total*
to include or count as part of a group
Example: *She numbers among the top students in her class.*
to list or enumerate items or individuals
Example: *Number the parents who come to collect their cash grant, in batches of one hundred.*

nurse /nˈɜːs/

to provide medical care or attention to someone who is ill or injured
Example: *Fay nursed her grandmother through her final days.*
to breastfeed a baby
Example: *The mother nursed her new-born in the quiet corner of the room.*
to foster or encourage the development or growth of something
Example: *Gary nursed his ambition to become a professional athlete.*
to hold or cradle something gently
Example: *Beth nursed the injured bird in her hands until it recovered.*

nuzzle /nˈʌzəl/
to gently rub or press one's nose or face against someone or something, often as a sign of affection or comfort
Example: *Daisy nuzzled the palm of Ellea's hand, as she stroked her mane.*

Oo

obey /əʊbˈeɪ/
to comply with or follow the commands, orders, or instructions of someone in authority
Example: *Children obey your parents in the Lord.*

object /əbˈdʒɛkt/
to express opposition or disagreement with something
Example: *Chad vehemently objected to being pulled from the squad.*

oblige /əblˈaɪdʒ/
to compel or require someone to do something, typically because of a legal, moral, or social duty
Example: *As parents, you are obliged to provide for the well-being of your children.*

observe /ɒbzˈɜːv/
to watch or notice something carefully
Example: *Donna observed a bird building a nest in the tree outside her window.*
to follow or abide by a law, rule, or custom
Example: *It is important to observe traffic laws while driving.*
to celebrate or commemorate a particular event or occasion
Example: *We will observe Veterans Day with a ceremony at the memorial.*
to perform a scientific or systematic study or analysis
Example: *Scientists observe the behaviour of animals in their natural habitat.*

obsess /ɒbsˈɛs/

to preoccupy or consume one's thoughts or feelings excessively, often to the point of being unhealthy or detrimental
Example: *Dexter was obsessed with winning the male skateboarding championship.*

obtain /ɒbtˈeɪn/
to acquire or get something
Example: *Reagan obtained twelve passes at the 2023 CAPE examination.*

occupy /ˈɒkjʊpˌaɪ/
to reside or live in a place
Example: *The doctors occupy the house next door.*
to fill or take up space
Example: *The large sofa occupies most of the living room.*
to hold or control
Example: *The army occupies the territory to maintain peace.*
to engage or involve someone's attention or time
Example: *His studies occupy most of his free time.*
to be in a position or job
Example: *Amy occupies a key position in the company.*

occur /əkˈɜː/
to happen, take place, or come into existence
Example: *It never occurred to me to change the seating arrangements.*

offend /əfˈɛnd/
to cause someone to feel upset, insulted, or displeased
Example: *It was not my intention to offend the visiting team of cricketers.*

offer /ˈɒfɐ/

to present or propose something for someone to accept or reject
Example: *She offered him a cup of coffee while they discussed the project.*
to provide or make available for use
Example: *The hotel offers complimentary breakfast to its guests.*
to express willingness or readiness to do something
Example: *He offered to help carry the groceries.*
to present for consideration or judgement
Example: *The lawyer offered evidence to support his case.*
to make a bid or proposal in a competition or auction
Example: *Henry offered the highest bid for the painting.*

officiate /əfˈɪʃɪˌeɪt/
to perform an official duty or function, typically in a formal or ceremonial context
Example: *The committee requested that the President of the club officiate the ceremony.*

ogle /ˈɒɡəl/
to look at someone or something amorously or with desire, often in a way that is considered impolite or inappropriate
Example: *I saw him ogling the pretty waitress.*

ooze /ˈuːz/
to flow or seep out slowly
Example: *The sap oozed from the tree trunk after it was cut.*
to exude or emit something in a gradual and natural manner
Example: *The wound oozed blood for several minutes before clotting.*
to display or convey a certain quality or characteristic
Example: *Her confidence oozed from every word we spoke.*
to give an impression or appearance of something
Example: *The old house oozes charm and character.*

open /ˈəʊpən/
to unfasten or unlock something so that it can be accessed
Example: *Deon opened the door and stepped outside.*
to start or begin a business, event, or activity
Example: *The new restaurant will open next week.*
to reveal or disclose information
Example: *The detective opened the investigation into the missing person case.*
to spread out or expand
Example: *The flower petals opened in the warmth of the morning sun.*

operate /ˈɒpərˌeɪt/
to control or manage the functioning of a machine, system, or organisation
Example: *Jerry operates the machinery in the factory.*
to perform a surgical procedure
Example: *The surgeon will operate on the patient's knee tomorrow.*
to function or work in a particular way
Example: *The computer operates using advanced software.*
to conduct or carry out a task or activity
Example: *The detective operates undercover to gather information.*
to control or direct something for a particular purpose
Example: *The manager operates the business efficiently to maximise profits.*

opine /əʊpˈaɪn/
to express an opinion or to state one's beliefs on a matter
Example: *The entire team opined that the manager was unfit and should be replaced.*

oppose /əpˈəʊz/

to resist, reject, or be against someone or something
Example: *There was no one to oppose the marriage of the obviously drunk couple.*

opt /ˈɒpt/
to make a choice or decision, especially by selecting one option over others
Example: *The young couple opted to wait two years before starting a family.*

orate /ˈɔːreɪt/
to speak in a formal or eloquent manner
Example: *My three-year-old son left us in stitches when he began orating like his grandfather, the Bishop.*

order /ˈɔːdɐ/
to request or instruct someone to do something
Example: *The teacher ordered the students to sit down and be quiet.*
to arrange or command something to be done in a specific way
Example: *The sergeant ordered the troops to march in formation.*
to request or obtain something from a supplier or service
Example: *He ordered a new book from the bookstore.*
to command or direct someone to be placed in a particular state or condition
Example: *The doctor ordered bed rest for the patient.*
to arrange or organise something in a particular sequence
Example: *Berry ordered the items on the shelf by size.*

organise /ˈɔːgɐnˌaɪz/
to arrange or plan something systematically or methodically
Example: *Every year we organise a fundraiser for charity.*

orient /ˈɔːriənt/
to align or position something according to a specific direction or point
Example: *The map helps orient travellers to their destination.*
to familiarise or adapt someone to a new situation or environment
Example: *The orientation session helped new employees orient themselves to the company's policies.*
to focus or direct attention toward a particular objective or goal
Example: *The training program aims to orient participants toward career advancement.*
to determine one's position or direction in relation to surroundings
Example: *The compass helps hikers orient themselves in the wilderness.*
to establish or maintain one's bearings or sense of direction
Example: *Sam paused to orient himself before proceeding with the task.*

originate /ərˈɪdʒɪnˌeɪt/
to come into existence or to have a specific beginning
Example: *The moon walk dance originated with Michael Jackson.*

ornament /ˈɔrnəmənt/
to decorate or adorn something with ornaments or embellishments
Example: *A variety of flowers ornament the display in the art gallery.*

oscillate /ˈɒsɪlˌeɪt/
to move or swing back and forth in a regular rhythm or pattern
Example: *Most days, it is too hot to allow the fan to oscillate.*

outdo /aʊtˈduː/
to surpass or exceed in performance, achievement, or quality
Example: *The younger Nicholson sibling desperately tried to outdo the older one.*

outline /ˈaʊtlaɪn/
to give a summary or a general overview of something, typically in a concise or simplified form
Example: *The professor requested an outline of an essay on Kamau Brathwaite, not an essay.*

outmanoeuvre /aʊtməˈuːvɐ/
to outwit, outsmart, or surpass someone in a strategic or tactical manner
Example: *Mark Vieira outmanoeuvred the younger drivers to win the South Dakota Grand Prix meet.*

outwit /aʊtwˈɪt/
to defeat or overcome someone through cleverness, intelligence, or cunning
Example: *Melissa had once again outwitted her grandpa at their weekly game of chess.*

overbalance /ˌəʊvəbˈɑləns/
to lose one's balance and fall, typically due to being off-balance or unstable
Example: *The heavily obese passenger overbalanced while crossing the bridge from the dock to the boat.*

overbear /ˌəʊvəbˈeə/
to overcome or dominate someone or something by force or authority
Example: *His loud voice overbore the protests of the crowd.*
to be too much to bear or to overwhelm
Example: *The intensity of the grief overbore her, and she could not hold back her tears.*
to influence or sway someone's decision or opinion forcefully
Example: *His commanding presence overbore any objections from his colleagues.*
to bear down upon or press heavily

Example: *The storm overbore the weak defences of the coastal town.*

overcome /ˌəʊvəkˈʌm/
to successfully deal with or defeat a problem, obstacle, or difficulty
Example: *The team overcame a two-goal deficit to win the match.*
to prevail over someone or something, typically in a contest or competition
Example: *Despite the odds, she overcame her opponents and won the election.*
to overpower or overwhelm someone emotionally
Example: *He was overcome with joy when he received the good news.*

overcompensate /ˌəʊvəkˈɒmpənsˌeɪt/
to take excessive or extreme measures to counteract a perceived deficiency or compensate for something
Example: *Her aunt overcompensated by never missing events, because Petra she had lost both parents in an accident.*

overdo /ˌəʊvədˈuː/
to do something excessively or to an excessive degree
Example: *Whoever decorated the entrance, overdid it with the streamers.*

overdraw /ˈoʊvɚˌdrɔ/
to withdraw more money from a bank account that the account holds, resulting in a negative balance
Example: *Deon accidentally overdrawn his checking account by forgetting to record a recent purchase.*
to depict or represent something in an exaggerated or excessive manner
Example: *The artist tended to overdraw facial expressions, in her portraits.*
to overuse or exhaust a resource or supply

Example: *We must be careful not to overdraw our natural resources.*

overflow /ˈoʊvɚˌfloʊ/
to fill or cover something completely, often beyond its capacity
Example: *After the heavy rain, the river overflowed its banks and flooded the surrounding area.*
to have an excessive amount of something
Example: *Her heart overflowed with joy when she received the good news.*
to exceed or surpass a limit or boundary
Example: *His love for her seemed to overflow all bounds of reason.*

overhear /ˌoʊvəhˈiə/
to unintentionally hear something that was not intended for one's ears
Example: *I overhear too many things when I sit at the back of the class.*

overlook /ˈoʊvɚˌlʊk/
to fail to notice or consider something
Example: *The manager overlooked the mistakes in the report and praised the team for their effort.*
to have a view of from above
Example: *Their hotel room overlooked the ocean, offering a stunning view of the sunset.*
to provide supervision or be responsible for
Example: *The security guard overlooks the parking lot to ensure safety.*
to forgive or excuse something
Example: *Arty chose to overlook his rude behaviour because she knew he was under stress.*

overpower /ˌoʊvəpˈaʊɐ/

to overcome, overwhelm, or defeat someone or something with superior force or strength
Example: *Juan overpowered Roc in the ring to become the champion wrestler of our school.*

overtake /ˌəʊvətˈeɪk/
to pass someone or something that is moving slower
Example: *Do not overtake on bridges.*
to catch up with or surpass someone or something in progress
Example: *The White's building project overtook the Carter's building project in its penultimate stage.*
to happen suddenly or unexpectedly, often surpassing someone or something else
Example: *Pat was overtaken by grief when she saw Nedd in the coffin.*

overthrow /ˈoʊvɚˌθroʊ/
to remove forcibly from power, to defeat or depose someone or something
Example: *Azad left when he realised that the plot was to overthrow the government.*

overturn /ˌəʊvətˈɜːn/
to cause to turn over or flip upside down
Example: *The strong wind overturned the picnic table.*
to invalidate or reverse a decision, ruling, or judgement
Example: *The Supreme court overturned the Magistrate court's verdict and ordered a new trial.*
to overthrow or defeat someone or something, typically in a sudden or unexpected way
Example: *The new evidence overturned the long- standing theory.*
to bring about a significant change or transformation
Example: *The discovery of a new technology could overturn the entire industry.*

owe /ˈəʊ/
to be under obligation to pay or repay something
Example: *The players owe the coach an apology.*

own /ˈəʊn/
to possess or have something as one's own
Example: *Almost every home in Guyana owns a bicycle.*

Pp

pace /ˈpeɪs/
to walk back and forth
Example: *He paced nervously in the waiting room.*
to set the speed or rate of something
Example: *She paced herself during the marathon.*
to measure distance by counting steps
Example: *He paced out the dimensions of the room.*
to serve as a guide or example for
Example: *His success paced the ambition of his peers.*
to mark off a route or area by walking it
Example: *The soldiers paced the perimeter of the camp.*
to keep up with someone or something mentally or emotionally
Example: *Amy struggled to pace herself with the fast- talking presenter.*
to be consistent with
Example: *Justin's actions did not pace with his words, causing confusion.*

pack /pˈɑk/
to put items into a container or luggage
Example: *Pack only the necessities for the camporee.*
to fill completely
Example: *Pack the jars with the gooseberry jam, as it tends to settle over the course of the journey.*
to arrange and organise
Example: *Mum told Gevon to pack up his toys immediately after using them.*

pad /ˈpɑd/
to line or cushion with soft material

Example: *The footman padded the sides of the carriage with cushions to make the journey comfortable for his mistress.*

to walk quietly

Example: *Whiskers padded softly across the room to her favourite spot.*

to add unnecessary words or material

Example: *Gem's heavily padded speech of praise for the Director after her promotion, brought him under suspicion.*

to protect with padding

Example: *In the 80s and 90s, the boys in my school padded their pants when they expected to be flogged.*

to tamper or distort

Example: *The scorer padded the scores of his daughters' team to make them emerge the victors of the rounders match.*

paddle /pˈadəl/

to move a boat through water using a paddle

Example: *The girls paddled furiously and nipped the boys on the finish line of the canoeing meet.*

to walk with shallow steps, often making a splashing sound

Example: *The villagers paddled out of their streets to the main road as the flood waters continued to rise steadily.*

to spank lightly with a flat object

Example: *Years ago, parents paddled children on their bottom as a means of punishment for misbehaviour.*

to struggle or work inefficiently

Example: *Workers who turn up sick, paddle through the day creating more work for their co-workers rather than performing their duties.*

to beat or throb rhythmically

Example: *Examinees paddling their fingers on the desk during an exam should be asked to leave.*

to navigate or manoeuvre through a situation or environment

Example: *Zeke paddled his way out of the marshes with skill and expertise.*

paint /pˈeɪnt/
to apply colour to a surface using a brush or similar tool
Example: *We will paint our house this year for Christmas.*
to depict or describe vividly with words
Example: *The mother had painted a picture of peace and tranquillity in the home.*
to represent or describe in a particular way
Example: *Paint a good picture of me to your mother, please.*

palaver /pəlˈɑːvɐ/
to talk or discuss at length, often in a tedious or idle manner
Example: *They palaver for hours about trivial matters.*
to negotiate or bargain
Example: *The diplomats palaver over the terms of the treaty.*
to flatter or cajole to persuade
Example: *Sam palavered his way into getting a discount at the store.*

pale /pˈeɪl/
to become lighter in colour or shade
Example: *The child paled immediately when the stranger walked through the door.*
to lose significance or importance
Example: *The Mona Lisa pales in comparison to Isaiah's new painting.*
to appear weak or lacking in vitality
Example: *The strength of the pride of lions, pales next to the herd of mature bull elephants.*
to cause to become pale in colour or shade
Example: *The paintings paled from exposure to sun.*

palm /pˈɑːm/
to hold or conceal in the palm of one's hand
Example: *Susan palmed the coin before showing it to the audience.*
to pass off or dispose of by deceit
Example: *Walter palmed off the counterfeit painting as an original.*
to touch or stroke with the palm of the hand
Example: *Heather palmed his cheek affectionately.*
to hit or strike with the palm of the hand
Example: *Johnson palmed the basketball to fake out the defenders.*

palpate /pˈalpeɪt/
to examine or explore by touching or feeling, typically referring to the examination of a part of the body for medical purposes
Example: *The stomach of the dog was palpated until he regurgitated the ball he had swallowed.*

pamper /pˈampɐ/
to indulge with excessive attention, comfort, or luxury
Example: *The twins pampered their mother with a spa treatment for her birthday.*

panic /pˈanɪk/
to feel sudden, overwhelming fear or anxiety, often causing confusion or hysteria
Example: *The zoologist panicked when he realised the cage with the ocelots was unlocked.*
to react impulsively or irrationally due to fear or anxiety
Example: *The entire neighbourhood panicked when the earthquake occurred.*

pant /pˈɑːnt/

to breathe quickly and with difficulty due to exertion or excitement
Example: *Ziggy panted loudly after his daily run with Jeremiah.*
to long eagerly or desperately for something
Example: *Jeff panted after Louise with a lovestruck expression, but she never even noticed him.*

parade /pərˈeɪd/
to walk or march in a public procession, often in celebration or demonstration
Example: *The victorious soccer team paraded proudly through the streets of the city.*
to display or show off something, often in a proud or boastful way
Example: *Lou paraded his medal deliberately in front of his rival.*

paraphrase /ˈpærəfrˌeɪz/
to restate the meaning of something using different words
Example: *Paraphrase the article on the President's visit to the Netherlands.*

pardon /ˈpɑːdən/
to forgive someone for a mistake or offence
Example: *Pardon me for stepping on your toe, please.*
to excuse someone from a punishment or penalty
Example: *Every year several prisoners are pardoned and given a chance to start over.*
to excuse or overlook a minor offence or mistake
Example: *After winning the competition, the dancers were more willing to pardon the botch to their costume by the designer.*

park /ˈpɑːk/
to place or leave a vehicle, usually temporarily, in a particular location
Example: *This is where I park every day.*
to set aside or reserve a place for a specific purpose

Example: *The medical students parked their lab coats on the front row seats to reserve their spots, while they used the bathroom.*

parrot /pˈarət/
to repeat or mimic someone's words or actions without understanding their meaning
Example: *His younger brother parroted his every word.*

parry /pˈari/
to deflect or ward off a blow, attack, or criticism
Example: *The Chairman of the company effortlessly parried the questions posed by the reporters.*
to skilfully evade or avoid a question or topic
Example: *The seasoned actress parries the questions from the paparazzi with ease; but the inexperienced actress struggles over her responses.*

part /pˈɑːt/
to separate or divide into pieces or sections
Example: *The hairdresser parts my hair into four before she starts braiding it.*
to leave or separate from someone or something
Example: *The lovestruck couple had parted two days before their intended wedding.*

participate /pɑːtˈɪsɪpˌeɪt/
to take part in an activity, event, or situation
Example: *The students were eager to participate in the science fair, showcasing their experiments and research projects.*
to be involved or actively contribute to something
Example: *Emily actively participates in volunteer work, dedicating her time helping those in need in her community.*

to share in or have a role in something
Example: *Everyone in the family is expected to participate in the annual holiday tradition of decorating the Christmas tree.*

pass /pˈɑːs/
to move past or go by someone or something
Example: *She quietly passed her mother's room hoping she was not seen.*
to transfer from one place or person to another
Example: *The role of proprietor is passed on to the eldest son in the Williams' family.*
to succeed or achieve a required standard in an examination, test, or course
Example: *Sacha passed her cosmetology exam with a perfect score.*
to die
Example: *The passing of a pet brings much grief to loving owners.*

pat /pˈat/
to lightly touch or tap someone or something with the palm of one's hand as a gesture of affection or encouragement
Example: *Marcus affectionately patted the head of the huge mastiff owned by his brother.*
to lightly tap or stroke something to flatten or shape it
Example: *Kareem patted his flattop hairstyle with his Physics book as he walked to class.*
to lightly strike or slap something, often to remove dust or dirt
Example: *Mum never sits without patting the seat first.*

patch /pˈatʃ/
to mend or repair something by applying a piece of material
Example: *Sam patch the hole in his jeans with a piece of denim fabric.*
to cover or fix a problem or deficiency temporarily

Example: *They patched the leak in the roof with a tarp until they could afford to have it repaired properly.*

patrol /pɐtrˈəʊl/
to keep watch over an area by regularly walking or travelling around it
Example: *The soldiers patrol the compound for eight hours every night.*
to move through an area in search of someone or something
Example: *The police patrolled the city looking for the escaped criminal.*

patronise /pˈatrənˌaɪz/
to treat someone in a condescending manner, often displaying a sense of superiority
Example: *The bride's wealthy father patronised the groom in the presence of the guests.*
to support or be a regular customer of a business, organisation, or establishment
Example: *The students patronise the Home Economics Department's fundraising event.*
to be a benefactor or sponsor of someone or something
Example: *The owner of the chain of boutiques patronises the school his daughter attends every year by supplying each child with a backpack.*

pause /pˈɔːz/
to temporarily stop an action, activity, or movement
Example: *Donna paused for a moment to catch her breath before continuing with her run.*
to hesitate or wait before proceeding
Example: *Justin paused before answering the question, carefully considering his response.*
to interrupt briefly, often for dramatic effect or to allow for reflection

Example: *The speaker paused during her speech, allowing the audience to absorb her powerful message.*

paw /pˈɔː/
to touch or strike something with a paw, typically a cat or a dog
Example: *Ziva pawed furiously at the screen door as the cat passed by.*
to clumsily or eagerly handle or manipulate something with the hands
Example: *The inexperienced sculptor pawed desperately at the wood trying to fix the damage she had caused.*

pay /pˈeɪ/
to give someone money in exchange for goods, services, or work done
Example: *Chase pays for lunch for both girls.*
to give someone what is due, in terms of punishment or reward
Example: *They will pay for breaking the antique vase.*
to suffer the consequences or experience the result of one's actions
Example: *He is paying for his infidelity even today, for the children refuse to visit him.*

peck /pˈɛk/
to strike or pick at something with a beak, as birds often do
Example: *The roosters pecked at each other through the fence.*
to give light, quick kisses or taps with the lips
Example: *The baby gurgled in glee every time his mum pecked him on the nose.*
to nibble or eat in small, hesitant bites
Example: *The twins peck at the horrible tasting cookie; waiting for a chance to throw it over the fence.*

pedal /ˈpɛdəl/
to operate a pedal, typically on a bicycle or a musical instrument
Example: *Anisa pedalled furiously against the wind to win the 1500 m girls open cycle race.*

peek /pˈiːk/
to look quickly or furtively, especially from a hidden or concealed position
Example: *The guide took a quick peek at the list of destinations for the morning tour.*

peel /pˈiːl/
to remove the outer layer or skin from something, typically a fruit or vegetable
Example: *Kim carefully peeled the apple before slicing it into pieces for a snack.*
to come off in thin strips or layers
Example: *The paint on the old house began to peel, revealing the wood underneath.*
to strip away or separate gradually
Example: *Luke had to peel away the layers of tape to reveal the contents of the package.*

peep /pˈiːp/
to look quickly and furtively, especially through a small opening or from a hidden position
Example: *A peep through the keyhole confirmed their worst fears.*
to emit a faint or high-pitched sound, typically associated with chicks or small birds
Example: *The peeping of the baby chicks filled the air when we stepped on the chicken farm.*
to make a brief or cautious comment or observation
Example: *"Joshua did it!" Tyrell peeped. As mum raised her hand holding the leather strap.*

peer /ˈpɪr/
to look closely or intently, especially with difficulty
Example: *Lorna peered through the fog, trying to make out the shapes ahead on the road.*

to be equal to someone or something in quality, status, or ability
Example: *Her academic achievements allowed her to peer with confidence in her classmates.*
to appear slightly or gradually, as if coming into view
Example: *The first stars began to peer in the evening sky as twilight fell.*

pelt /pˈɛlt/
to attack someone or something by repeatedly throwing things at them
Example: *Some naughty boys pelted stones at donkeys grazing in the field.*
to move quickly and with determination
Example: *We were pelting towards the principal's office to complain but turned back when we saw the boys in the corridor.*
to beat or strike repeatedly, as with blows or missiles
Example: *The soldiers pelted the concrete structure with a steady stream of bombs before it finally collapsed killing the terrorists.*

perceive /pəsˈiːv/
to become aware of, understand, or interpret something through the senses or the mind
Example: *The perceived allegations of corruption within the firm was cause for concern.*

perch /pˈɜːtʃ/
to sit or rest on something, especially a high or narrow object
Example: *The bird perched on the branch.*
to be situated in a high or elevated position
Example: *The house perched on top of the hill.*
to position oneself in a place temporarily
Example: *Susan perched on the edge of her seat.*
to secure a foothold or position precariously
Example: *The cat perched on the edge of the fence.*

perfect /pɚˈfɛkt/
to make something as good as possible; to improve or refine something until it is flawless
Example: *Tina spent years perfecting her craft.*
to complete or accomplish something successfully
Example: *The cook perfected his recipe for chocolate cake.*
to become skilled or proficient in something
Example: *With practice, Dawn perfected her tennis serve.*

perform /pəfˈɔːm/
to carry out a task, duty, or function
Example: *He performs his role as both mother and father with ease and dignity.*
to execute a piece of music, a play, or another form of entertainment in front of an audience
Example: *Every time she performed this season the theatre was left in awe.*
to achieve or execute something successfully
Example: *Dancer and Wayne performed the jump with much room to spare, despite our fears.*

perk /pˈɜːk/
to become or make more lively, cheerful, or interesting
Example: *The waiting audience immediately perked up when Kunchie walked onto the stage.*
to provide someone with special benefits or advantages as part of their job or status
Example: *Emily enjoys perking her staff at Christmas for their work all year round.*

permit /pɚˈmɪt/
to allow or authorise someone to do something
Example: *The teacher permitted the students to leave early.*
to grant someone the right or ability to do something

Example: *The ticket permits entry into the museum.*
to tolerate or accept something
Example: *The rules do not permit smoking in this area.*

persist /pəsˈɪst/
to continue firmly or obstinately in an opinion or a course of action despite difficulty or opposition
Example: *If you persist in coming into my yard, I will call the police.*

perspire /pəspˈaɪə/
to sweat, typically because of heat or physical exertion
Example: *The children perspired heavily in bulky Mashramani costumes.*

persuade /pəswˈeɪd/
to convince someone to do or believe something through reasoning or argument
Example: *I regret being persuaded to purchase the beach front property.*

peruse /pərˈuːz/
to read or examine something carefully and thoroughly
Example: *Jake perused the list intently hoping to see his name.*

pester /pˈɛstɐ/
to annoy persistently or repeatedly
Example: *Nyasha pesters her brother incessantly.*

pet /pˈɛt/
to stroke or caress an animal affectionately
Example: *Donna loves to pet her dog while watching TV.*
to treat with special favour or kindness, often indulgently

Example: *The boss tends to pet his favourite employee, giving him all the best assignments.*
to become upset or sulky, especially over a trivial matter
Example: *Do not pet about not getting the front seat; it is not a big deal.*
to kiss or caress amorously
Example: *Marvin leaned in to pet Susan's cheek before leaving for work*
to stroke or smooth gently or lovingly
Example: *Ariel petted the fabric of her new dress, admiring its softness.*

philosophise /fɪlˈɒsəfˌaɪz/
to engage in the activity of discussing or contemplating philosophical ideas or principles
Example: *My dad always philosophised in our discussions on theology.*

phone /fˈəʊn/
to make a telephone call
Example: *Phone him now to find out whether he is coming or not.*

photograph /fˈəʊtəɡrˌɑf/
to take a picture with a camera
Example: *Sherwin patiently photographed the entire Year Two kindergarten class.*

pick /pˈɪk/
to select or choose from a group or set
Example: *Grethel picked a red apple from the basket.*
to pluck or gather by hand
Example: *Fred picked flowers from the garden for his mother.*
to remove something with a quick light motion

Example: *She picked the lint off her sweater before leaving the house.*
to clean or remove unwanted items from
Example: *Jerry picked the bones from his fish before eating it.*
to play a stringed instrument by plucking the strings
Example: *He picked a cheerful tune on his guitar.*
to break up or loosen something with a tool or instrument
Example: *The burglar picked at the lock with a bobby pin to try to open the door.*
to provoke or irritate someone
Example: *Stop picking on your little brother; it is not nice.*
to excel or perform well in a task or activity
Example: *Emma really picked up her game in the second half of the match.*

picture /pˈɪktʃɚ/
to visualise or imagine something in one's mind
Example: *Close your eyes and picture a peaceful forest.*
to represent or depict in a visual form
Example: *Gail pictured herself living in a cosy cottage by the sea.*
to capture an image of something with a camera
Example: *Abe pictured the beautiful sunset with his camera.*
to portray or present something in a particular way
Example: *The advertisement pictured the product as a solution to all household pests.*

pierce /pˈiəs/
to make a hole or opening in something with a sharp object
Example: *The teacher pierced the paper with a needle to hang it on the wall.*
to penetrate or pass through something with force
Example: *The bullet pierced the window, shattering it into pieces.*
to enter or affect deeply or sharply

Example: *His words pierced her heart, leaving her feeling hurt and betrayed.*

pile /pˈaɪl/
to arrange or stack something in a heap or mound
Example: *She piled the books neatly on the shelf.*
to load or fill something with a large quantity of things
Example: *The hungry tourist piled his plate high with food at the buffet.*
to increase in amount or quantity
Example: *The work piled up as the deadline approached.*

pilot /pˈaɪlət/
to operate or control an aircraft, ship, or vehicle
Example: *He piloted the aeroplane through turbulent weather conditions.*
to guide or steer something through a difficult or dangerous situation
Example: *The supervisor piloted the company through its restructuring process.*
to serve as a guide or leader
Example: *The experienced hiker piloted the group through the treacherous mountain terrain.*
to conduct a trial or test of something
Example: *The company piloted its new software with a select group of users before releasing it to the public.*

pin /pˈɪn/
to attach or fasten something with a pin
Example: *I helped Sarah to pin her bun up neatly.*
to mark or identify something with a pin
Example: *When it was my turn, I pinned St. Lucia on the map as my honeymoon destination.*
to hold someone or something in a particular position or place

Example: *Thumb tacks effectively pins the backdrop in place for the photoshoot.*
to attribute or ascribe something to someone or something
Example: *His colleagues pinned the missing firearm on him causing him to lose his job.*

pinch /pˈɪntʃ/
to squeeze or compress something between the thumb and fingers
Example: *Wendy pinched her cheeks to give them a rosy colour.*
to grasp hold onto something tightly between surfaces, typically causing discomfort or pain
Example: *The new shoes pinched her toes, so she had to take them off.*
to steal or take something quickly and stealthily
Example: *The pickpocket pinched the woman's wallet while she was distracted.*
to be in a situation where there is a shortage or lack of something, especially money
Example: *They had to pinch pennies to afford the rent.*

pinpoint /pˈɪnpɔɪnt/
to identify or locate precisely, often by using a specific point or detail
Example: *The aerial team soon pinpointed the vessel lost at sea.*

pioneer /paɪənˈiə/
to be the first to develop or explore something new or innovative
Example: *Marie Curie pioneered research on radioactivity.*
to initiate or lead the way in a particular field or activity
Example: *The company pioneered the use of renewable energy in their manufacturing process.*
to settle or establish in a new place or area
Example: *The settlers pioneered the frontier, building homes and farms in the wilderness.*

pipe /pˈaɪp/
to convey or transport (liquid, gas, etc.) through pipes
Example: *The city pipes water from the reservoir to homes and businesses.*
to produce sound resembling that of a pipe instrument
Example: *The wind piped through the cracks in the old window frames.*
to supply with pipes or a pipe system
Example: *The house is piped for natural gas heating.*
to speak in a high-pitched or shrill voice
Example: *"That was my part!" Mary piped from the audience.*
to decorate with piping, as on clothing or upholstery
Example: *The seamstress piped the edges of the pillow with contrasting fabric.*

pitch /pˈɪtʃ/
to throw or toss something with force
Example: *Vaughn pitched the frisbee with great force, but Boxer still caught it easily.*
to set up or erect something, such as a tent or a campsite
Example: *Pitching the tent is dad's favourite part of camping.*
to present or propose something, especially in a persuasive or compelling manner
Example: *We allow the boys to each pitch an idea for a summer business, then everyone pitches in to make the best idea a reality.*

pity /pˈɪti/
to feel sympathy or compassion for someone, mostly in a situation of suffering or distress
Example: *Desma pitied her because she had lost her grandmother.*

pivot /pˈɪvət/
to turn or rotate on a central point

Example: *A hidden camera was set on pivot to capture all angles of the room of the suspect.*
to change direction or strategy abruptly
Example: *The antelope pivoted suddenly causing the wild dogs to crash into the bushes directly in the path.*
to serve as a central or crucial point or axis
Example: *By the age of eight Darrel was pivoting easily during his one-on-one basketball sessions with his coach.*

placate /plɛkˈeɪt/
to make someone less angry or hostile by giving them what they want or soothing their feelings
Example: *Exhausted, Malcolm tried to placate his angry wife with flowers and chocolate.*

place /plˈeɪs/
to put something in a particular position or location
Example: *Alie usually places the key in a slot in the wall of the wooden house.*

plait /plˈeɪt/
to braid or weave together strands of material, typically hair or fabric
Example: *Plaiting bread is no longer a frequently practised activity in home baking.*

plan /plˈɑn/
to decide on and arrange in advance what is to happen or how something is to be done
Example: *The girls plan to surprise Shanell at work for her birthday.*

plant /plˈɑnt/
to place (a seed, bulb, or plant) in the ground so that it can grow

Example: *Adrian and Tinny planted a mango seed, which they watered every day.*

play /plˈeɪ/
to engage in an activity for enjoyment or recreation
Example: *At the Rose Hall Town Nursery School, the students are allowed to play freely.*
to perform in a theatrical production or in a musical composition
Example: *Dion played the role of Timon in the production of the "Lion King" put on by his old school.*
to manipulate (a situation), typically in a skilful or underhand way
Example: *At the end of the heist, they realised that Joe had played them all, for the jewellery and cash were gone.*
to operate (a device or instrument) to produce music or sound
Example: *Rayel can play the steelpan well.*
to take part in (a sport)
Example: *The gang enjoys playing a good game of cricket at every outing.*
to behave in a particular way or have a particular effect or outcome
Example: *Mrs. Samuels does not play when it is time for practical in her Home Economics class.*

plead /plˈiːd/
to make an emotional appeal or earnest request
Example: *The eager teens pleaded for a chance to ride the Ferris wheel.*
in legal contexts, to enter a formal statement of guilt or innocence in response to a charge
Example: *Pleading the case on behalf of the defendant was Prosecutor DeFreitas.*

please /plˈiːz/
to give satisfaction, pleasure, or enjoyment to; make glad or contented
Example: *The delicious meal pleased everyone at the party.*

to be agreeable or acceptable to
Example: *The proposal pleased most of the committee members.*
used as a polite expression of request or an indication of agreement
Example: *Please pass the salt.*

pledge /plˈɛdʒ/
to make a solemn promise or commitment
Example: *The team pledged to retrieve the body of their fallen comrade.*
to give as security for the performance of an act
Example: *The stranger pledged a sterling performance on the piano for the opening night.*
to drink a toast to someone or something
Example: *The glasses clinked as the men pledged their support for Ray's new business venture.*

plod /plˈɒd/
to walk or move slowly and heavily, especially with much effort or difficulty
Example: *The farmer plodded through the mud to free the ram caught by its horns.*

plonk /plˈɒŋk/
to put or place something heavily or unceremoniously
Example: *The students planked the textbooks onto the table in front of the librarian.*
to move or walk with heavy, clumsy steps
Example: *The sound of Wayne planking along on his crutches echoed eerily through the silent house.*

plop /plˈɒp/
to fall, drop, or be placed with a soft, splashing sound
Example: *After work, Ave looks forward to plopping down on her bed and burying her head under her pillows to sleep.*

plot /plˈɒt/
to plan or scheme secretly, especially something harmful or unlawful
Example: *They had been plotting his demise for a long time.*
to mark or delineate the outline or main features of something
Example: *The team met to plot the route for the hike on Father's Day.*
to develop the sequence of events or actions in a story
Example: *Agatha Christie had skilfully plotted the novel to keep readers on the edge of their seats.*

pluck /plˈʌk/
to pull something quickly to remove it or extract it forcefully
Example: *Deborah patiently plucked each new strand of grey hair she saw alone her hairline.*
to take or seize something suddenly or unexpectedly
Example: *The bully plucked Lisa's lunch money out of her hand as she stood in line at the canteen.*

plug /plˈʌg/
to fill or close a hole or gap with a plug or stopper
Example: *Darcia plugged the hole in the boat to stop it from sinking.*
to insert a device into an outlet or socket to connect it to a power source
Example: *Please plug in the charger to recharge my phone.*
to promote or advertise something, often persistently
Example: *The company is trying to plug its new product through various marketing campaigns.*
to mention or recommend something, often in a casual manner
Example: *She subtly plugged her friend's business in the conversation.*

plump /plˈʌmp/
to drop or fall heavily or suddenly
Example: *The ripe mango plumped to the ground from the tree.*
to make something swell or become fuller in shape

Example: *Adding extra stuffing made the pillow plump and comfortable.*

to express strong support or preferences for someone or something

Example: *The audience plumped for the proposal with the loudest applause.*

plunge /plˈʌndʒ/

to jump or dive quickly and forcefully into something, typically water

Example: *The swimmer severely injured his neck when he plunged into the river.*

to fall or drop suddenly and steeply

Example: *The jeep plunged over the cliff and into the sea after the rail gave way along the side of the road.*

to undertake or engage in something with enthusiasm or determination

Example: *The students plunged excitedly into preparations for the Talent Competition.*

point /pˈɔɪnt/

to direct or aim something in a particular direction

Example: *A kind man pointed the way to the Inniss's home.*

to emphasise or draw attention to something

Example: *The concerned councillor pointed out how precariously the old house on the Singh's property was leaning.*

to be oriented or directed in a particular way

Example: *My uncle points me in the direction of my dream every time I become disheartened.*

to have a specific purpose or significance

Example: *Spanish and Mandarin classes are pointing me in the direction of being an interpreter.*

poke /pˈəʊk/

to push or prod with a finger or a pointed object

Example: *Jess poked the play button on the cassette player to see if it worked.*

to make a quick, sharp movement or thrust
Example: *I poke a hole in my belt as my waist was too small for the available holes.*
to jab or nudge someone in a playful or teasing manner
Example: *She pokes fun at his mascot costume every time she sees him in it.*

polish /ˈpoʊlɪʃ/
to make something smooth and shiny by rubbing or buffing
Example: *At cadet camp, the children learn to polish and shine their shoes.*
to remove imperfections or errors from something
Example: *Polish, then print your essay and submit it.*

ponder /ˈpɒndɚ/
to think about or consider something deeply and carefully
Example: *Devya pondered her options carefully before deciding on her career choice.*
to reflect on or mull over a topic or idea
Example: *In her quiet time, she will ponder on the actions of her peers.*

pontificate /pɑnˈtɪfəˌkeɪt/
to speak or express opinions in a pompous or dogmatic manner, often without considering opposing views
Example: *As the lone female Lieutenant Colonel, she had an opportunity to pontificate her vast knowledge of military matters but chose rather to be humble in her delivery.*
to act as a pontiff or potential authority, especially within a religious context
Example: *As the new Catholic priest in the parish, Father Charles will be pontificating about the importance of love and compassion as he believes the community is lacking in both.*

pop /pˈɒp/
to make a short, sharp, explosive sound
Example: *Whenever the substitute teacher attempts to speak, Ebrahim pops a bubble.*
to move or appear suddenly or unexpectedly
Example: *Parents are encouraged to pop in unexpectedly at school occasionally.*
to appear briefly or momentarily
Example: *The head popped in at the window, then disappeared altogether.*
to burst or break suddenly due to pressure or force
Example: *He popped the champagne in celebration of the historic win.*

pore /pˈɔː/
to examine or study something closely and attentively
Example: *She pored over her notes before the exam.*
to be absorbed in reading or studying something intently
Example: *Gerald spent the afternoon poring over his favourite novel.*
to be covered in or filled with small openings
Example: *The sponge was designed to be porous, allowing water to pass through easily.*
to flow or seep steadily through small openings
Example: *Water began to pore through the cracks in the roof during the storm.*

pose /pˈəʊz/
to assume a particular position, especially in front of a camera or artist
Example: *The family posed smilingly in front of the camera for the portrait.*
to present a problem, challenge, or question
Example: *The girls always pose better questions than the boys during the questions and answers segment.*

to pretend to be someone else; to assume a false identity
Example: *Josiah's brother posed as his father for the PTA meeting.*

position /pəz'ɪʃən/
to place or arrange something in a particular location or orientation
Example: *The investigating team positioned the drone directly over the home of the suspected terrorist.*
to place or establish someone or something in a particular role, rank, or status
Example: *Mr. Jules was positioned as Chief Education Officer by the Minister of Education himself.*
to determine or clarify one's stance or viewpoint on a particular issue
Example: *The prosecutor clearly positioned his argument on the matter before the court.*
to adopt or assume a particular posture or stance
Example: *The workmen positioned the planks under the beams of the house to hold it up.*

possess /pəz'ɛs/
to own or have control or ownership of something
Example: *I possess several businesses along the Corentyne Coast.*
to have or exhibit certain qualities or attributes
Example: *Ms. Layne possesses several degrees, including one in Education.*
to be controlled or influenced by something, often a feeling or emotion
Example: *Several celebrities claim they become possessed by an entity before they perform.*
to have knowledge or mastery of something
Example: *Artie the magician possessed the ability to make one's hand disappear before their eyes.*

post /p'əʊst/
to display or publish something publicly, especially on the internet or a bulletin board

Example: *Posting on social media can have several drawbacks.*
to assign someone to a particular position or duty
Example: *The sentry posted on duty had a hard time staying awake.*
to announce or advertise something publicly
Example: *The restaurant posts a different menu every day.*

postulate /ˈpɑstʃəˌleɪt/
to suggest or assume something as a basis for reasoning, discussion, or belief
Example: *The exchange student from Peru postulated experiencing a home with Islamic beliefs as his reason for attending the university in Saudi Arabia.*

pounce /pˈaʊns/
to suddenly and vigorously seize or attack something or someone
Example: *The cat pounced on the unsuspecting mouse only to realise it was a toy.*

pound /pˈaʊnd/
to strike or hit repeatedly with force
Example: *The lady in white pounded frantically on the door of the Jones' house.*
to move with heavy, thudding steps
Example: *We could hear the students pounding down the stairs as soon as the bell rang.*
to crush or pulverise something by hitting or pressing it forcefully
Example: *Nigel pounds his cherries with his little fist before eating them.*

pour /pˈɔː/
to cause a liquid to flow or stream out of a container, often in a steady or continuous manner
Example: *It is better to pour the milk out of the jug that has a spout.*

to express or convey a large amount of something, such as emotions or words
Example: *Nickella poured out heartbreak about losing the race between snobs and snivels to her father.*
to rain heavily or continuously
Example: *It is pouring on the West Side this morning.*

pout /pˈaʊt/
to protrude the lips in a sulky or discontent way, often as an expression of unhappiness or annoyance
Example: *Cintya pouted and folded her arms in annoyance as the boys made silly jokes.*

practise /prˈæktɪs/
to perform or engage in an activity regularly or repeatedly to improve or maintain proficiency
Example: *The hip hop dance team practised every day in preparation for the semi-final competition.*

praise /prˈeɪz/
to express admiration, approval, or commendation for someone or something
Example: *The diver received high praise for her swift action in retrieving the toddler from the river.*

prance /prˈɑːns/
to move with high steps, especially in a lively and spirited manner
Example: *Aria pranced proudly in her ballet swan costume as her team awaited their turn on stage.*

prattle /prˈætəl/
to talk at length in a foolish or inconsequential way, often in a chattering or gossip manner

Example: *Emmanuel prattled excitedly about planets and galaxies on the way to the space museum.*

pray /pr'eɪ/
to communicate with a deity or spiritual being, typically through words or thoughts, often as a form of worship, supplication, or request for guidance, help, or blessings
Example: *I have no time or place to pray; I just pray.*

preach /pr'iːtʃ/
to deliver a sermon or religious message, often with the intention of teaching, exhorting, or persuading others to adopt certain beliefs or principles
Example: *The new young pastor preaches with much passion, unlike the older pastor.*
to deliver a passionate or fervent speech or message about a particular topic or cause
Example: *At Monday's assembly, the Senior Mistress preached about the harms of vape and marijuana to the young mind.*

precede /prɪs'iːd/
to come before something else in time, order, or position
Example: *Not surprisingly, the cheerleading team preceded the football team in the parade.*

predict /prɪd'ɪkt/
to forecast or foretell an event or outcome based on available information or evidence
Example: *Tazim had predicted rain and it was indeed pouring outside.*

preen /pr'iːn/

to groom oneself carefully or to pridefully admire and attend to one's appearance
Example: *Sarafina preened in front of the mirror as she admired her new outfit and hairstyle.*

prefer /prɪfˈɜː/
to like, choose, or favour one thing over another
Example: *They were astonished that she preferred the Hawkins bike over the pink Mercedes Benz.*

prepare /prɪpˈeə/
to make ready or put in proper condition for a particular purpose or activity
Example: *Many long, hard hours are used to prepare assessments for students.*

prescribe /prɪskrˈaɪb/
to recommend or order the use of something, typically a medication or treatment, to address a medical condition or problem
Example: *The doctor prescribed antibiotics to treat the bacterial infection.*
to specify or recommend a particular course of action or behaviour
Example: *The therapist prescribed relaxation techniques to help manage stress.*
to authorise or order something officially
Example: *The government agency prescribed safety regulations for the construction site.*
to set or establish a rule, principle, or standard
Example: *The coach prescribed a strict training regimen for the athletes to follow.*

present /ˈprɛzənt/
to show, offer, or bring something to someone's attention

Example: *The evidence presented to the judge was insufficient to gain a conviction.*

to give or bestow something

Example: *The appreciative parents present their children's teacher with a huge bouquet of flowers.*

to introduce or bring forth something or someone

Example: *For today's program, Pauline will present the facilitator to the participants.*

to appear or manifest

Example: *In the midst of the feigned exorcism, the dead aunt presented herself much to the horror of terrified teens.*

preserve /prɪsˈɜːv/

to maintain or keep something in its original state or condition

Example: *More effort needs to be made to preserve the historic wooden buildings in Guyana.*

to protect or save something from harm or decay

Example: *The roses at the flower shop are very well preserved.*

to prepare and store food or other perishable items in a way that prevents spoilage

Example: *The Indonesians have a unique method of preserving fish and other seafood.*

to maintain or uphold a particular tradition, culture, or way of life

Example: *Storytelling, especially by the elderly, is a great way to preserve the culture of a people.*

press /prˈɛs/

to apply force or pressure

Example: *The medic pressed his hand against the wound to stem the flow of blood.*

to push or squeeze something firmly

Example: *After five minutes of pressing the sides of the bulging suitcase together, they finally got it closed.*

to urge or demand persistently

Example: *The investigative reporter continued pressing for answers in the hit and run case.*
to iron or smooth out wrinkles
Example: *The steam iron pressed the troublesome fabric effortlessly.*

pressure /prˈɛʃɐ/
to apply force or influence to persuade or compel someone to do something
Example: *Her Chinese relations were pressuring her to marry and return to Beijing.*

presume /prɪzjˈuːm/
to suppose something to be true without having definite proof
Example: *They presumed she was innocent because of her dainty appearance; they never learned.*

pretend /prɪtˈɛnd/
to act as if something is true when it is not
Example: *Hadiyah and Jarielle were pretending to be nurses.*

prevaricate /prɪvˈɑrɪkˌeɪt/
to speak or act in an evasive way, typically to avoid giving a direct answer or to deceive
Example: *Contractors often prevaricate the actual cost of projects they are assigned.*

prevent /prɪvˈɛnt/
to stop something from happening or to hinder its occurrence
Example: *Washing your hands thoroughly helps to prevent infections.*

prick /prˈɪk/
to puncture lightly with a sharp point or object

Example: *The naughty boy pricked the balloon when the girl was not looking.*
to cause a sharp, stinging pain
Example: *The point of the compass pricks harder than you would expect.*

primp /prˈɪmp/
to spend time making minor adjustments to one's appearance, especially in a fussing or self-conscious manner
Example: *The nervous girls primped their hair and touched up their lipstick when the agent walked in.*

print /prˈɪnt/
to reproduce text or image on paper or other material using a printing press or printer
Example: *They printed flyers to advertise the event.*
to produce copies of a document or image
Example: *Heather printed out the report for her meeting.*
to publish or make available in written or printed form
Example: *The newspaper printed an article about the local election.*
to leave an impression or mark
Example: *The dog's paw prints were visible in the mud.*

prise /prˈaɪz/
to use force or leverage to open or move something that is tightly closed or held
Example: *Anxiously, the young men prised open the lid of the crate from which came the thudding.*

probe /prˈəʊb/
to investigate or explore something thoroughly, especially by asking questions or examining closely

Example: *The student government body was probing the case of the missing tennis rackets from the game room.*

proceed /prəsˈiːd/
to continue with a course of action or to move forward
Example: *The parade will proceed along the Main Street to the parade ground.*

process /ˈprɔˌsɛs/
to perform a series of actions or operations on something to achieve a result
Example: *We need to process the data before we can analyse it.*
to deal with or handle something according to a set procedure
Example: *The bank will process your loan application within one week.*
to undergo a series of changes or developments
Example: *The film needs to be processed before it can be viewed.*
to deal with information or experiences mentally or emotionally
Example: *Drew needed time to process the news of her friend's death.*

proclaim /prəklˈeɪm/
to announce or declare something publicly or officially
Example: *King Nebuchadnezzer proclaimed that everyone should worship Daniel's God.*

procrastinate /prəkrˈɑːstɪnˌeɪt/
to delay or postpone doing something, especially out of habitual laziness or a tendency to avoid tasks
Example: *Because we procrastinate, we missed our submission deadline.*

procure /prəkjˈɔː/

to obtain or acquire something, typically through effort or initiative
Example: *They were finally able to procure the property after many months of battle in court.*

prod /prˈɒd/
to poke, jab, or urge someone or something to act or move forward
Example: *The jockey prodded the horse, but he refused to move forward.*

produce /ˈproʊdus/
to make or manufacture something
Example: *The bakery produces fresh bread every morning.*
to bring forth or generate something, often because of effort or creativity
Example: *V.S. Naipaul produces novels that captivate readers around the world.*
to create or bring into existence
Example: *The musician produces music that resonates with audiences.*
to yield or provide a result or outcome
Example: *His efforts produced positive changes in the community.*
to present or make available for others to see, hear, or experience
Example: *The theatre company produces plays throughout the year.*

profess /prəfˈɛs/
to declare openly or publicly, especially one's beliefs, opinions, or feelings
Example: *We listened in disbelief as the janitor professed his love for the principal over the intercom.*

proffer /prˈɒfɚ/
to offer or present something for acceptance or consideration, typically in a formal or courteous manner

Example: *He gallantly proffered his handkerchief, but she brushed it aside.*

prognosticate /prəgnˈɒstɪkˌeɪt/
to predict or forecast future events or outcomes
Example: *One cannot prognosticate the stock ratings for tomorrow based on the ratings for today.*

progress /proʊˈgrɛs/
to advance or move forward, especially towards a goal or objective
Example: *The rescuers made slow progress down the mountainside with the injured rock climber.*

prohibit /prəhˈɪbɪt/
means to formally forbid something by law, rule, or authority
Example: *The workmen were prohibited from entering the property until the dispute was settled by the court.*

project /prəˈdʒɛkt/
to plan or estimate something for the future
Example: *For the new season, we project at least three sessions of home care for the orphanage.*
to display or show an image or video onto a surface
Example: *The image of the lost dog was projected onto the huge screen in the National Park.*
to extend outward or protrude
Example: *The piece of wood from the broken frame, projected out from beneath the cloth.*
to convey a particular quality or impression
Example: *The sentry at the palace gates, projects an image of calm demeanour, but he must be annoyed at being stared at and poked by tourists.*

promenade /ˌprɒmənˈɑːd/
to take a leisurely walk, especially in a public place for pleasure or to be seen
Example: *The newlyweds promenaded along the beach, holding hands.*

promise /prˈɒmɪs/
to assure someone that one will do, give, or arrange something
Example: *I promise to take great care of your pets.*

promote /prəmˈəʊt/
to support or encourage the progress, growth, or development of something
Example: *St. Joseph's High School does a great job of promoting their Athletics Championship.*

prompt /prˈɒmpt/
to cause or bring about an action or reaction
Example: *Their dishonesty prompted the organisers to cancel the competition.*

prong /prˈɒŋ/
the action of piercing or poking with a fork-like or pointed object
Example: *The chef pronged the turkey to check for doneness.*

pronounce /prənˈaʊns/
to make the sound of a word in the correct way
Example: *The announcer pronounces the words carefully in the spelling bee competition.*
to declare or announce formally or officially
Example: *Pastor Charles pronounced them man and wife.*

proofread /prˈuːfriːd/

to examine or read over written material for errors and make corrections

Example: *Before final submission, it is important to proofread thoroughly.*

prop /prˈɒp/
to support, hold up, or bolster something in a particular position
Example: *The plank propping up the beam slipped, and the entire building collapsed.*

propel /prəpˈɛl/
to drive, push, or cause to move forward or onward
Example: *A strong gust of wind will propel Kevin's toy helicopter into the air.*

prophesy /prˈɒfəsi/
to predict or foretell future events, often with a sense of divine inspiration or insight
Example: *Noah had prophesied the destruction of the world by a flood, and it had come to pass.*

propose /prəpˈəʊz/
to suggest or put forward a plan, idea, or intention for consideration or discussion
Example: *The student government body proposes a student government run strictly by the students.*

proposition /ˌprɒpəzˈɪʃən/
to offer or suggest something for consideration or acceptance
Example: *Our school's Parent Teacher Association propositions that the proceeds from the concert go solely towards equipping each classroom with a smartboard.*

prostrate /ˈprɑstreɪt/
to lay oneself flat on the ground, especially face downwards, as a sign of humility, submission, or adoration
Example: *It is no longer a common site to see a person prostrate themself before a leader.*

protect /prətˈɛkt/
to keep safe from harm or danger
Example: *Bodyguards are employed to protect their charges with their own lives.*

protest /ˈproʊˌtɛst/
to express strong objection or disagreement
Example: *Oran protested vehemently when he was accused of cheating in the race.*

prove /prˈuːv/
to demonstrate the truth or existence of something, typically by providing evidence or arguments
Example: *The swim team vowed to prove that their teammate was innocent.*

provide /prəvˈaɪd/
to furnish or supply something
Example: *Her parents provide her with hot meals every day.*

provoke /prəvˈəʊk/
to incite or stimulate a reaction or feeling, often intentionally
Example: *I felt satisfied when the dog bit him after being relentlessly provoked.*

prowl /prˈaʊl/

to move around stealthily, often in search of prey or with a sense of stealth
Example: *Bandits had been observed prowling the area, casing the homes, over the past two weeks.*

pry /prˈaɪ/
to inquire too closely into someone's personal affairs
Example: *Try to not pry into the private affairs of your staff.*
to force open with a lever or similar tool
Example: *A crowbar is needed to pry open the door of the locked shed.*

publicise /pˈʌblɪsˌaɪz/
to make something known to the public, often through various means of communication
Example: *The summer swim program is being nicely publicised through social media.*

pucker /pˈʌkɐ/
to gather into small folds or wrinkles, especially on the surface of something like skin or fabric
Example: *When Jan pulled the loose string it puckered up the front of her skirt.*

puff /pˈʌf/
to emit or blow out air or smoke forcefully
Example: *The professor puffed on his cigarette, releasing a cloud of smoke.*
to swell or expand in a rounded or bulging shape
Example: *The pastry puffed up beautifully in the oven.*
to breathe heavily or audibly due to exertion or excitement
Example: *After running for a while, she was puffing and panting.*
to speak boastfully or self-importantly

Example: *David puffed about his accomplishments during the interview.*
to add substance or volume, often in a deceptive or exaggerated manner
Example: *Advertisements often puff up the benefits of their products.*

pull /pˈʊl/
to exert force to move something towards oneself or away from something
Example: *Sam pulled the rope to lift the heavy box.*
to remove something by force
Example: *Amy pulled the weeds out of the garden.*
to draw or attract someone or something in a particular direction
Example: *The magnet pulled the metal paper clips towards it.*
to take action to cause someone or something to be removed or repositioned
Example: *The stranger pulled the child away from the busy street.*
to extract or obtain information, resources, or support from someone or something
Example: *The detective tried to pull information from the reluctant witness.*

pummel /pˈʌməl/
to repeatedly strike someone or something with force, typically with the fists
Example: *Gaistrie pummelled his chest and wept bitterly when she heard of his betrayal.*

pump /pˈʌmp/
to operate a pump to move liquid or gas from one place to another
Example: *The mechanic pumped air into the flat tire to inflate it.*
to move rhythmically or forcefully, often in a repetitive motion
Example: *The sprinter pumped his arms as he ran to increase his speed.*

to cause something to increase rapidly or forcefully
Example: *The government pumped money into the economy to stimulate growth.*
to extract or draw out, often with force or effort
Example: *The doctor pumped the poison out of the patient's stomach.*
to question or extract information from someone
Example: *The detective pumped the suspect for information about the crime.*

punch /pˈʌntʃ/
to strike someone or something with the fist
Example: *The boxer landed a solid punch and floored his opponent.*
to create a hole or opening in something by forcefully pressing a pointed object into it
Example: *The students frequently ask to borrow the perforator to punch their assignments.*
to hit or press a button or keys, typically to operate a machine or device
Example: *Devya punched angrily at the keys of the laptop as he retyped the essay that had been deleted.*
to make a strong impression or impact
Example: *Seeing Shelly with her new best friend punched a hole in Sarah's heart.*

puncture /pˈʌŋktʃɐ/
to pierce or make a hole in something, especially a tire or skin
Example: *While riding to school, a shard of glass punctured my bike.*
to weaken or damage someone's pride, confidence, or reputation
Example: *The slanderous statements by the media punctured the young man's sterling record on his job.*

punish /pˈʌnɪʃ/
to impose a penalty on someone for wrongdoing or to discipline them for their actions

Example: *Perpetrators of cyberbullying should be punished by revoking access to social media if there is a repeat in the offence more than twice.*

purchase /pˈɜːtʃɪs/
to buy or acquire something by paying money for it
Example: *The teachers purchased lovely tokens for the students.*

purr /pˈɜː/
the soft, low, continuous sound made by a contented cat
Example: *Minx purred contentedly as Roy rubbed her ear.*

purse /pˈɜːs/
to pucker or contract, typically the lips, in a particular way
Example: *She pursed her lips in disapproval when she heard the news.*
to gather or contract into folds or wrinkles, typically fabric or skin
Example: *Her brows pursed with concern as she listened to the troubling news.*
to hold or carry something in a purse or similar container
Example: *William pursed the coins in his hand before dropping them into the donation box.*

pursue /pəsjˈuː/
to follow or chase someone or something to catch or reach them
Example: *Two police officers on bikes pursued the young man who had snatched the woman's purse.*
to engage in an activity or course of action to achieve a goal
Example: *At the age of 70, Mrs White is currently pursuing her high school diploma.*
to continue or proceed with a course of action or line of thought
Example: *Justin will pursue a career in football, despite his slim chances of making it professionally.*

push /pˈʊʃ/
to exert force against something to move it away
Example: *She pushed the shopping cart down the aisle.*
to press or move something forward or away from oneself
Example: *The secretary pushed her chair back from the table.*
to advocate or promote the adoption or acceptance of
Example: *The organisation is pushing for stricter environmental regulations.*
to try to achieve or obtain something
Example: *The team is pushing to meet the deadline for the project.*
to cause someone or something to move or progress in a particular direction
Example: *The coach pushed the team to give their best performance.*

put /ˈpʊt/
to place or set something in a particular position or location
Example: *Luke put the keys on the table in the living room.*
to cause something to be in a particular condition or state
Example: *The caterer put the food in position before the guests arrived.*
to express or convey in speech or writing
Example: *The manager put forth his opinion during the meeting.*
to assign or attribute something to someone or something
Example: *They put the blame on the stranger for the mistake.*
to apply effort or force to accomplish something
Example: *The students put their skills to use in solving the problem.*

putter /ˈpətɚ/
moving or acting aimlessly or casually
Example: *My granny putters around her garden at least three times a week.*

Qq

quack /kwˈɑk/
to make the characteristic sound of a duck
Example: *Charisse could only quack a hoarse reply from her severely parched throat.*

qualm /kwˈɑːm/
to have doubts or reservations about something
Example: *I qualm at the thought of group projects.*
to hesitate or feel uneasy
Example: *The decision by the university to review the use of AI qualmed many students who had become dependent on the use of AI.*

qualify /kwˈɒlɪfˌaɪ/
to meet the requirements or conditions; to be eligible
Example: *She qualified for the scholarship with her outstanding grades.*

quantify /kwˈɒntɪfˌaɪ/
to measure or express the quantity of something
Example: *The scientists needed to quantify the amount of water in the sample.*

quarantine /kwˈɒrɑːntˌiːn/
to isolate or restrict the movement of people or animals to prevent the spread of disease
Example: *My family was quarantined and enjoyed our time together immensely.*

quarrel /kwˈɒrəl/

to have an angry argument or disagreement
Example: *My mother quarrels when we walk into the house with our shoes.*

quash /kwˈɒʃ/
to suppress forcibly
Example: *In the blink of an eye, the Olympic champion's dreams were quashed as she stumbled and fell on the track.*
to put an end to something by authority
Example: *The Chairman quickly quashed rumours that he disliked working with females when he appointed Daniella as his Permanent Secretary.*

quell /kwˈɛl/
to suppress or put an end to something (usually a rebellion or uprising)
Example: *Alie has a knack for quelling disagreements amongst the children.*

quench /kwˈɛntʃ/
to satisfy or extinguish (thirst, desire, or fire)
Example: *Nothing quenches the thirst like a tall glass of cool water.*

query /kwˈiəri/
to ask a question, especially to request information
Example: *We should all query the unsubstantiated promotions.*

question /kwˈɛstʃən/
to inquire about something
Example: *Adrian questioned the soldiers about the use of each equipment on display at their booth.*
to express doubt or uncertainty
Example: *Zahir questions the sincerity of his offer of friendship, for he was best friends with his arch enemy.*

quibble /kwˈɪbəl/
to argue or raise objections about a trivial matter
Example: *It would be that they had quibbled unnecessarily over who should speak first, as neither of them were allowed to speak.*

quicken /kwˈɪkən/
to make something happen faster
Example: *The spin cycle quickens the process of drying clothes that have been washed.*
to accelerate
Example: *Yashminee felt her heartbeat quicken, when the voice over the intercom boomed that exam results were in.*

quiet /kwˈaɪət/
to make or become silent or less noisy
Example: *One look from the headmistress quiets the class.*

quintuple /kwˈɪntuːpəl/
to increase fivefold or multiply by five
Example: *The workers' wages quintupled when the company expanded to the international market.*

quip /kwˈɪp/
to make a clever or witty remark
Example: *"If she spent as much time on her studies as she did on her hair, she'd be a scholar." Noel quipped.*

quit /kwˈɪt/
to stop doing or leave something
Example: *Do not quit!*

quiver /kwˈɪvɐ/

to tremble or shake with a slight rapid motion
Example: *The children quivered with fear as the dark shadow loomed closer.*

quiz /kwˈɪz/
to test someone's knowledge or understanding of a subject
Example: *After every lesson, Ms. Samuels quizzes her students on what was taught.*

quote /kwˈəʊt/
to repeat or cite a passage, speech, or opinion
Example: *The head nurse quotes Florence Nightingale at every opportunity she gets.*

Rr

race /rˈeɪs/
to compete in a contest of speed
Example: *The cars raced around the track at incredible speeds.*
to move or progress swiftly or hurriedly
Example: *Harry raced to catch the bus before it left.*
to engage in a competition or rivalry
Example: *The two siblings raced to finish their homework first.*

radiate /rˈeɪdiˌeɪt/
to emit or send out rays or waves, especially light or heat
Example: *Every sunrise, light radiates from the crack in the wall.*
to spread out from a central point in all directions
Example: *A sharp pain radiated from his chest and spread out towards his ribs.*
to give off or exhibit a particular quality or feeling strongly
Example: *The toddler's face radiated with glee when she spotted her nanny.*

rage /rˈeɪdʒ/
to express or feel intense anger or fury
Example: *The angry child raged at Simon for spoiling her painting.*
to proceed or spread with great violence or intensity
Example: *The matador watched in shock as the angry bull raged towards the gatekeeper.*
to be or become popular or prevalent to an intense or widespread degree
Example: *Her quick rage to fame was unprecedented.*
to act or speak in an uncontrolled way
Example: *The indisciplined athlete raged at the referee for calling a foul.*

rain /rˈeɪn/
the action of water falling from the sky in the form of droplets
Example: *I love when it rains, and I do not need to leave the house.*

raise /rˈeɪz/
to lift or move something to a higher position
Example: *The flood waters raised by four inches over the last 8 hours.*
to increase the level, amount, or value of something
Example: *The teachers demanded a raise of pay to their salaries.*
to bring up or rear children or animals
Example: *Laura was raised in Lethem, Guyana.*
to cause to arise, appear, or come into existence
Example: *The tide raised the car that had been submerged for more than a decade.*

rake /rˈeɪk/
to gather, collect, or move with a rake
Example: *Raking leaves is the only chore Vickram enjoys doing.*
to search or comb through something thoroughly
Example: *Bandits raked through the chest of jewels looking for the famed Star of India.*
to criticise or blame severely
Example: *The marketing team raked Jason for leaking valued information to the competition.*

rally /rˈɑli/
to come together for a common purpose or cause
Example: *The community rallied to support the victims of the natural disaster.*
to recover or rebound after a setback
Example: *The team rallied in the final quarter and won the game.*
to revive or inspire enthusiasm, support, or spirits

Example: *The coach's halftime speech rallied the team to give their best efforts.*
to assemble or organise for a political or social cause
Example: *The union rallied its members to demand better working conditions.*
to engage in a competitive event, especially in motorsports
Example: *The drivers rallied through the rugged terrain in the off-road race.*

ram /rˈam/
to forcefully strike or collide with something
Example: *A black SUV suddenly rammed our car from behind.*

ramble /rˈambəl/
to walk or talk in a long-winded or wandering manner, often without a clear direction or purpose
Example: *The vagrant rambled on about his wife and children being captured by a UFO.*

rank /rˈaŋk/
to assign a position or level in a hierarchy or classification
Example: *Ben ranks as one of the top performers in the company.*
to hold or be assigned a particular position or status
Example: *The city ranks among the wealthiest in the country.*
to have a particular level of importance or significance
Example: *The safety of the students ranks as the school's top priority.*
to arrange or classify in a particular order or sequence
Example: *The website ranks its products by popularity and price.*
to compare or evaluate someone or something in relation to others
Example: *Marriott hotel ranks among the top-rated accommodations in the city.*

ransack /rˈansak/

to search through something thoroughly or aggressively, often causing disorder or damage in the process
Example: *Thieves had ransacked our home looking for my dad's research.*

rant /rˈɑːnt/
to speak or write in a loud, passionate, and often angry or exaggerated manner
Example: *Before I could stop myself, I was ranting about the importance of preserving the planet.*

rap /rˈap/
to strike a quick, sharp blow with something
Example: *He rap his knuckles on the door to get their attention.*
to talk or converse in a casual or informal manner
Example: *The friends often rap about their plans for the weekend.*
to perform or engage in rap music
Example: *Bob Marley raps about social issues and personal experiences in his songs.*
to criticise or reprimand someone sharply or forcefully
Example: *The teacher rap the student's knuckles with a ruler for misbehaving.*

rasp /rˈɑːsp/
to grate or scrape with a rough, harsh sound
Example: *The metal legs of the chairs rasped noisily on the floor each time the students stood.*

rate /rˈeɪt/
to assign a value or score to something based on its quality or performance
Example: *The hotel was rated five stars for its exceptional service and amenities.*

to consider or evaluate someone or something based on a particular criterion
Example: *The teacher rated the students' essays based on clarity, grammar, and content.*
to establish a standard or scale for measuring or comparing
Example: *The government set a minimum wage rate for workers in certain industries.*
to have a particular level of importance, significance, or value
Example: *Safety rates as the top priority for the construction project.*

ratify /rˈatɪfˌaɪ/
to officially approve or confirm something, typically by a formal process or legal means
Example: *Morgan's biological children refuse to ratify the ownership of their family home to their dad's wife.*

rationalise /rˈaʃənəlˌaɪz/
to justify or explain something logically or to reorganise something to make it more efficient or logical
Example: *Vaughn desperately tried to rationalise his reason for cheating on his finals.*

rattle /rˈatəl/
to make a series of rapid, sharp sounds, often in a noisy or uneven manner
Example: *The windows rattled in the strong wind.*
to cause someone to feel nervous, unsettled, or anxious
Example: *The unexpected noise rattled her concentration during the exam.*
to shake or disturb something, often causing noise or disruption
Example: *She rattled the keys in her pocket as she walked.*
to speak or express something in a rapid or disjointed manner

Example: *George rattled off the names of all the countries he had visited.*
to criticise or rebuke someone, often in a harsh or forceful way
Example: *The coach rattled the players after their disappointing loss.*

ravage /rˈavɪdʒ/
to cause severe and extensive damage or destruction to something
Example: *Hurricane Irma had ravaged the tiny island of Tortola.*

rave /rˈeɪv/
to speak or write about something enthusiastically or in an exaggerated manner
Example: *Josh raved about his new girlfriend to everyone.*
to talk incoherently, often due to extreme emotion or excitement
Example: *The new 100m sprint Olympic record holder raved breathlessly about her success.*
to attend or participate in a lively and energetic party or social gathering
Example: *It was only the first night of the summer vacation, but they had already raved an entire night.*

re-evaluate /riːɪvˈalju:ˌeɪt/
to assess or examine something again, often with the intention of making changes or updates based on new information or perspectives
Example: *My scores did not match my consistent performance, so they decided to re- evaluate me.*

reach /rˈiːtʃ/
to extend or stretch out to touch or grasp something
Example: *The baby reached out and grabbed a fistful of Charisse's locks.*
to arrive at or come to a particular place, condition, or state

Example: *Her temper had reached breaking point by the end of his report.*

to make contact or communication with someone
Example: *They tried reaching out to her father to no avail.*

to achieve or accomplish something
Example: *He had one more level to go, to reach the highest level of taekwondo.*

to extend or cover a distance or range
Example: *Sargassum reached from one end of the Cane Garden Bay beach to the other.*

reacquaint /rˈiːkweɪnt/
to become familiar with someone or something again, especially after a period of absence or lack of contact
Example: *Omia and the girls will get reacquainted after being apart for more than a year.*

react /rɪˈakt/
to respond or behave in a particular way in response to a stimulus, situation, or event
Example: *Jan's skin reacted to the new medication by developing a rash.*

read /ˈrɛd/
to look and comprehend meaning of written or printed matter by interpreting the characters or symbols
Example: *At three years old, Emmanuel was reading the signs in the Pier Park in Tortola.*

readjust /rˌiːədʒˈʌst/
to make small changes or adaptations to something to improve its function or effectiveness, especially after a period of change or disruption

Example: *The teachers readjusted the timetable to accommodate the new teachers.*

ready /rˈɛdi/
to prepare or make something ready for use or action
Example: *Ready the horses! We are going to the race.*

reaffirm /rˌiːɐfˈɜːm/
to assert or confirm something strongly, especially beliefs, decisions, or agreements, often after a period of doubt or challenge
Example: *The dealer reaffirmed that he ordered one hundred Toyota Rush.*

realign /rˌiːɐlˈaɪn/
to adjust or reorganise something, typically to bring it into better alignment or to adapt it to new circumstances
Example: *Dad will realign the wheels of the truck today before he leaves on vacation.*

realise /rˈiəlaɪz/
to become aware of or understand something
Example: *She did not realise how much time had passed until she looked at the clock.*
to achieve or make something real or concrete
Example: *After years of hard work, she finally realised her dream of starting her own business.*
to convert assets or investments into cash or money
Example: *They realised the value of their property by putting it on the market.*
to bring something into existence or make it happen
Example: *The team realised their potential by winning the championship.*
to bring or come to a conclusion or decision

Example: *After much deliberation, they realised that they needed to make a change.*

rearrange /ˌriːərˈeɪndʒ/
to change the position, order, or layout of something
Example: *The rearranged conference room was now suited to persons with and without wheelchairs.*

reason /ˈriːzən/
to think logically and draw conclusions based on facts, evidence, or sound judgement
Example: *The coastguards reasoned that with the increased incidents of unlawful entries to the island, there was a need for more patrol vessels.*

reassert /ˌriːəsˈɜːt/
to state or declare something firmly or confidently again, often after it has been challenged or doubted
Example: *The Guyana Amazon Warriors reasserted themselves as the champions of the CPL T20 cricket.*

reassess /ˌriːəsˈɛs/
to evaluate or review something again, typically to adjust or updates based on new information or changed circumstances
Example: *After reassessing the damages caused to the building, the team decided to rebuild the entire structure.*

reassure /ˌriːəʃˈɔː/
to give someone confidence or alleviate their doubts or fears
Example: *The rescue team reassured the family of Ziggy's safety by sending a video of him smiling.*

reattach /ˌriːətˈatʃ/

to rejoin or re-secure something that was previously detached or separated
Example: *Artie's arm was reattached by the robotics team yesterday.*

rebuff /rɪbˈʌf/
to reject or refuse someone or something in an abrupt or ungracious manner
Example: *Malcolm rebuffed claims that he had given up cricket to play soccer.*

rebuke /rɪbjˈuːk/
to express sharp disapproval or criticism towards someone for their actions or behaviour
Example: *Before handing down the sentence, the judge rebuked the young couple for preventing their two-year-old from getting medical care.*

recall /rɪˈkɔl/
to remember or recollect something from the past
Example: *She recalled the events of her childhood with fondness.*
to officially order the return of a product because of a fault or defect
Example: *The company recalled the faulty airbags in thousands of cars.*
to remove someone from a position or job
Example: *The board of directors decided to recall the CEO due to a lack of performance.*
to bring or summon something back into one's mind or attention
Example: *The smell of cookies baking recalled memories of her grandmother's kitchen.*
to bring something back from a specific location or destination
Example: *The bomb was recalled from entering the building in the nick of time.*

recap /rɪˈkɑp/

to summarise or review the main points of something
Example: *At the end of his presentation on substance abuse, Matthew recapped the session with a game.*

receive /rɪsˈiːv/
to be given or presented with something, usually as a gift, payment, or delivery
Example: *Pensioners receive barely enough to cover meals for the month.*

reciprocate /rɪsˈɪprəkˌeɪt/
to respond to a gesture or action with a similar one
Example: *His kindness of three years ago was reciprocated when the woman he had saved from the fire bought him a house.*

recite /rɪsˈaɪt/
to repeat aloud from memory or to read aloud with expression
Example: *Liam recited the words of the poem brilliantly with no error.*

reckon /rˈɛkən/
to consider or regard something in a particular way, often in terms of estimation or judgement
Example: *The team reckoned that they needed a chopper to transport the injured miner to increase his chances of survival.*

reclaim /rɪklˈeɪm/
to retrieve or recover something that was lost
Example: *Descendants of the displaced Akawaio tribe had come to reclaim the lands of their ancestors.*
to restore land to a better condition
Example: *More land is to be reclaimed along the shorefront of the island of Tortola.*

to assert ownership or control over something
Example: *Omari presented relevant evidence and was able to reclaim his belt buckle.*

recline /rɪklˈaɪn/
to lean or lie back in a relaxed or comfortable position, typically in a chair or on a piece of furniture
Example: *Mom reclines in her favourite chair after a long day at work.*

recognise /rˈɛkəgnˌaɪz/
to identify someone or something as familiar or known
Example: *We all recognise him from the circus.*

recoil /riˈkɔɪl/
to suddenly spring or flinch back in fear, horror, or disgust
Example: *Maggie recoiled when her hand touched the slimy, green blob.*

recollect /ˌrɛkəˈlɛkt/
to recall or remember something from memory
Example: *If I recollect correctly, there were five fire extinguishers, not three.*

recommend /rˌɛkəmˈɛnd/
to suggest or endorse something as suitable, desirable, or advisable
Example: *The doctor recommended that her grandmother take short walks every day to improve her circulation.*

reconcile /rˈɛkənsˌaɪl/
to restore friendly relations between two or more parties or to make two or more things compatible or consistent

Example: *The couple reconciled their differences and have now been married for twenty-seven years.*

reconsider /ˌriːkənˈsɪdə/
to think about something again, especially to change one's previous opinion or decision
Example: *The owners of the house are reconsidering selling since property prices skyrocketed last week.*

record /rəˈkɔrd/
to make a permanent document or audio/video representation of something
Example: *Her sorority sisters recorded her singing unbeknownst to her and sent it to the AGT team.*

recount /rɪˈkaʊnt/
to tell or narrate in detail, typically an event or story
Example: *Jenny recounted the details of her ordeal like it had happened yesterday.*

recover /rɪˈkəvə/
to regain something lost
Example: *I recovered my missing files in a drawer in the storeroom.*
to return to a normal state after an illness, injury, or setback
Example: *Greg is recovering much faster than we all expected him to.*

recruit /rɪkrˈuːt/
to enlist or bring in new members or participants to a group, organisation, or cause
Example: *Cadet Chase did a great job of recruiting new members to the school's cadet program.*

recuperate /rɪkjˈuːpərˌeɪt/
to recover health or strength after an illness or injury
Example: *Kamal is recuperating nicely after his bout of illness.*

redden /rˈɛdən/
to become red or to make something red in colour
Example: *The constant blast of wind had reddened her cheeks on the back of the motorbike.*

redirect /rˌiːdaɪrˈɛkt/
to change the direction or route of something to a different destination or purpose
Example: *Traffic was being redirected because there had been an accident along Mandela Avenue.*

rediscover /rˌiːdɪskˈʌvɐ/
to discover or find something again, especially after it has been lost or forgotten
Example: *Following several years of memory loss, Frank rediscovered his talent of playing the saxophone.*

reduce /rɪdjˈuːs/
to make something smaller, lesser, or to bring it down to a lower level
Example: *I will reduce the size of the font so the entire document will fit the page.*

reel /rˈiːl/
to stagger or sway unsteadily, usually because of dizziness or intoxication
Example: *After spinning around in circles, she reeled and nearly fell over.*
to wind something onto a reel or spool
Example: *Justin reeled the fishing line, hoping to catch a big fish.*

to react with shock or disbelief
Example: *Arnold reeled at the news of his friend's sudden death.*
to draw back or retract, as if being pulled in
Example: *The company reeled in its spending after facing financial difficulties.*

refer /rɪfˈɜː/
to direct someone's attention or thoughts to something else, typically for further consideration or action
Example: *The matter was referred to the Welfare Department for further investigation.*

reference /rˈɛfrəns/
to mention or allude to something for support or clarification
Example: *He referenced the Bible in his debate against female pastors and elders of the church.*

refill /riˈfɪl/
to fill something again after it has been emptied
Example: *Jessie had refilled his water bottle thrice and it was only 10 o'clock.*

refine /rɪfˈaɪn/
to improve or perfect something by making small changes or adjustments
Example: *Wendy had taken the negative criticisms and refined herself almost beyond recognition.*

reflect /rɪflˈɛkt/
to think deeply or carefully about something, or to show an image or likeness of something
Example: *It is customary to reflect on the day's proceedings, after a day of work.*

refocus /rɪfˈəʊkəs/
to adjust one's attention or efforts back onto a specific task or goal
Example: *Since the trials are over, David will refocus on his dance career.*

refrain /rɪfrˈeɪn/
to abstain or hold back from doing something
Example: *Althea refrained from the sharp retort on the tip of her lips.*

refuse /rɪfˈjuz/
to decline to accept or do something
Example: *The children refused to have their dog euthanized just because he had lost a leg.*

refute /rɪfjˈuːt/
to prove a statement, theory, or argument to be false or incorrect
Example: *The family refuted the claim by officers that Jared reached for a weapon in his waist.*

regain /rɪgˈeɪn/
to recover or obtain something that was lost or taken away
Example: *Michelle regained consciousness but could not recognise her surroundings.*

regale /rɪgˈeɪl/
to entertain or delight someone with something, often by providing them with enjoyable experiences or stories
Example: *Every day I am regaled with stories of Ms. Nikki and the Year 2 Winners.*

regard /rɪgˈɑːd/
to consider or view something in a particular way

Example: *Paulette regards her nieces with much love and admiration.*

regret /rɪgr'ɛt/
to feel sorrow or remorse about something that has happened or that one has done
Example: *Tazim regretted his outburst almost immediately.*

regulate /r'ɛgju:l‚eɪt/
to control or adjust something according to a set of rules or standards
Example: *Updated mandates regulated the treatment of the asylum seekers to Canada.*

rehabilitate /rɪhəb'ɪlɪt‚eɪt/
to restore someone or something to a normal or healthy condition after illness, injury, or wrongdoing
Example: *After undergoing surgery to his leg, Andrew was rehabilitated through a series of therapy sessions.*

reign /r'eɪn/
to hold royal office; to rule as a monarch
Example: *King Charles reigns as the new monarch after the death of his mother Queen Elizabeth.*

reinforce /r‚i:ɪnf'ɔ:s/
to strengthen or support something, often by adding more material or additional support
Example: *The men reinforced the shutters after the hurricane was upgraded to category five.*

reintroduce /r‚i:‚ɪntrədj'u:s/
to bring something back into use or existence after it has been absent or removed

Example: *Some cities have reintroduced the use of patrol police officers on bicycles.*

reiterate /rˌiːˈɪtərˌeɪt/
to say or do something again, typically for emphasis or clarity
Example: *The commander reiterated the importance of packing the bare necessities for the patrol.*

reject /rɪˈdʒɛkt/
to refuse to accept, believe, or agree with something or someone
Example: *The presidential candidate rejected claims of bribery and corruption.*

rejoice /rɪdʒˈɔɪs/
to feel or express great joy or happiness
Example: *The members of the band rejoiced when they heard they were receiving new equipment and uniforms.*

relate /rɪˈleɪt/
to make a connection between two or more things
Example: *There is no proof that the case of the missing windows is related to the case of the missing door frames.*
to tell a story or give an account of something
Example: *She related her experience on her trip to China with much enthusiasm.*

relax /rɪˈlɑks/
to become less tense, anxious, or stressed
Example: *Soothing sounds of the sea relaxes her better than soft music does.*

relay /ˈriˌleɪ/
to pass on or communicate information or a message to someone

Example: *The teller was given the information to relay to the manager.*

release /rɪˈlis/
to set free or make something available to the public
Example: *The butterflies should be released back into the garden.*

relent /rɪˈɛnt/
to soften in attitude, temper, or determination, especially after being stubborn or strict
Example: *Her dad relented when he heard how talented she was on the piano.*

relinquish /rɪˈɪnkwɪʃ/
to voluntarily give up or let go of something
Example: *Kurt relinquished ownership of the trucking company after he decided to leave the state.*

relish /rˈɛlɪʃ/
to appreciate or enjoy something
Example: *The children relished the grated cheese on top of their pancakes.*

rely /rɪˈaɪ/
to depend on or trust in someone or something for support, help, or fulfilment
Example: *The family relied heavily on each other for support when Ms. Marie died.*

remain /rɪmˈeɪn/
to stay in the same place or condition
Example: *They were taken aback by the pristine condition the body had remained in after five years.*

to continue to exist
Example: *Of the five pups in the litter, only two remain.*
to be left over after others have gone
Example: *They were surprised to find that the Vanderstoops had remained in their old neighbourhood.*

remark /rɪˈmɑrk/
to say or mention something as a comment or observation
Example: *The spectators remarked on the skill of the young basketball player.*

remember /rɪmˈɛmbɐ/
to have in or be able to bring to one's mind an awareness of something from the past
Example: *"I remember my kindergarten days like it was yesterday," said Keimaul.*

remind /rɪmˈaɪnd/
to cause someone to remember something, often by bringing it to their attention
Example: *Every day the students are reminded to not loiter in the corridors.*

reminisce /rˌɛmɪnˈɪs/
to indulge in enjoyable recollection of past events or experiences
Example: *Dereck reminisced on his beautiful years with his wife as he sat overlooking the Pitons.*

remonstrate /rˈɛmənstrˌeɪt/
to make a forcefully reproachful protest
Example: *Yashminee remonstrated the punishment given to the class for being undisciplined on the claim that the allegations were false.*

remove /rɪmˈuːv/
to take away or eliminate something from a place or position
Example: The council is removing Mr. Wilson as town clerk and appointing Mr. Scott instead.

rend /rˈɛnd/
to tear or split apart violently
Example: The wrestler rends the championship belt in anger when he lost the match.

render /rˈɛndɐ/
to provide or care
Example: The company will render a report on its quarterly earnings.
to represent or depict
Example: The artist rendered the scene with detail.
to cause to become or make
Example: Prolonged exposure to the sun can render skin cells damaged.
to translate into another language or form
Example: The novel was rendered into several languages.
to melt down or extract something
Example: The chef rendered the fat from the meat.

reorganise /rɪˈɔːgɐnˌaɪz/
to organise again or rearrange in a different way
Example: It took twenty minutes to reorganise placement of the flags on the field.

repack /rɪpˈak/
to pack something again or in a different way
Example: We repacked our suitcases using the new method and had much room to spare.

repair /rɪˈpɛr/
to fix or mend something that is broken or damaged
Example: *The men repaired the broken koker just in time before the rainy season started.*

repeat /rɪpˈiːt/
to say or do something again
Example: *Prayers were repeated for families lost at sea.*

repel /rɪpˈɛl/
to drive away or force back
Example: *The strong scent of Jeyes fluid is used to repel snakes when the flood waters rise.*
to cause a feeling of strong dislike or distaste in
Example: *His grotesque appearance repelled the crowd of onlookers.*
to resist the effect of
Example: *The mosquito coil was not successful in repelling mosquitoes outdoors.*

repent /rɪˈpɛnt/
to feel regret or remorse for one's actions or sins and to resolve to change one's ways
Example: *They repented of their wrong doings and were forgiven.*

rephrase /rɪfrˈeɪz/
to express or say something in a different way, often to clarify or convey the meaning more effectively
Example: *Dad rephrased his question and mum finally responded.*

replace /rɪplˈeɪs/
to take the place of something or someone that is removed, lost, or no longer adequate

Example: *They are replacing all the patrol horses with high powered mountain bikes.*

reply /rɪpˈlaɪ/
to respond to something that has been said or written
Example: *Brenda replies promptly to emails received from the care home.*

report /rɪˈpɔrt/
to provide information about something
Example: *The journalist reported on the earthquake that struck the region.*
to present oneself or be present in a particular place, especially for work or duty
Example: *The soldiers reported for duty at dawn.*
to make an official statement or complaint about someone or something
Example: *The employee reported his co-worker's misconduct to the supervisor.*
to give a detailed account of something
Example: *The witness reported what she saw to the police.*

reposition /rɪpəzˈɪʃən/
to change the position or placement of something, often with the intention of improving its effectiveness or function
Example: *The antennae is repositioned after heavy winds because it affects the function of the television channels.*

represent /ˌrɛprɪˈzɛnt/
to depict or stand for something
Example: *Three brothers are representing the county of Berbice in the Cycling Athletics Championship.*

repress /rɪˈprɛs/
to suppress or restrain something, typically a feeling, desire, or action
Example: *Jessie repressed the urge to scream as she felt the gun dig into her rib.*

reprimand /ˈrɛprɪmˌɑːnd/
to scold or admonish someone, usually formally or officially
Example: *The students were reprimanded for cutting classes.*

reproach /rɪprˈəʊtʃ/
to express disapproval or disappointment towards someone for their actions or behaviour
Example: *Reproaching children publicly may result in rude, explosive responses because they are embarrassed.*

reproduce /rɪprədjˈuːs/
to produce offspring
Example: *Christians believe they have been given a mandate to get married and reproduce.*
to make a copy of something
Example: *Sounds made in wide enclosed spaces often reproduce the sound through an echo.*

repudiate /rɪpjˈuːdɪˌeɪt/
to reject or refuse to accept something as true, valid, or binding
Example: *In a surprising twist of events, each witness repudiated claims that they had seen the man commit the gruesome act.*

repulse /rɪpˈʌls/
to drive back or reject with disgust or horror
Example: *The sight of blood repulses me.*

request /rɪkwˈɛst/
to ask for something politely or formally
Example: *She requests an extension of time to complete tasks given.*

rescind /rɪsˈɪnd/
to revoke, cancel, or repeal something, especially an official agreement, law, or decision
Example: *The team's visa was rescinded, and they were denied access to the country.*

rescue /rˈɛskjuː/
to save someone or something from a dangerous or harmful situation
Example: *Maxwell's dog rescues countless tourists every year during the summer holidays.*

research /ˈrisɝtʃ/
to systematically investigate or study a subject to discover facts or reach new conclusions
Example: *We are researching the effects of global warming on the Arctic Region.*

resent /rɪˈzɛnt/
to feel bitterness or indignation at a perceived unfairness, insult, or injury
Example: *To date, she resents her father for leaving the family.*

reside /rɪˈzaɪd/
to live in a particular place or to be situated
Example: *A young couple now resides in the old mansion at the end of the street.*

resign /rɪˈzaɪn/

to voluntarily leave a job or position, typically by formally notifying one's employer or superior
Example: *Joe had resigned abruptly, leaving a huge void in his place on the board.*
to accept something reluctantly because it cannot be avoided
Example: *I resign myself to the fact that a person will change only if he or she sees it fit to do so.*

resist /rɪsˈɪst/
to withstand the action or effect of something
Example: *Everyday Pinky resists the urge to give up on the book she was writing.*
to refuse to accept or comply with something
Example: *A young man was shot while resisting arrest.*
to refrain from giving in to temptation or pressure
Example: *The urge to bite into the chocolate muffin was great but Ray resisted the temptation.*

resolve /rɪˈzɑlv/
to come to a firm decision about something
Example: *The agricultural department resolved to have the students each rear two chicks for their project.*
to solve or settle a problem, dispute, or conflict
Example: *The matter was resolved legally in court.*
to have determination or strong willpower to accomplish something
Example: *Michael had resolved to swim across the Berbice River, and he just did.*

respect /rɪspˈɛkt/
to have a feeling of deep admiration for someone or something based on their qualities, achievements, or abilities
Example: *The staff respects the manager and complies with her decisions.*
to treat someone with politeness and consideration

Example: *The commander was respected by each officer saluting when he entered the room.*
to adhere to or comply with something, such as rules, agreements, or standards
Example: *Children ought to respect the rules of their home.*

respond /rɪspˈɒnd/
to reply or react to something, often in words or actions
Example: *Kindergarteners often respond with nods rather than words.*
to react favourably or effectively to a stimulus or situation
Example: *Brad nodded his response to Casey's question.*

rest /rˈɛst/
to relax or cease from activity or work
Example: *Mom rests in the hammock after a day's work before starting her evening chores.*
to be supported or based on something
Example: *The woman's claim rests on the belief that her father is still alive.*
to remain or be left in a particular state
Example: *His remains were rested next to his wife's in the family's burial chambers.*

restate /rɪstˈeɪt/
to state or express something again often in a different way or with emphasis
Example: *The accuser restated her claims of abuse by the judge much to the consternation of the courtroom.*

restrain /rɪstrˈeɪn/
to prevent someone or something from doing something or acting in a certain way

Example: *The young mother desperately tried to restrain the toddler from touching the fruit display.*

to control or hold back someone or something physically

Example: *The court Marshall restrained the enraged father when the murder accused walked into the courtroom.*

to limit or restrict someone or something

Example: *The decision restrains him from playing hockey for the next two years.*

restructure /rɪstrˈʌktʃɐ/
to organise, alter, or change the structure of something, often to make it more efficient or effective
Example: *The schools on the coast are being restructured to accommodate the new CVQ program.*

resume /rɪˈzum/
to begin again or continue after a pause or interruption
Example: *School for the Christmas term resumes on September 2, 2024.*
to take up or occupy again
Example: *Production of Volkswagens may resume soon.*

retaliate /rɪtˈalɪˌeɪt/
to respond to an action or attack with a similar action, especially in return for harm or injury inflicted
Example: *When Mr. Jones retaliated to the taunts by firing shots into the air, it sparked a block feud that lasted for an entire day.*

retch /rˈɛtʃ/
to make an involuntary effort to vomit or to gag
Example: *I can hear him retching every morning at 4 o'clock.*

retell /rɪtˈɛl/

to tell a story or recount an event again, often in one's own words or with slight changes
Example: *Camp guides retell stories of past camp experiences around the fire on the first night at camp.*

retire /rɪtˈaɪə/
to withdraw or remove oneself from active duty, work, or employment, especially upon reaching a certain age
Example: *My grandmother retired at the age of sixty.*
to move back or withdraw from a position or place
Example: *The team retired to their hiding places when they heard vehicles approaching.*
to take oneself to bed, typically for sleep or rest
Example: *She will retire early tonight for tomorrow promises to be a long, hard day.*

retort /rɪtˈɔːt/
to respond sharply or angrily to a remark or criticism
Example: *Malachy retorts sharply at Jude for criticising his model plane.*

retract /rɪtrˈakt/
to withdraw, take back, or revoke something previously stated, published, or done
Example: *The newspapers were made to retract the article written on Allison Hinds as the information was defamatory.*

retreat /rɪtrˈiːt/
to withdraw or move back, especially from a different or dangerous situation
Example: *The soldiers retreated hastily from the borders of the country when the jets flew overhead.*
to go to a quiet, secluded place for relaxation or meditation

Example: *The first family retreated to their home in the woods to get away from prying eyes.*
to change one's opinion or position on a matter
Example: *Jess retreated her position on the case and worked to arrive at an amicable solution.*

retrieve /rɪtrˈiːv/
to get or bring back something that was lost, stolen, or misplaced
Example: *The stolen car was retrieved from the back-lands in Rose Hall Town.*

return /rɪˈtɜ·n/
to go or come back to a place where one was before
Example: *After completing college she returned to work in the family business.*
to give, put, or send something back to its original place or owner
Example: *Return products that you are dissatisfied with, without hassle using my company.*
to revert to a previous state or condition
Example: *In the morning, the tide had returned the dinghy to the position we had struggled to move it from the night before.*

reveal /rɪvˈiːl/
to make something known or visible that was previously hidden or secret
Example: *He was shocked when they revealed the identity of his biological parents.*

revel /rˈɛvəl/
to take great pleasure or delight in something
Example: *The teachers revelled in the students' success at their exams.*
to engage in lively and noisy festivities or celebrations

Example: *There is great revelling at the carnival parade on the first Monday in August.*

revere /rɪvˈiə/
to regard with deep respect, admiration, or awe
Example: *Despite the accusations against him, his congregation revered him.*

reverse /rɪvˈɜːs/
to go backward or turn in the opposite direction
Example: *Halfway up the hill we were forced to reverse as there was a huge fallen tree blocking the way.*
to change to the opposite state, condition, or effect
Example: *Castor oil used correctly, reverses many conditions that prescribed medication does not heal, is the claim of many persons suffering from chronic illnesses.*
to overturn or annul a decision, ruling, or outcome
Example: *The judges reversed their decision and awarded the top spot to Martha Francis.*
to cause something to move or operate in the opposite direction
Example: *Reverse into park; it makes leaving the venue easier when the lot becomes crowded.*
to flip or turn something over to its opposite side or position
Example: *When this side of the card is full, reverse it and write on the other side.*

revert /rɪvˈɜːt/
to return to a previous state, condition, or behaviour
Example: *With no guidance at home, Jack soon reverted to his old habit of stealing.*
to go back to a former owner or state
Example: *Control of the business reverts to the Hernandez family if the debt is not paid by the end of the month.*

review /ˌrɪvˈju/
to examine or assess something carefully
Example: *The Board of Directors reviews the annual financial report more meticulously than they do the quarterly report.*
to give a critical appraisal or evaluation of something
Example: *After several complaints were filed, a team reviewed the grades issued to the students graduating with high honours.*
to study, revise, or refresh one's memory of something
Example: *Our group quickly reviews the notes before heading in to do our presentation.*
to look back on or recall past events or experiences
Example: *In tribute to our mum, we reviewed her years as a teacher using photos on the projector.*

revise /rɪvˈaɪz/
to reconsider, amend, or alter something, especially written or printed material, to make corrections or improvements
Example: *The building plans for the city mall were revised and adjustments made to the proposed parking lot.*

revoke /rɪvˈəʊk/
to officially cancel or withdraw something, such as a law, privilege, or agreement
Example: *Justin's rights to visitation of his children were revoked after he lost his temper and smashed his fist into a wall at their mum's home.*

reward /rɪwˈɔːd/
to give something, typically in recognition of one's effort, achievement, or behaviour
Example: *The company rewards shoppers who spend $100,000 and above with gift certificates.*

reword /riˈwɜ-d/
to express or rewrite something using different words but with the same meaning
Example: *Students were advised to avoid rewording essays written by AI and write their own thoughts.*

rhapsodise /rˈɑpsədˌaɪz/
to speak or write about something with great enthusiasm or emotion, often in an exaggerated or extravagant manner
Example: *After the performance, many patrons rhapsodised about the brilliance and elegance of the performance by the characters.*

rhyme /rˈaɪm/
to have or produce a similarity of sound, especially at the ends of words
Example: *Rhyming is not a necessary aspect of poetry writing.*

rid /rˈɪd/
to free or relieve someone or something of something undesirable or unwanted
Example: *After years of struggle, she was finally able to rid herself of the bad habit of chewing gum.*

riddle /rˈɪdəl/
to fill or spread throughout something with holes or openings
Example: *The crazed student riddled the doors to the gym with bullets in his attempt to gain access to the students supporting the students' election campaign.*
to solve or explain something that is difficult or puzzling
Example: *Josh walked in and riddled out the answer to the problem that had been puzzling us all morning.*

ride /rˈaɪd/

to sit on and control the movement of an animal, vehicle, or device for transportation
Example: *She learned how to ride a bike when she was five years old.*
to travel in a vehicle as a passenger
Example: *He rides the bus to work every morning.*
to move or be carried in a particular direction on something, such as a wave or current
Example: *The surfer rode the wave all the way to the shore.*
to experience or endure something
Example: *The company is currently riding a wave of success after the release of their latest product.*

ridicule /rˈɪdɪkjˌuːl/
to mock or make fun of someone or something in a scornful or contemptuous way
Example: *Mrs Smith's constant ridiculing of the children makes her their least liked teacher.*

riffle /rˈɪfəl/
to flip through the pages of a book, magazine, or stack of papers quickly and casually
Example: *I watched her riffle through the pages of the book to find the note I had placed there.*
to shuffle or mix playing cards by repeatedly dividing them into two parts and interleaving them together
Example: *The magician riffled the pack of cards three times before asking Simon Cowell to pick a card.*

rifle /rˈaɪfəl/
to search through something quickly and thoroughly, often in a disorderly or indiscriminate manner
Example: *He hurriedly rifled through the drawer trying to find his report booklet.*

to steal or take something, especially by searching through it quickly
Example: *On Friday nights when her dad comes in from work, Denise rifles through his pockets looking for loose change.*

ring /rˈɪŋ/
to produce or emit a clear, resonant sound, typically by striking or vibrating something
Example: *The bell rang loudly, signalling the end of the school day.*
to encircle or surround something
Example: *The trees ringed the edge of the meadow, providing shade and shelter.*
to call someone or communicate with them by telephone
Example: *Sarah rang her friend to invite her to the party.*
to have a particular characteristic or quality
Example: *His words rang true, and everyone believed him.*

rinse /rˈɪns/
to clean or wash something with water, typically by pouring water over it or immersing it briefly
Example: *Mum likes to rinse the dishes herself after my sister has washed them.*

rip /rˈɪp/
to tear or pull something apart forcefully
Example: *The bride accidentally ripped her dress on a nail.*
to move quickly or forcefully
Example: *The wind ripped through the trees, bending them sideways.*
to criticise or speak sharply to someone
Example: *Deon ripped into his opponent's argument during the debate.*
to steal something

Example: *Thieves ripped off the jewellery store, stealing valuable items.*

riposte /rɪpˈɒst/
to make a quick and clever reply, especially in response to a criticism or challenge
Example: *He quickly riposte in response to her callous comments about his workers.*

rise /rˈaɪz/
to move upward or ascend
Example: *From the distance we could see black smoke rising in the air.*
to increase in amount, level, or value
Example: *The water level rose quickly as the rain continued to pour.*
to stand up or assume an upright position
Example: *We rise in respect at the entrance of notable public figures.*
to originate or come into existence
Example: *Her sudden rise to fame shocked the locals who thought her a plain Jane.*
to revolt or rebel against authority
Example: *United they rise to protest the injustices being meted out to their counterparts.*

risk /rˈɪsk/
to expose someone or something to danger, harm, or loss
Example: *Why risk your life for such a meagre wage?*

roam /rˈəʊm/
to move about or travel aimlessly or without a fixed destination
Example: *The lost sheep roamed aimlessly until the shepherd found him.*

roar /rˈɔː/
to make a loud, deep, or prolonged sound, like that of a lion or a strong wind
Example: *Hurricane Beryl roared through the Windward Islands causing much destruction in Grenada.*
to shout or speak loudly, often in anger or excitement
Example: *The stadium erupted in a loud roar when Shamar Joseph took the winning wicket.*

roast /rˈəʊst/
to cook food, especially meat, by exposing it to direct heat, typically in an oven or over an open flame
Example: *My siblings and I are roasting beef and potatoes for dinner this evening.*
to criticise or ridicule someone or something severely and publicly
Example: *The public roasted the referee for his inconsistent ruling in the match.*
to subject something to intense heat, often for the purpose of drying or toasting
Example: *We will roast the meat to preserve them for our summer camp.*

rob /rˈɒb/
to take property unlawfully from someone or some place, typically by force or threat
Example: *The supermarket was robbed three times in the past month.*

rock /rˈɒk/
to move back and forth or sway from side to side
Example: *Rocking Zavion in the hammock is the fastest way to get him to sleep.*
to shock or deeply disturb someone emotionally
Example: *The news of the accident rocked her to the core.*
to wear or carry something, often with pride or confidence

Example: *The contestants each rocked locally designed evening gowns.*

roll /rˈəʊl/
to move forward by turning over and over
Example: *The ball rolled down the stairs.*
to form into a rounded or cylindrical shape
Example: *Martha rolled the dough into a ball.*
to turn over in one's mind or think about something deeply
Example: *Ethan rolled the idea around in his mind for a while.*
to flow or move in a smooth, continuous motion
Example: *The waves rolled gently onto the shore.*
to start or cause to move, operate, or progress
Example: *Zack rolled the dice to see who would go first.*

romp /rˈɒmp/
to play or frolic in a lively and carefree manner
Example: *We watched the dogs romp happily in the open field.*
to win or be successful easily and convincingly
Example: *The school's soccer team romped to victory winning the match 4 - 0.*

rot /rˈɒt/
to decay or decompose due to the action of bacteria, fungi, or other organisms
Example: *The fish is rotting because it has been exposed all day to the direct sun.*
to deteriorate or decline in quality or condition
Example: *We were surprised to discover that the furniture in the room was badly rotted.*

rotate /rəʊtˈeɪt/
to turn or cause to turn around a central axis or point

Example: *My nephew is fascinated at how the planets rotate around the sun.*
to alternate or take turns in a sequence or cycle
Example: *The chores are rotated among the children in the home.*
to change or shift positions in a regular or systematic manner
Example: *The school's cafeteria has a rotating system for the daily menu.*

round /rˈaʊnd/
to shape into a round or curved form
Example: *The sculptor uses his bare hands to round off the edges of bowls and cups he makes.*
to go or pass around something in a circular direction
Example: *When Bolt rounded the corner in the 200m sprint race, the crowd cheered wildly.*
to make something more complete or whole by adding or adjusting
Example: *I will round off the sale by adding two more mangoes to the parcel.*
to approximate a particular number by increasing or decreasing it to the nearest whole number or specified place value
Example: *The children of Ms. Dow's class are learning to round numbers.*
to finish or complete a task or activity
Example: *Cassie rounded off the necklace she was making with a heart-shaped bead.*

rouse /rˈaʊz/
to wake someone from sleep or to stir them from a state of inactivity
Example: *Amy tried to rouse her brother from his deep sleep.*
to cause someone to become excited, interested, or emotionally aroused
Example: *The coach's inspiring speech roused the team to victory.*

rub /rˈʌb/
to move one's hand or an object back and forth against a surface with pressure
Example: *Josh rubbed the nape of his neck to ease the tension he felt in his neck.*
to cause friction by moving against something
Example: *The rubbing of the rope against the edge of the wall will cause it to break after a while.*
to be an annoyance or source of irritation
Example: *Joe's friends rubbed him about missing all the goals in the game the day before.*

ruffle /rˈʌfəl/
to disturb the smoothness or neatness of something by causing it to become wrinkled or disordered
Example: *The hen ruffled her feathers and clucked protectively as the farmer approached her pen.*
to cause someone to feel uneasy or flustered
Example: *The boss's comments about tardiness ruffled Sandra's feathers as she was always late for work.*
to flip through the pages of a book, typically quickly and casually
Example: *Annie ruffled the pages of the book in search of her assignment.*

ruin /rˈuːɪn/
to destroy or severely damage something
Example: *The newly erected billboard was ruined after the storm.*
to cause someone to lose their wealth, reputation, or happiness
Example: *Marrying without a prenup can ruin a wealthy person.*
to spoil or render useless or ineffective
Example: *Fifteen years of sterling service was ruined by one thoughtless act.*

rule /ˈruːl/

to govern or control with authority
Example: *The President rules with an iron fist, much to the dismay of his citizens.*
to establish or enforce regulations or guidelines
Example: *The committee rules the distribution of cash grant with very strict guidelines for parents.*
to be predominant or the norm in a particular situation
Example: *Ruling the school for a day seemed like an easy task to the PTA body, until they executed it.*
to make a formal decision or judgement
Example: *The panel ruled that the presumed offence was null and that the claims could not be substantiated.*

rumble /rˈʌmbəl/
to make a continuous deep, resonant sound, like distant thunder
Example: *Thunder rumbled in the distance reminding us of the approach of the hurricane.*
to move with a low, continuous, and somewhat menacing noise
Example: *In the wee hours of the morning, we can hear the enormous trucks rumbling through the once quiet village of Port Mourant.*

ruminate /rˈuːmɪnˌeɪt/
to think deeply about something, often for a prolonged period
Example: *The Toshaos from several communities ruminate over the proposed development to the villages that the government has earmarked.*

rummage /rˈʌmɪdʒ/
to search through something untidily or thoroughly, typically by moving things around
Example: *It is a sad sight to see the homeless rummaging through the garbage bins for food.*

run /rˈʌn/
to move swiftly on foot
Example: *She likes to run in the park every morning.*
to operate or function
Example: *The car runs smoothly after the mechanic fixed it.*
to be in charge or manage something
Example: *Sam runs his own business.*
to extend or stretch in a particular direction
Example: *The fence runs along the perimeter of the property.*
to flow or move continuously in a specified direction
Example: *The river runs through the valley.*

rush /rˈʌʃ/
to move quickly or hurriedly
Example: *Julia rushed to catch the bus before it left.*
to do something in a hurry or with urgency
Example: *Derick rushed through his homework so he could go out with his friends.*
to cause someone to feel a sudden sense of urgency or excitement
Example: *The news of the sale rushed her to the store to get the discounted items.*
to attack or assault suddenly and forcefully
Example: *The robbers rushed into the bank, demanding money.*
to fill or flow quickly or suddenly
Example: *The water rushed out of the broken pipe, flooding the yard.*

rustle /rˈʌsəl/
to make a soft, muffled, cracking sound, like the sound of leaves or paper being moved or stirred
Example: *Leaves rustle in the gentle breeze creating a soothing effect to the calm morning.*
to move or act in a quiet, secretive, or furtive way
Example: *Wil nervously rustled the sheaves of paper on his desk as the teacher looked intently at him.*

Ss

sack /sˈak/
to dismiss or fire someone from their job
Example: *The police officers were sacked for causing the death of the young man by unlawfully opening fire at him.*
to plunder or loot
Example: *Criminal minded citizens often sack business in the aftermath of a devastating hurricane.*
to tackle or tackle aggressively in sports, especially American football
Example: *Ray Lewis is famous for his ability to sack his opponents effortlessly.*
to criticise or condemn harshly
Example: *The social worker sacked the Petersons for their negligent treatment of the children in their care.*

sail /sˈeɪl/
to travel on water in a ship or boat, using sails
Example: *Sailing on the open sea under a starlit sky is a beautiful experience.*
to move swiftly and gracefully, often with a sense of purpose
Example: *Sabrina sailed through her dance routine with the grace of a gazelle.*

salivate /sˈalɪvˌeɪt/
the physiological response of producing saliva in the mouth, especially when anticipating food or as a reaction to something appetising
Example: *The scent of bread coming from the bakery caused the hungry children to salivate.*

salute /səlˈuːt/

to greet or show respect to someone, usually by raising one's hand to the forehead or performing a similar gesture
Example: *The corporal saluted smartly as the Lieutenant passed by.*

salvage /sˈalvɪdʒ/
to rescue or retrieve something from loss or destruction, especially from a wreckage or disaster
Example: *The team of divers salvaged a crate of gold coins from the truck that ran off the Demerara Harbour Bridge.*
to save or recover usable materials or items from something that is no longer in use
Example: *The mechanic salvages the engines of old vehicles for his hobby of building go karts.*
to restore or make something usable or valuable again
Example: *Maxwell's venture of salvaging his brother's old BMX bike, has now become a business of salvaging bicycles for sale.*

sashay /sˈaʃeɪ/
to walk or move in a confident, casual, and often ostentatious manner, typically with exaggerated hip movements
Example: *The contestants sashayed down the runway in pairs, wowing the audience.*

satirise /sˈatɪrˌaɪz/
to use humour, irony, or exaggeration to criticise or ridicule someone or something, often in a literary or artistic work
Example: *The columnist satirised the pronouns adopted by the LBGTQIA community, and his column was given to another writer in the company.*

satisfy /sˈatɪsfˌaɪ/
to fulfil or meet a need, desire, or expectation
Example: *Several small meals satisfy me better than one big meal.*

to provide enough or sufficient quality or quantity
Example: *Most parents give an allowance that will satisfy a little more than the basic needs of their children.*
to fulfil a condition or requirement
Example: *Her qualifications satisfied the criteria needed for the job with the firm, but her attitude was a turn off.*

saturate /sˈatʃərˌeɪt/
to soak or fill completely with a substance
Example: *We saturated the heap of dried grass with water before lighting it to create smoke to combat the mosquitoes.*
to completely fill a space or area to its maximum capacity
Example: *For T20 cricket finals, the Guyana National Stadium is saturated with fans from every walk of life.*
to completely imbue or permeate with a particular quality or attribute
Example: *He was so saturated with his own ego that missed several opportunities to bond with his family and repair the damage that had been done through the separation.*

saunter /sˈɔːntɐ/
to walk in a slow, relaxed, and casual manner, often with an air of leisure or indifference
Example: *The room was hazy when he sauntered in, but she could recognise that walk even in a pitch-dark room.*

savage /sˈavɪdʒ/
to attack violently or ferociously
Example: *The lioness savaged the doe, working together to rip her apart limb by limb before inviting the cubs to eat.*
to condemn or criticise harshly
Example: *The media has a poor track record for savaging persons before a matter is properly investigated.*
to treat someone or something brutally or mercilessly

Example: *Many times, teenage girls savage other girls who do not conform to their proposed standard of deportment and attire.*

save /sˈeɪv/
to rescue or preserve someone or something from harm, danger, or loss
Example: *A kind man saved the stranded pups from a life on the street by taking them home to his farm.*
to keep or set aside for future use or purposes
Example: *Kelon's mum saved all his paintings and drawings from kindergarten to high school.*
to prevent something from being wasted or used unnecessarily
Example: *We save water when we do not leave the tap running while brushing our teeth.*
to store or preserve data or information electronically
Example: *Google docs automatically saves your documents while you are working.*
to except or exclude
Example: *Of the seven pups in Ziva's litter, all have died save Ziggy and Zoe.*

savour /sˈeɪvɐ/
to enjoy or appreciate something slowly and with great pleasure, often by lingering over it
Example: *Andy sat on the porch, savouring the tranquillity of the evening.*
to taste or perceive with relish or enjoyment
Example: *They savour the unique flavours of the local cuisine while travelling.*
to enjoy or appreciate something intellectually or emotionally
Example: *As a literature enthusiast, Grethel savoured every word of the classic novel.*

saw /sˈɔː/

to cut something using a saw
Example: *My brothers argued over whether the tree should be cut or sawed.*
to perceive or notice something
Example: *I saw the pain in her eyes when her friends revealed over the intercom at lunch that she was adopted.*

say /sˈeɪ/
to express something verbally; to utter words
Example: *Many men have difficulty saying how they feel about varying situations.*
to state or affirm in writing or speech
Example: *In her letter she said that she will not be returning to her home country, India.*
to indicate or suggest without stating
Example: *I will say what I want to say when the time is right.*

scale /skˈeɪl/
to climb up or over; ascend
Example: *Oran scaled every rung on the high jump bar.*
to change the size of something while maintaining its proportion
Example: *The owner of the building project requested that the architect scale the building plan to suit his new idea.*
to remove the scales from
Example: *Scaling the fish is a part of the package offered by fish vendors in the fish market.*
to estimate or measure the size or magnitude of something
Example: *Students of the Industrial Tech class were tasked with scaling the main building that occupies the GUYSUCO Training School.*

scamper /skˈampɐ/
moving quickly with small, light steps, often in a playful or hurried manner

Example: *The startled mouse quickly scampered away when the lights were put on in the kitchen.*

scan /skˈɑn/
to examine closely or quickly
Example: *He walked through the doors and scanned the room in search of the fugitive.*

scare /skˈeə/
to cause fear or alarm in someone or something
Example: *A loud pounding on the door just before sunrise scared us out of our sleep.*

scatter /skˈatɐ/
to throw or distribute things over an area, or to disperse things in different directions
Example: *The farmer scattered seeds on the newly ploughed beds on his farm.*

schedule /ʃˈɛdjuːl/
to plan or arrange an event, task, or appointment to occur at a specific time
Example: *The distribution of filaria tablets was scheduled for report card distribution day.*

scheme /skˈiːm/
to plan or devise a systematic or strategic course of action
Example: *Most politicians have a managerial team that schemes the operation of their campaign leading up to elections.*
to engage in secretive or dishonest plotting or planning
Example: *I could hear them scheming in the next room to skip school to attend the Neyo concert.*

school /skˈuːl/
to educate or teach someone, typically in a formal setting
Example: *Denzel's father schools him along with his older siblings in preparation for handing over the reins of the company to one of them someday.*

scoff /skˈɒf/
to speak or act contemptuously or mockingly about something, often showing disbelief or disdain
Example: *Those of us who had scoffed at Esau's dream of owning a car dealership sat mum at the opening ceremony that we had been invited to.*

scold /skˈəʊld/
to reprimand or criticise someone angrily, typically for their behaviour or actions
Example: *The campers were scolded for the untidy manner that they left the campsite in.*

scoop /skˈuːp/
to lift or gather something with a scoop or similar utensil
Example: *Walter scooped a spoonful of ice cream into his bowl.*
to obtain or acquire something ahead of others
Example: *The reporter scooped the story before anyone else could.*
to dig out or hollow out with a scooping motion
Example: *The excavator scooped away the earth to reveal the buried cars.*
to win or achieve something decisively or unexpectedly
Example: *The team scooped victory in the final minutes of the game.*

scoot /skˈuːt/
to move quickly or hastily, often in a short, swift motion

Example: *Before anyone could stop him, the child had scooted out of the park into the path of oncoming traffic.*

scorch /skˈɔːtʃ/
to burn or char the surface of something, usually because of intense heat
Example: *The fire had destroyed several buildings and scorched a few others.*

score /skˈɔː/
to achieve or win points in a game or competition
Example: *The soccer team scored three goals in the first half of the game.*
to make a mark or cut into a surface
Example: *Gerald scored his initials into the tree trunk.*
to obtain or secure something, often with effort
Example: *Burt scored a job at the company after months of searching.*
to orchestrate or arrange music
Example: *The composer scored the symphony for a full orchestra.*

scorn /skˈɔːn/
to reject, disdain, or treat with contempt or derision
Example: *The members of the executive board of the company scorned the proposal put forward by the data entry clerk, but the boss loved the idea.*

scour /skˈaʊə/
to clean or polish something thoroughly, typically by scrubbing
Example: *Scouring pots and pans is not a favoured chore for me.*
to search or comb an area or place thoroughly to find something
Example: *The rescue team scoured the wooded area searching for the missing child.*

scowl /skˈaʊl/
to frown or look displeased or angry, often by contracting the eyebrows
Example: *When she is not scowling, Emma is a very pretty girl.*

scramble /skrˈæmbəl/
to move quickly and awkwardly using hands and feet
Example: *The hikers scrambled up the steep slope.*
to mix or stir something quickly and haphazardly
Example: *She scrambled the eggs in the frying pan.*
to compete or struggle for something urgently or in disorder
Example: *Reporters scrambled to get the latest information on the breaking news story.*
to cause confusion or disorder
Example: *The power outage scrambled the computer system.*

scrape /skrˈeɪp/
to rub or scratch a surface with something sharp or rough, often resulting in the removal of material
Example: *The grating sound of metal against metal filled the air as they scraped the paint off the old Wrangler jeep.*
to make a harsh or grating noise by rubbing or dragging something against a surface
Example: *The children trembled in fear as the intruder scraped a sharp object along the kitchen window.*
to barely manage to achieve or obtain something
Example: *The students who could not scrape 50% were assigned a stream instead of being allowed to choose one.*

scratch /skrˈætʃ/
to mark or damage the surface of something by scraping it with something sharp or abrasive
Example: *Janice scratched her initials into the top of her desk as the class prepared to leave school for higher learning.*

to produce a sound or noise by dragging something sharp or rough across a surface
Example: *Ziggy scratched his side loudly as the bite from the ant irritated him.*
to cancel or eliminate something from a list, plan, or schedule
Example: *Miah reluctantly scratched Kevin's name off the list of campers for the 2024 expedition to Jamaica.*

scrawl /skrˈɔːl/
to write something quickly and carelessly, often with poor handwriting or in an untidy manner
Example: *Jack unsuspectingly scrawled his signature on the incriminating document.*

scream /skrˈiːm/
to make a loud, high-pitched cry or noise, often as an expression of fear, excitement, pain, or anger
Example: *We could hear piercing screams coming from several stories above ours.*

screech /skrˈiːtʃ/
to make a loud, high-pitched, and often harsh or unpleasant sound
Example: *There was a long loud screech followed by the sound of a terrible impact.*

screw /skrˈuː/
to fasten or tighten something by turning a screw or similar object
Example: *My task was to screw on the covers of the bottles.*
to manipulate or exploit someone for one's own advantage
Example: *He only realised that it was a bogus company after they had screwed him over.*
to mess up or ruin something
Example: *Jada is known for screwing up our parties, so she was not invited.*

scribble /skrˈɪbəl/
to write or draw something quickly and carelessly, often in a messy or illegible way
Example: *Our Math professor scribbled the solution to the problem on the chalkboard much to the dismay of the class who had been hoping he would explain it instead.*

scribe /skrˈaɪb/
to write or inscribe something, typically in a formal or official capacity
Example: *Dana was designated the job of scribing the plans for the group assignment.*
to serve as a professional copyist or recorder of documents or information
Example: *The company's secretary scribes for all the general meetings held by the company.*
to mark or score a surface with a sharp tool or instrument
Example: *To the teacher's dismay, the students had scribed their names on the tops of each desk.*

scrub /skrˈʌb/
to clean something by rubbing it hard with a brush or abrasive material
Example: *As a child we scrubbed the steps with wire brushes to make them clean.*
to cancel or eliminate something, often because of a change in plans
Example: *The soccer match scheduled to begin this evening was scrubbed because the field was flooded.*

scrunch /skrˈʌntʃ/
to squeeze or crush something into a compact shape
Example: *The crusher scrunched the Tundra truck like it was nothing.*
to make a noise or sound by crushing or rubbing something
Example: *We could tell Antoine was coming as he scrunched along the path stepping on each soda can that he passed.*

to contract or draw together tightly, often in a facial expression
Example: *The child scrunched her face expectantly as when she saw the syringe in the doctor's hand.*

scrutinise /skrˈuːtɪnˌaɪz/
to examine or inspect something closely or thoroughly, often with great attention to detail
Example: *Greg took his time to scrutinise the map and commit the entrance and exit routes to memory.*

scuff /skˈʌf/
to scrape or scratch the surface of something, often causing damage or abrasion
Example: *The nervous boy scuffed at the ground anxiously not realising he was bruising the polish.*
to walk or shuffle with a dragging or shuffling motion, often resulting in noise
Example: *We could hear the children scuffing along the path on their way home from the hike.*

scurry /skˈʌri/
to move hurriedly with short, quick steps, often in a busy or anxious manner
Example: *Scurry along quickly! You have five minutes before the bell rings.*

scuttle /skˈʌtəl/
to move quickly with short, hurried steps, especially while trying to avoid being noticed
Example: *Mum caught Alexis trying to scuttle past the living room after she came in late from the concert.*
to sink a ship deliberately by creating holes or openings in its hull
Example: *The captain ordered an investigation into the scuttling of his ship the Lady Marianne.*

to put an end to or thwart a plan or project
Example: *News of his management of funds in his previous job quickly scuttled Jim's chances of being employed by Mr. Cole.*
to run or move quickly in a haphazard or uncoordinated way
Example: *The lizard scuttled away when the shadow of the hawk fell across the yard.*

seal /sˈiːl/
to close or fasten securely with a seal or closure device
Example: *We ensured that we sealed the lids of the barrels properly to prevent losing any of our valuables.*
to make something airtight or watertight by applying a sealant or adhesive
Example: *One part of our bottled juice production is sealing the bottles properly.*
to affix a stamp or mark on a document to make it official or legally binding
Example: *The King sealed the proclamation with orders that it should be read thirty days after he died.*
to confirm or finalise something
Example: *The CEOs of the two companies shook hands to seal the deal.*

seam /sˈiːm/
to join or sew together pieces of fabric or material along a line of stitching
Example: *The seamstress seamed the sides of the skirt with double stitches.*
to close or seal something by joining two edges together
Example: *The secretary seamed the letter twice before stamping it and placing it into an envelope.*

search /sˈɜːtʃ/

to look for something carefully or thoroughly
Example: *The task force is conducting a search for twenty missing persons on the island of Grenada in the aftermath of Hurricane Beryl.*
to investigate or probe into something to uncover information
Example: *Investigators continue to search for the truth in the case of the murder of Monica Reece committed more than three decades ago.*

section /sˈɛkʃən/
to divide or separate something into distinct parts or categories
Example: *The vendor deftly sectioned the huge watermelon into fifty pieces as requested by the teacher.*

secure /sɪkjˈɔː/
to make something safe or free from danger
Example: *Valiant efforts to secure the property by battening down the windows proved futile as the ferocious winds ripped through the shutters and tore the house apart.*
to obtain or acquire something, typically after effort or difficulty
Example: *Amidst much adversity, he was able to secure a spot in the 2024 Paris Olympic Games.*
to fasten or attach something firmly in place
Example: *Learning from his mishap a year ago, Damien secures his handbrake well before exiting the vehicle.*
to ensure or guarantee something
Example: *The tickets in Simmone's hand and the smile on her face was evidence that our spot for the concert had been secured.*

see /sˈiː/
to perceive with the eyes; to observe
Example: *I see several lines of cars along the highway.*
to understand or comprehend mentally

Example: *I see more than meets the eye in this situation.*
to meet or visit someone socially or professionally
Example: *We are going to see my friend Vanessa who is in the country on vacation.*
to accompany or escort someone to a location
Example: *The plan is to see her to the Brazilian border, and no further.*
to foresee or predict future events
Example: *It was plain for everyone except them to see that they were meant to be together.*

seek /sˈiːk/
to attempt to find or obtain something, or to try to achieve a goal
Example: *Monique is seeking a summer job to offset her expenses for the upcoming school year.*

seem /sˈiːm/
to express an impression or opinion about something without stating it as a fact
Example: *Your section manager seems to think that you are no longer interested in this job.*

send /sˈɛnd/
the act of causing something to go or be taken to a destination or recipient
Example: *Alie sends her flowers even when there is no special occasion.*

seep /sˈiːp/
the slow movement of a liquid or gas through a porous material or small openings
Example: *The syrup for the cinnamon rolls boiled up and began to seep out from beneath the lid of the pot.*

seethe /sˈiːð/
to be filled with intense but unexpressed anger, or to be in a state of extreme agitation or excitement
Example: *Adrian seethed with rage as he heard the accusations filed against him.*

seize /sˈiːz/
to take hold of suddenly and forcibly
Example: *Shawn seized Shaundel by the shoulders and demanded answers to his questions.*
to capture or apprehend
Example: *Three motorcyclists were seized and taken into custody as they attempted to flee the scene of the burglary.*
to take control of something
Example: *The bank seizes the properties of homeowners who are unable to pay their mortgages.*
to take hold
Example: *He seized the arm of the chair to prevent himself from falling.*

select /sɪlˈɛkt/
to choose or pick out from a group based on specific criteria
Example: *Of the entire cricket team, five of the players selected were from Berbice.*

sell /sˈɛl/
to exchange goods or services for money
Example: *Many Indonesians sell fish as a means of making a living.*

sense /sˈɛns/
to perceive or become aware of something
Example: *Mike sensed the hostility when he walked into the room but was not deterred by it.*
to detect or recognise

Example: *Tyrese senses that he knows the guy from somewhere but cannot remember from where.*
to have a feeling or intuition about something
Example: *Tiara sensed that something was off with the customer and pressed the alarm just as he whipped out the revolver and aimed it at her chest.*

sentence /ˈsɛntəns/
to declare a punishment for someone convicted of a crime
Example: *The man had been sentenced to fifteen years in prison for a crime he had not committed.*
to express a thought or idea in a particular way
Example: *Pauline is sentenced to deliver the charge at the graduation; she is not ecstatic about it.*

separate /ˈsɛpɚˌeɪt/
to divide, disconnect, or set apart from others
Example: *Emmanuel has learned to separate the clothes for laundering according to their colour scheme.*

serenade /ˌsɛrɪnˈeɪd/
to perform music or sing for someone, especially outdoors or under their window as a gesture of romantic affection
Example: *The contestants were serenaded by the sweet sound of Carlvin Burnette's voice.*

serve /sˈɜːv/
to provide a service
Example: *The job of the police is to serve and protect the citizens of the country.*
to present food or drinks
Example: *As soon as we were served, we wolfed down our meal as we were very hungry.*
to fulfil a duty or function

Example: *The young maid had served her mistress for 30 years before she became ill and died.*
to spend a specified period in prison or the military
Example: *After serving time in prison, he became a mentor for troubled teens.*

service /sˈɜːvɪs/
to maintain or repair something
Example: *The washer repair man finally came to service the washing machine after three months of waiting.*
to provide assistance or help
Example: *The cadets will service the home for the elderly by mowing the lawn, and power washing the exterior as part of their community service requirement.*
to perform duties as part of one's job
Example: *I will service the Rose Hall Town and Williamsburg communities in my rounds as the community nurse.*

set /sˈɛt/
to put something in a particular place or position
Example: *Setting the table for breakfast has become an easy task for the children.*
to establish or arrange something
Example: *It did not take long to set a date for our wedding.*
to cause something to start or be in motion
Example: *The operator set the Ferris wheel in motion, much to the delight of the children.*

settle /sˈɛtəl/
to resolve or reach an agreement
Example: *They quickly settled their disagreement when they realised the delay was costing them money.*
to establish oneself in a place

Example: *Having lived in the valley for over a decade, they were quite settled and not inclined to move to a new location.*
to come to rest
Example: *The divers plan was to have the submarine settle one mile away from the sunken vessel and then approach it by swimming the remainder of the way.*

sever /sˈɛvɐ/
to cut off or separate something, often in a sudden or forceful manner
Example: *When they recognised how dishonest he was they severed ties with him.*

sew /sˈəʊ/
to join or repair fabric or other materials by using a needle and thread
Example: *Paulette enjoys sewing the buttons onto the tiny children's clothes.*

shade /ʃˈeɪd/
to protect from direct sunlight
Example: *The grove of trees shaded the picnickers from the glaring sunlight.*
to darken or colour slightly
Example: *Shading the edges of the drawing in a darker hue really enhanced the overall appearance of the portrait.*
to cast a shadow
Example: *We sat shading in the shadow cast by the dilapidated building and listened to 'Nansi stories told by my grandmother.*

shake /ʃˈeɪk/
to move back and forth or up and down
Example: *The young artist mixed his paint by shaking them up in several one litre bottles.*
to cause to tremble

Example: *We figured something was wrong, as every time Shania sees Fred, she shakes violently and stops speaking.*
to mix by agitating
Example: *The students shake the ingredients when they are mixing a Margarita or a Daiquiri.*

shamble /ʃˈambəl/
to walk or move in an awkward, unsteady, or clumsy way
Example: *The veteran shambled along favouring the leg that he had been shot in.*

shape /ʃˈeɪp/
to form, mould, or give a particular form or structure to something
Example: *The sculptor carefully shaped the clay into a wine jar.*
to influence, direct, or determine the course or outcome of something
Example: *The President's disrespect of the religion of the Mayan civilisation, shaped his defeat at the General Election the following year.*

share /ʃˈeə/
to divide or distribute something among others
Example: *The generous multi billionaire shares his wealth by building homes for the needy.*
to partake in something together with others
Example: *Our family shares a Christmas dinner at our parents' home every year.*

sharpen /ʃˈɑːpən/
to make something, typically a tool or object, more effective, precise, or acute
Example: *We were made to sharpen our pencils every Sunday in preparation for school the following day.*

shatter /ʃˈatɐ/
to break into many small pieces, typically with a loud noise
Example: *The vase shattered into a million tiny pieces revealing the wedding band we all thought was lost.*

shave /ʃˈeɪv/
to remove hair from the body, typically by using a razor or other cutting instrument
Example: *The middle of his head had been shaven clean in preparation for his surgery.*

shear /ʃˈiə/
to cut or remove the hair or wool from an animal, typically using scissors or electric clippers
Example: *Farmer Brown shears his sheep the old- fashioned way, though it takes him thrice as long as the other farmers do to shear theirs.*

sheathe /ʃˈiːð/
to encase or cover something, especially a blade or weapon, with a protective covering or case
Example: *The ninja sheathed his sword and proceeded to fight with his bare fists.*

shed /ʃˈɛd/
to discard
Example: *In the morning we discovered that the caterpillar had shed its cocoon for a beautiful pair of butterfly wings.*
to emit or give off
Example: *The mysterious canister shook violently and started shedding a foul green odour.*
to remove or lose something
Example: *By the end of the eighth week, Vicky had shed 20 pounds.*

shelter /ʃˈɛltɐ/
to provide protection or refuge from danger, harsh conditions, or adverse circumstances
Example: *Canada is known for providing shelter to destitute people seeking refuge from their homeland.*

shield /ʃˈiːld/
to protect or defend someone or something from harm or danger
Example: *Without a second thought, Jamal shielded Kenisha from the spray of bullets*

shift /ʃˈɪft/
to move or change position
Example: *Within two hours, the storm had shifted its position and was heading towards Puerto Rico.*
to transfer or exchange
Example: *When Dan is nervous, he shifts his weight from one foot to the next.*
to alter or adjust
Example: *With new reports of corruption within the government, votes may be shifting in favour of the opposition, ANC.*

shine /ʃˈaɪn/
to emit light
Example: *"Shine the light in the direction the shouts are coming from." Trevor instructed.*
to be bright or glowing
Example: *When she emerged from the prayer room, her face was shining like she had had a divine encounter.*
to excel or perform exceptionally well
Example: *The grade 6 students and teachers of Cumberland Primary shine this year at the NGSA examinations.*

shirk /ˈʃɝk/

to avoid or neglect a duty or responsibility, often out of laziness or a desire to evade work
Example: *On arriving at the bank of the river, I realised that we had all shirked our duties for the morning in favour of a quick dip in the river.*

shiver /ʃˈɪvɐ/
to tremble or shake involuntarily, typically as a response to cold, fear, or excitement
Example: *Megan shivered and wrapped her arms around her shoulders as she waited for the much-needed blanket that June had offered.*

shock /ʃˈɒk/
to cause a sudden and intense feeling of surprise, disbelief, or distress
Example: *We were shocked to find on our arrival at the knighting ceremony, that the King had already knighted Keimaul Thornton.*

shoot /ʃˈuːt/
to discharge a projectile from a weapon
Example: *Today we are heading to the Timehri ranges to learn to shoot.*
to take a photograph
Example: *Mr. Wiggins was shooting a handsome family for their family portrait when we walked into the studio.*
to move quickly and suddenly
Example: *For the third time today, the team watched David blaze up the ramp on his bike and shoot himself into a somersault.*

shop /ʃˈɒp/
to visit stores or browse online in search of goods or services to purchase
Example: *Of late, many people prefer to shop online.*

shorten /ʃˈɔːtən/
to make something shorter or to reduce its length or duration
Example: *The production manager shortened the play to two and a half hours and the audience seemed to appreciate that.*

shoulder /ʃˈəʊldɐ/
to carry a burden or responsibility
Example: *Nigel shouldered the responsibility of running the business when his father was out of the country.*
to push or press against something using the shoulder
Example: *The boys shoulder their way through the crowd, making a path for the girls to follow.*
to take on or accept something willingly
Example: *Tamica willingly shoulders the responsibility of caring for her siblings since her mum has fallen ill.*

shout /ʃˈaʊt/
to speak loudly or to call out loudly, often in a forceful or intense manner
Example: *The children learning to swim shouted joyfully every time they accomplished a task.*

shove /ʃˈʌv/
to push forcefully or roughly
Example: *The prisoner was shoved into the cell and the door banged shut.*

shovel /ʃˈʌvəl/
to lift and move (a load, typically of earth, snow, or coal) with a shovel
Example: *My heart swelled, for the children had shovelled a path through the snow for their grandparents to walk.*

show /ʃˈəʊ/

to display or exhibit
Example: *The Castellani House will be showing art pieces done strictly by students today.*
to demonstrate or reveal
Example: *At the science fair, the students showed how the robot they had built works.*
to provide evidence or proof
Example: *The weeping teen took off his shirt and showed his scared back to us to substantiate his tales of being flogged at the orphanage.*

showcase /ʃˈəʊkeɪs/
to exhibit or display something in a prominent or impressive way, often to highlight its quality or importance
Example: *The Guyana National Museum will be holding a special viewing in August showcasing Guyana's wildlife creatures.*

shower /ˈʃaʊɚ/
to rain heavily
Example: *It showered heavily yesterday, resulting in the cancellation of the picnic planned for the day.*
to bathe under a spray of water
Example: *With only a short time to leave the house, Pat quickly showers, dons a track suit and leaves the house.*
to give someone a large number of gifts or compliments
Example: *The outgoing principal was showered with gifts from both the staff and student population.*

shred /ʃrˈɛd/
to tear or cut into small pieces, especially in a vigorous or forceful manner
Example: *Xhara angrily shredded the letter of dismissal she found on her desk.*

shriek /ʃrˈiːk/
to make a loud, sharp, piercing cry or sound, typically expressing fear, excitement, or pain
Example: *The startled climber let out a frightened shriek as the ground gave way beneath her.*

shrink /ʃrˈɪŋk/
to become smaller in size or volume
Example: *With every purchase we make, the amount in the container seems to shrink a little.*

shrug /ʃrˈʌg/
to raise and lower the shoulders slightly, usually to indicate uncertainty, indifference, or lack of concern
Example: *Vibert shrugs in response to questions he wants to avoid answering.*

shudder /ʃˈʌdɐ/
to tremble or shake involuntarily, often as a reaction to fear, cold, or disgust
Example: *Vanessa shuddered as she remembered the cold, expressionless eyes of the assailant.*

shuffle /ʃˈʌfəl/
to walk with a dragging or shuffling gait
Example: *The old woman shuffles along from her home to the park and back every morning.*
to mix or rearrange items randomly
Example: *Simon Cowell shuffled the deck of cards he had been given by the magician.*
to move something in a furtive or evasive manner
Example: *The skilled host shuffles the pieces on the chic-chic board and waits for the players to choose a hand.*

shush /ʃʌʃ/
to silence or quiet someone by making a "shushing" sound or gesture
Example: Meg tried to shush the crying baby but was greeted with louder wails.

shut /ʃʌt/
to close something, typically a door, window, or container
Example: The sudden burst of wind shut the door, causing a loud bang.

sidestep /sˈaɪdstɛp/
to avoid or dodge something, usually by stepping sideways
Example: Rihanna deftly sidestepped the question from a nosy reporter about a third pregnancy.

sidle /sˈaɪdəl/
to move sideways in a cautious or furtive manner, often with the intention of avoiding attention
Example: The team had almost successfully sidled past the sleeping Coach Janice when Cindy's cell phone started ringing.

sift /sˈɪft/
to examine or sort through something methodically, typically to separate out what is wanted from what is not
Example: It is customary for us to sift the flour before making pastries.

sigh /sˈaɪ/
to emit a long, audible breath, often expressing tiredness, relief, or disappointment
Example: Whatever it was that he was dreaming, this was the third time Ziggy has sighed in the past five minutes.

sign /sˈaɪn/
to write one's name on a document
Example: *Each of the residents except the Alexanders signed the agreement to relinquish ownership of their riverfront property.*
to communicate using sign language
Example: *The mute guitarist signed his intent to leave the party and was gone before we had a chance to respond.*
to indicate or mark something
Example: *The couple signed their love for each other with double hearts etched into the bark of the jamun tree.*

signal /sˈɪgnəl/
to communicate or indicate something, often using signs, gestures, or actions
Example: *The stranded mountain climber signalled to the rescue plane with his shirt that he had tied to the end of a piece of stick.*

silence /sˈaɪləns/
to make someone or something quiet or to suppress noise or sound
Example: *One look from her mum as she walked through the door, silenced the wails of the screaming child.*

simmer /sˈɪmɐ/
to cook something gently over low heat, just below boiling
Example: *The big pot of stewed peas was left to simmer while the rice boiled on the other burner.*
to be in a state of slow, restrained activity
Example: *Because the neighbours made a noise nuisance complaint, the party slowly simmered down, and the guests trickled out one after the other.*

simper /sˈɪmpɐ/

to smile or speak in a silly, affected, or self-conscious way
Example: *It is disgusting to see her simper every time Kevin speaks to her.*

simplify /sˈɪmplɪfˌaɪ/
to make something easier to understand or do by reducing its complexity
Example: *While most online forms have been simplified over the past two years, the customs forms seem to have gotten more complicated.*

sin /ˈsɪn/
to commit an act that goes against moral or religious principles
Example: *I am convinced that I sin every time that I think about the people who murdered my mum.*

sing /sˈɪŋ/
to produce musical sounds with the voice, typically in rhythm and often with melody
Example: *Allison hails from a family of good singers but cannot herself sing.*

sink /sˈɪŋk/
to descend or submerge below the surface of a liquid
Example: *Jerry sadly watched his favourite action figure sink to the bottom of the trench.*
to decline or fall
Example: *The records held by the former Olympians are holding up better than the new records which keep getting sunk every few years.*

sip /sˈɪp/
to drink (a liquid) slowly by taking small mouthfuls

Example: *Come over let us sip some wine and reminisce on the good old days.*

sit /sˈɪt/
to be seated or to take a position on a surface, typically with one's weight supported by a chair, bench, or the ground
Example: *I like to sit and gaze at the starlit sky*

size /sˈaɪz/
to determine or specify the dimensions or proportions of something
Example: *The children secretly sized their mum's finger while she slept to help their dad with his marriage proposal.*
to classify or categorise based on size
Example: *The cadets sized themselves then awaited further instructions from the drill instructor.*

sketch /skˈɛtʃ/
to make a rough drawing or outline of something
Example: *Larry sketched a beautiful image of their dog Rover.*

skewer /skjˈuːɐ/
to pierce or impale with or as if with a skewer (a long pin of wood or metal)
Example: *Mark skewered the bandit with his knees as he waited for the arrival of the police.*
to criticise or ridicule sharply and effectively
Example: *Public servants skewered the government for lack of wages and poor working conditions.*

ski /skˈiː/
the act of gliding over snow on skis
Example: *Skiing down the mountain can be dangerous but thrilling.*

skid /skˈɪd/
to slide or slip sideways, often due to loss of traction
Example: *After the heavy rains, many vehicles skid off the road, causing massive traffic jams.*
to deviate or veer suddenly from a straight or intended path
Example: *The cyclist skidded off the track, narrowly escaping a collision with another cyclist.*

skim /skˈɪm/
to move or pass swiftly and lightly over or along a surface
Example: *The rock skimmed the surface of the lake in a neat duck and drake manoeuvre.*
to read, glance through, or survey hastily or superficially
Example: *The man skimmed through the newspaper before purchasing it.*

skip /skˈɪp/
to move or proceed with quick steps to escape notice
Example: *The teenager skipped quickly across the road to avoid being hit by an oncoming car.*
to omit or disregard, especially routinely or without justification
Example: *Many students skipped section two of the mathematics paper.*
to leap or jump lightly over
Example: *Mary skipped over the muddy puddle in the road.*
to absent oneself from school or another commitment without permission
Example: *She skipped breakfast to avoid being late for work.*

skitter /skˈɪtɐ/
to move lightly and quickly or to dart rapidly
Example: *The crab skittered across the sandy shore and disappeared into a tiny hole.*

skulk /skˈʌlk/
to move stealthily or to keep out of sight, typically with a sinister or cowardly motive
Example: *The bandit skulked into the nearby bushes along the path, waiting for the perfect moment to attack.*

slam /slˈɑm/
to shut forcefully
Example: *Drivers warned passengers not to slam the car doors.*
to criticise severely
Example: *Teachers slammed principals for the lack of support with regards to the number of students in a classroom.*
to hit or strike with great force
Example: *The boxer slammed his opponent with a right jab, sending him to the ground.*
to move with great force or speed
Example: *The hurricane winds slammed against the hotels along the beaches with tremendous force.*

slander /slˈɑːndɐ/
to make false spoken statements damaging to a person's reputation
Example: *The man sued his son for slandering his reputation.*

slap /slˈɑp/
to strike with the palm of the hand
Example: *The woman slapped the cup out of the man's hands.*
to apply forcefully
Example: *The carpenter slapped the loose piece of wood into place.*
to put or place something quickly and carelessly
Example: *The student slapped the books one by one on the desk.*
to criticise or rebuke harshly
Example: *The teacher slapped the students about their poor performance in Mathematics.*

slash /slˈɑʃ/
to cut with a sweeping stroke, usually with a sharp object
Example: *The city council workers slashed the grass in the neighbourhood.*
to reduce drastically
Example: *The company decided to slashed wages to avoid bankruptcy.*
to criticise or attack harshly
Example: *After they each had a go at slashing at her without knowing the truth, she calmly told her side of the story.*

slather/slˈɑːðɐ/
to spread or apply generously
Example: *The little girl slathered her toast with peanut butter and jelly.*

slay /slˈeɪ/
to kill violently or with great efficiency
Example: *The man slayed his wife with a single blow to her head.*
to impress or amuse greatly
Example: *Comedians are known for slaying the audience with hit jokes.*
to criticise or insult someone skilfully
Example: *During the election debate, the politicians slay each other with their arguments.*

sleep /slˈiːp/
to rest with eyes closed, typically at night for a period
Example: *The baby sleeps longer in his mother's arms than in his crib.*

slice /slˈaɪs/
to cut something into tin, flat pieces
Example: *Mother sliced the block of cheese into smaller pieces.*

to make a deep cut or incision
Example: *The dentist sliced into the man's gum to remove the broken tooth.*
to hit or strike with slicing motion
Example: *At the netball game, the player sliced the ball across the court to secure the win.*
to divide or separate something into parts or sections
Example: *She sliced the macaroni pie into equal parts.*

slick /slˈɪk/
to make smooth or glossy
Example: *She uses gel to slick back her hair.*
to make something neat and tidy
Example: *The room was slicked for the arrival of the guests.*
to make something slippery or smooth in order deceive or trick
Example: *To capture the ants, mother slicked the counter with an oily substance.*
to move smoothly and quickly, often with skill or deception
Example: *The player was slick on the throw of the ball in the net.*

slide /slˈaɪd/
to move smoothly along a surface, typically with little or no friction
Example: *James and Mark slide down the rail with ease.*
to pass or go smoothly or easily
Example: *He slides effortlessly under the sheet without waking the baby.*
to decline gradually or to move into a worse state or condition
Example: *Mary slides deeper into unconsciousness during the surgery.*
to introduce or insert discreetly or surreptitiously
Example: *The boy secretly slid his test paper under the desk to avoid submitting it.*

sling /slˈɪŋ/

to throw or hurl with a swinging motion
Example: *He slings his towel over his shoulder while entering the bathroom.*
to suspense or hang something loosely and freely
Example: *The kite slings between the wires, as it swayed gently in the breeze.*
to support or carry something with a strap or harness
Example: *The photographer slings his camera before joining the tour bus.*
to criticise or insert someone harshly
Example: *The government slings criticism at the public servants for protesting for better working conditions.*

slink /slˈɪŋk/
to move stealthily or furtively, often due to guilt or shame
Example: *The furtive slink away from the crowd to avoid being caught.*

slip /slˈɪp/
to lose one's footing or balance unintentionally
Example: *Jane slips into the dirty water puddle.*
to move smoothly and quietly in a particular direction
Example: *The dog slips through the door quietly, before anyone notices him.*
to make a mistake or an error
Example: *Mr. John's documents slip into the wrong pile of papers.*
to decline or decrease gradually
Example: *Each month his account slips into arrears.*
to insert or to include something discreetly or surreptitiously
Example: *He slips the drug into her drinks as soon as she turns away.*

slit /slˈɪt/
to make a long, narrow cut or opening in something
Example: *Maria slits the box open to remove the laptop.*

slither /slˈɪðɐ/
to move smoothly and sinuously like a snake
Example: *The snake slithers across the lawn before disappearing into the nearby bushes.*

slobber /slˈɒbɐ/
to let saliva or mucus drip from the mouth in an uncontrolled manner, often due to excitement or excessive drooling
Example: *The dog slobbers all over the ground when he sees his favourite food.*

slosh /slˈɒʃ/
to move with a slashing or swishing sound, typically due to liquid being moved around
Example: *The juice sloshes in the mug with every stir.*
to spill or splash liquid around in a careless or messy manner
Example: *The baby sloshes the milk all over the crib.*
to walk or move through water or mud with a splashing or squelching sound
Example: *The children slosh through the muddy puddle.*

slouch /slˈaʊtʃ/
to sit, stand, or walk with a drooping, hunched, or lazy posture
Example: *Miss Jane slouches in the chair during the staff meeting.*

slow /slˈəʊ/
to reduce speed or slow down
Example: *Daddy slows down as he approaches the red light.*
to delay or make slower
Example: *The accident on the intersection slows the traffic significantly.*
to become less rapid or intensive
Example: *As the hurricane weakens the winds slow to a gentler breeze.*

to make progress with less speed or momentum
Example: *At the Olympic games, the distance runner slows her paces as she reaches the finish line.*
to become sluggish or less energetic
Example: *After hours of hiking, they slow down and take a short rest.*

slumber /slˈʌmbɚ/
to sleep lightly or peacefully, often in a relaxed state
Example: *She slumbers peacefully on the beach chair in the gentle evening breeze.*

slump /slˈʌmp/
to drop or fall heavily or suddenly
Example: *She slumps herself in the rocking chair.*
to decline or to deteriorate rapidly, especially in terms of value, performance, or mood
Example: *His presentation took a slump during his climax.*
to sit, stand, or move in a slouching or drooping manner
Example: *His mother often tells him not to slump while standing.*
to sink or settle into a lower position
Example: *Marcus slumps to the ground in laughter.*

slur /slˈɜː/
to speak unclearly or indistinctly, often by running words together
Example: *Grandfather's speech slurred after an attack of stroke.*
to utter with a slur, implying disparagement or insinuation
Example: *The accused began to slur after a series of questioning.*
to pass over lightly or carelessly
Example: *The judge nonchalantly slurred over the details of the case, leaving the witnesses confused.*

slurp /slˈɜːp/
to eat or drink noisily, often by drawing in liquid or food with a noising sucking sound

Example: *Alvin often annoys his friends when he slurps his drink.*

smack /sm'ak/
to strike with an open hand, usually resulting in a sharp sound
Example: *His mother smacks him on the mouth for his disrespectful tone.*
to hit something with a sharp blow
Example: *Maria smacks the bee to the ground in an attempt to kill it.*
to make a sharp sound by coming into contact with something
Example: *The ball smacked against the window with a loud noise.*
to kiss with a loud, smacking sound
Example: *My dad playfully leans into mom and smacks her on the cheek.*

smash /sm'aʃ/
to break or shatter violently into pieces
Example: *The glass was smashed into tiny pieces when it fell to the floor.*
to strike or hit forcefully, causing damage
Example: *The car smashed into the lamp pole leaving many injured.*
to defeat decisively or overwhelming
Example: *Our girls' netball team smashed the competition winning the game by five nil.*
to crush or flatten something by applying force
Example: *Mark smashed the juice can with his bat until it was flattened.*

smear /sm'iə/
to spread or apply (a substance) thinly and evenly over a surface
Example: *Mother smears the peanut butter evenly on the bread.*
to cover or coat with a greasy, sticky, or dirty substance
Example: *Paul smears the wax on the counter in order to fill the tiny holes.*

to damage the reputation or character of someone by making false malicious statements
Example: *The principal tried to smear the teacher's reputation with the new parents.*
to move or spread in a messy or uneven way
Example: *The paint accidentally smeared the wall when the man slipped and fell.*

smell /smˈɛl/
to perceive or detect odours through the nose
Example: *The smell from the bathroom is unbearable.*
to emit or give off an odour
Example: *The atmosphere smells of freshly cut grass.*
to have a particular odour or scent
Example: *Her home smells of lavender and wild coffee.*
to have a particular quality that can sensed or perceive
Example: *Dad knew that something was not right as the details presented smelled fishy.*

smile /smˈaɪl/
to form ones features into a pleased, kind, or amused expression, typically with the corners of the mouth turned up
Example: *She smiles widely when she sees her friends.*
to express happiness, amusement, or friendliness through a smile
Example: *He smiled at the comment made by his mother.*
to show approval or agreement with a smile
Example: *The judges could not help but smile when she won the competition.*

smirk /smˈɜːk/
to smile in smug, self-satisfied, or mocking way
Example: *Mark smirked when he realised that he had outsmarted his friend in a game of tic-tac toe.*

smite /smˈaɪt/
to strike with a firm blow
Example: *He smote the ball over the pavilion for six.*
to inflict a heavy blow or defeat upon someone or something
Example: *The team was smitten when they lost the finals.*
to affect suddenly and strongly with a feeling or emotion
Example: *She was smitten with grief on hearing of the death of her baby.*
to punish or afflict severely
Example: *The storm smote the village leaving many homeless.*

smoke /smˈəʊk/
to emit smoke or visible vapour, typically from burning something
Example: *The food outlet chimney is always smoking.*
to inhale and exhale the smoke of tobacco or a drug
Example: *Father smoked several cigarettes while in the washroom.*
to preserve or treat (food, especially meat or fish) by exposure to smoke
Example: *The chef smoked the beef to give it a nice flavour.*

smooch /smˈuːtʃ/
to kiss and cuddle amorously
Example: *The couple cuddled and smooched each other on the beach.*

smooth /smˈuːð/
to make something flat, level, or free from roughness
Example: *The mason used a shovel to smooth the surface.*
to make something sleek, glossy, or shine
Example: *They used polish to smooth the coffee table and chairs.*
to make something operate or progress without difficulty or interruption
Example: *The principal worked hard to smooth things out for teachers and students.*

to calm or soothe someone's emotions or concerns
Example: *Father played soft music to smooth his autistic daughter's fear.*
to eliminate obstacles or difficulties from a situation
Example: *The coaches did everything to smooth out all the issues between the players.*

smother /smˈʌðɚ/
to suffocate or stifle someone or something by covering them completely
Example: *She smothered the fire by covering it with a wet towel.*
to cover or envelope something entirely
Example: *The sky was smothered with a thick layer of dust.*
to overwhelm or oppress someone with excessively love, attention, or control
Example: *Her new boyfriend smothered her with excessive love and attention.*
to suppress or extinguish a feeling, emotion, or thought
Example: *Tariq tried to smother his anger by taking deep breaths.*

smoulder /smˈəʊldɚ/
to burn slowly and without a flame, often producing smoke or heat
Example: *The late-night campfire smouldered long into the mornings.*
to show signs of suppressed anger, passion, or emotion
Example: *He was smouldered with anger as he watched his mom being beaten by the drunkard.*
to exist in a hidden or suppress state, ready to burst forth
Example: *The department's issues have been smouldering for months before it was exposed.*

smudge /smˈʌdʒ/
to blur or obscure something by smearing or spreading a substance over it

Example: *She smudges the ink over the prints.*
to make something dirty or untidy by smearing or staining it
Example: *The little boy smudged his clothes during his play in the park.*
to create a blurred or hazy effect on something
Example: *The dust on his windscreen smudged the view, making it difficult for him to drive.*
to cause something to become unclear or confused
Example: *Covid smudged many industrial plans leaving employees confused about the future.*

snake /snˈeɪk/
to move or extend in a winding or twisting way, resembling the movement of a snake
Example: *The stream snaked its way along the forest floor and culminated in a crystal-clear lake surrounded by huge boulders.*
to twist or wind in a sinuous manner
Example: *With Raven's encouragement, the trapped students began to snake their way under the tight opening at the back of the cave.*
to steal or move secretly or stealthily
Example: *Just as the last captive had snaked her way past the kidnapper, he woke with a start and snatched at her foot.*

snap /snˈap/
to make a sudden, sharp cracking sound
Example: *The twig snapped loudly in the eerily quiet orchard.*
to speak abruptly or sharply
Example: *When mum snaps, know she has had a tough day, for she is usually pleasant.*
to take photograph
Example: *Tyra snaps a selfie at almost every turn that she makes.*
to close or fasten something quickly and forcefully

Example: *My grandma quickly snapped her purse shut when she saw us approaching.*
to become irritable or lose one's temper suddenly
Example: *The twins always snap when they are mistaken for each other.*

snarl /snˈɑːl/
to make an aggressive growling or rumbling sound, typically as a warning or displace of anger
Example: *The ocelot snarled as the children approached its cage.*
to become tangle or knotted
Example: *Her knotty hair snarls the comb every time she attempts to comb her hair herself.*
to speak or say something in a surly or hostile manner
Example: *The cornered burglar snarled threats at the men as they slowly closed in on him.*
to become twisted or confused, especially in traffic or a complex situation
Example: *The tourists made a wrong turn and found themselves snarled in traffic for three hours.*

snatch /snˈatʃ/
to seize or grab something suddenly or forcefully
Example: *A young man leaned out of the speeding truck and snatched the handbags of the two shocked ladies.*
to take or steal something quickly and often stealthily
Example: *The monkeys bide their time, then snatches the fruit away from unsuspecting visitors.*
to obtain or achieve something quickly and unexpectedly
Example: *We watched in horror as the championship title was snatched away from us by our rival secondary school.*

sneak /snˈiːk/

to move in a quiet, stealthy, or furtive manner, especially to avoid being notice
Example: *Bold students sneak out of their dorms to attend the movies on school nights.*
to act or proceed secretly or surreptitiously
Example: *Everyday he sneaks one page out of the file containing information on the disappearance of his brother.*
to do something in sly or underhanded manner
Example: *When the teacher decided to search the room, Martin sneaked the stolen phone into Mandy's bag to avoid being caught.*

sneer /snˈiə/
to smile or laugh in contemptuous or mocking manner
Example: *As the search for the missing phone was being carried out, Mandy caught Martin sneering at her and figured out what he had done.*
to express scorn, disdain, or derision through facial expressions or remarks
Example: *Mandy sneered at Martin, convinced the teacher would not take his word over hers, in the case of the missing phone.*
to speak or laugh in a manner that shows lack of respect or disapproval
Example: *When confronted by the principal about the allegations of stealing and framing Mandy made against him, Martin sneered, "Prove it!"*

sneeze /snˈiːz/
to expel air involuntarily and forcefully through the nose and mouth due to irritation in the nasal passage
Example: *Many days during the springtime, Collette can be heard sneezing from allergies brought on by the season.*

snicker /snˈɪkɐ/

to laugh in a quiet, suppress, or disrespectful manner, often expressing amusement or derision
Example: *Loud snickers followed the monkey as he walked past the children with toilet paper stuck to his bottom.*

sniff /snˈɪf/
to inhale air audibly through the nose, usually to detect a smell or to clear the nasal passages
Example: *As the car entered the Stanleytown area, she took a sniff of the air and felt nostalgia overwhelm her, for she was home.*

sniffle /snˈɪfəl/
to sniff repeatedly, usually audibly and involuntarily, often due to having a runny or congested nose, or as a sign of crying
Example: *Jess was found with her arms wrapped around the neck of the golden retriever and sniffling loudly.*

snigger /snˈɪgɐ/
to laugh in a disrespectful or mocking manner, often quietly or under one's breath
Example: *The boys sniggered amongst themselves when they realised their opponents were grade nine girls.*

snip /snˈɪp/
to cut with small, quick strokes, especially with scissors or shears
Example: *I watched in fascination as ninety-year-old Mrs. Vanderstoop expertly snipped the roses from the rose bush in her garden of flowers.*
to remove something by cutting, often in a quick and precise manner
Example: *Taking a calming breath, the barber snips off the Cherokee plait that Tony had been growing since he was a young boy.*
to make a small, sharp sound resembling that scissor cutting

Example: *The scissors snipping loudly in the stonily quiet room, as the trainees were prepped for their first task, was the only sound that could be heard in the room.*

snipe /snˈaɪp/
to shoot at someone or something from a hidden position, especially with a firearm
Example: *In consternation we watched as the hostages that were released, were sniped one after the other as they exited the building.*
to make a sly or critical remark
Example: *It would appear that the young coach snipes at his players without care about how it affects their mental state before a game.*

snitch /snˈɪtʃ/
to inform on someone or report their wrongdoing to authorities, often in a secretive or betraying manner
Example: *Rebecca had been snitching on our operation from the first stage of planning.*
to steal or take something, especially in a sneaky or underhanded way
Example: *The children snitch mints from granny's table when they think she is not looking.*
to grab or snatch something quickly or eagerly
Example: *The hungry cat snitched the fish the cook offered her.*

snivel /snˈɪvəl/
to cry or whine in a weak, tearful, or self-pitying manner
Example: *A dishevelled looking woman sat snivelling on a chair on a corner of the room.*
to complain or express discontent in whining or sniffling manner
Example: *Mary sobbed and snivelled her distress over the flooded apartment to everyone she met.*
to sniffle or sob, often while complaining or seeking sympathy

Example: *Spying an opportunity to get Avinash's attention, Lisa snivelled and buried her head in his chest.*

snooze /snˈuːz/
to sleep lightly, especially for a short period of time, often during the day
Example: *Miah took videos of 'Team Kabisa' as they snoozed after a rowdy night of fun.*
to doze or nap briefly, usually unintentionally
Example: *It is not uncommon to find university students snoozing during lecture time on zoom.*
to relax or rest in a drowsy or a half-asleep state
Example: *D'Nae snoozes all the way through on our journey to Bartica.*

snore /snˈɔː/
to breathe during sleep with a harsh, noisy, or hoarse sound cause by vibration of the soft palate and other issues in the throat
Example: *Loud snoring could be heard coming from the female dorms of the training camp.*

snort /snˈɔːt/
to force air violently and noisily through the nostrils, often as a reaction to irritation, laughter, or disdain
Example: *All eyes turned on us as my friend snorted loudly in the middle of her fit of laughter.*
to inhale a drug, typically cocaine, through the nostrils audibly and forcefully
Example: *When the teens were found, it was obvious that they had been made to snort a considerable amount of cocaine.*
to express disdain or contempt through a loud or forceful snort
Example: *My grandma snorts in disgust every time we mention the name of her lawyer.*

snow /snˈəʊ/
to fall as or like snow
Example: *The children pressed their faces expectantly waiting for it to snow.*
to cover with or as if with snow
Example: *It had snowed the previous night and the entire mountainside was covered in white.*
to deceive or overwhelm with elaborate or excessive compliments or praise
Example: *The family snowed Ella with praise for her cooking in front of the guests, but none of them touched their food.*

snub /snˈʌb/
to rebuff, ignore, or reject someone in a disdainful or dismissive manner
Example: *Charmaine snubs the company's effort to sign her since they were the first to dismiss her earlier attempts at signing a record deal.*
to treat someone with disdain or contempt by ignoring them or refusing to acknowledge their presence
Example: *Lauren felt snubbed when Leah walked past her at the awards ceremony.*

snuff /snˈʌf/
to shorten or blunt (something), especially by cutting or trimming
Example: *The maids snuffed the wicks of the candles to be used for the wedding ceremony.*

snuffle /snˈʌfəl/
to breathe noisily or with difficulties especially through the nose often due to congestion or illness
Example: *I could hear him snuffling throughout the night because of his bad cold.*
to sniffle or snort repeatedly, often to clear the nasal passages

Example: *Jess kept snuffling as she was finding it difficult to breathe.*
to make a low, grunting, or sniffling sound, as a pig
Example: *We threw open the lid of the crate to find that the snuffling was coming from a young boy.*

snuggle /snˈʌgəl/
to move or lie closely together in a comfortable, affectionate manner, often for warmth or intimacy
Example: *The Carters found the two toddlers in their barn snuggled against the ewe who recently gave birth.*

soak /sˈəʊk/
to make or become totally with or saturated with liquid
Example: *We soaked the cloth in kerosene then proceeded to light the fire.*
to immerse something in a liquid to soften, clean, or treat it
Example: *They will soak the badly stained shirts overnight in bleach and wash them in the morning.*
to absorb liquid gradually
Example: *It takes time for the chickpeas to soak before they are ready to be cooked.*
to spend a long time in a particular activity or environment
Example: *The tourists spent all day on the beach, soaking up the sun.*

sob /sˈɒb/
to cry loudly while making convulsive gasps
Example: *The frightened girl sobbed loudly as they tried to get her to stay in the pool.*

sober /sˈəʊbɐ/
to make or become sober after intoxication or drunkenness
Example: *After a night of binge drinking, it took several hours for the group to sober up.*
to make or become serious, sensible, or rational

Example: *Josh sobered up immediately when his dad walked through the door.*

to make or become free from excess or extravagance

Example: *Losing his job has sobered Malik into becoming more careful in his spending and investments.*

to make or become calm or serious after excitement or excess

Example: *The task of caring for her sick mother had sobered the carefree young lady into becoming a responsible woman.*

socialise /sˈəʊʃəlˌaɪz/

interact or engage in social activities with others

Example: *Old Broom Lounge is a popular bar where you can socialise with friends and family.*

to participate in or attend social events or gatherings

Example: *The ExxonMobil training institute is geared towards training and socialising youths in Guyana for a wide variety of jobs now available in the country.*

to make or become prepared for interaction in a social setting

Example: *It is important to socialise our children by having them attend public functions and events where they must interact with both adults and children.*

to acclimatise or adapt social norms or expectations

Example: *Zhane is known for socialising well with persons from varying socio-economic backgrounds.*

soften /sˈɒfən/

to make or become less hard, form, or rigid

Example: *Jace added a little moisture to soften the mixture.*

to make or become less severe, harsh, or intense

Example: *Tamara's facial expression softened when her husband walked into the room.*

to make or become less stubborn, resistant, or inflexible

Example: *The hairdresser applied a water-based moisturiser to the client's hair to soften it in preparation for styling.*

to make or become less sharp, distinct, or pronounced
Example: *The candlelight softened the drab appearance of the restaurant, giving it a nice ambience.*

solve /sˈɒlv/
to find an answer or explanation to a problem or question
Example: *There may be several different ways to solve the same problem.*

somersault /sˈʌməsˌɒlt/
to perform a forward or backward roll in which the body makes a complete revolution, usually in the air
Example: *Several of the children somersaulted off the diving board and into the pool under the instruction of the swim coach.*
to turn or flip end over end
Example: *The minibus driver lost control of his bus and it somersaulted over the railway and into the sea.*

soothe /sˈuːð/
to calm, comfort, or alleviate pain or distress
Example: *The nanny's voice soon soothes the twins back to sleep and their parents resume having dinner.*

sort /sˈɔːt/
to arrange or organise items into groups based on correct characteristics, categories, or criteria
Example: *Adrian sorts his toys according to their colours and places them into their respective containers.*
to examine or sift through a collection of items to identify or select specific ones
Example: *The junior teachers will sort through the set of flashcards to find the ones suited to the kindergarteners.*
to separate or classify things according to type, quality, or size

Example: *It took two days to sort out the royal family of England's huge jewellery collection.*
to deal with or handle a situation or problem in a particular way.
Example: *On his visit to Region Six, the CEO promised to sort out the matter of salary discrepancies.*
to resolve or clarify a matter
Example: *The mix up of the salaries between the two Wendy Josephs was sorted out by the Regional Office.*

sough /sˈəʊ/
to make a soft, murmuring, or rustling sound, often like the wind through trees or foliage
Example: *Although the accident survivor had no visible external injuries, she soughed in her sleep all through the night.*

sow /ˈsoʊ/
to plant or scatter seeds in the ground for growth
Example: *This year we plan to sow corn; last year we tried grapes and had great results.*
to introduce or spread things, such as ideas, beliefs, or feelings, usually with the intention of promoting growth or development
Example: *The exchange students were encouraged to sow good seeds of friendship with their new families, as it may be rewarding years down the line.*
to cause or bring about a particular result or outcome, often with a negative connotation
Example: *The Changs' accusations and her hesitation, were enough to sow seeds of doubt in the minds of her prospective business partners.*

span /spˈan/
to extend across or cover a specific distance or period
Example: *The swarms of locusts spanned the expanse of fields as far as our eyes could see.*

to measure the distance or duration between two points
Example:	*The land surveyor spanned the tape from the marker post to the end of the neighbour's fence.*
to include or encompass a particular range or variety of things
Example:	*The services offered at the multicomplex hall span a wide variety of things including hairdressing, manicures and pedicures, and a boutique for shopping.*
the stretch or extend across something
Example:	*The Berbice Bridge spans the width of the Berbice River from Palmyra to Rosignol.*

spank /spˈɑŋk/
to slap someone's buttocks, usually as a punishment or in a playful manner
Example:	*In the 80s and 90s it was more common for children to be spanked than it is now.*

spare /spˈeə/
to refrain from harming, injuring, or using something or someone
Example:	*Considering the pleas of his classmates, the headmaster spared John from a spanking.*
to give or grant something to someone, especially when one has more than enough
Example:	*"I can only spare two sheets of drawing paper." Maggie said*
to set aside or reserve something for a particular purpose
Example:	*Jan had spared the last candle in case they needed it and now she was happy that she had done that.*
the save or avoid using something for later use
Example:	*Andre had spared his favourite candy bar to eat for dessert after dinner that evening.*
to omit or leave out something unnecessary or excessive

Example: *Parents were spared the trouble of purchasing fancy clothes for the graduation ceremony because the students were required to be in uniform.*
to free someone from an obligation or duty
Example: *Her husband's return spares Mrs. Smith from the task of chairing the meeting for the board of directors.*

spark /spˈɑːk/
to ignite or produce a small flame or spark
Example: *After hitting the rocks together for a while, they sparked and lit the kerosene- soaked pile of wood.*
to trigger or initiate something, especially a discussion or reaction
Example: *The drowning of the teen at the National Aquatic Centre sparked a discussion on safety at the poolside.*
to cause or create a sudden burst of energy, interest, or inspiration
Example: *Shemroy on his heels at the 50-metre mark on the track, sparked Darren's energy and he blazed to victory in the nick of time.*
to cause something to happen or develop suddenly or unexpectedly
Example: *Their mutual love for dogs sparked the unlikely friendship that developed into twenty years of owning a dog shelter.*
to provide a small amount of encouragement or motivation
Example: *Her mother's presence sparks her every time to perform her best.*

sparkle /spˈɑːkəl/
to shine brightly with small flashes of light
Example: *Her engagement ring sparkled and winked at her guests as they walked from table to table greeting everyone.*
to emit or reflect bright, lively, or vibrant light or colours
Example: *It was a beautiful night, with the stars sparkling in the blue-black sky.*
to be vivacious, lively, or full of energy

Example: *Moira's eyes sparkled as she sang and entertained her guests at her 50th birthday celebration.*
to be or become animated, lively, or enthusiastic
Example: *Liandra did a marvellous job as the host of the pageant sparkling across the stage with brilliant quips and an infectious smile, while clad in a gorgeous evening gown.*

spasm /spˈɑzəm/
to experience a sudden, involuntary contraction of muscles, typically causing pain or discomfort
Example: *Delon gripped his leg and sank to the track, as it began to spasm and convulse in the middle of his race.*

speak /spˈiːk/
to communicate verbally or orally
Example: *It is a blessing to be able to speak.*
to express one's thoughts, ideas, or opinions
Example: *I will speak freely when asked my opinion on integrated education for students in today's society.*
to utter words in a particular language or dialect
Example: *Most South American natives speak Spanish.*
to give a speech or deliver an address
Example: *President Obama had a knack for speaking in the most down to earth tones which always put his listeners at ease.*
to convey a message or convey information
Example: *Before Richard could stop him, Jaleel had already started speaking to the wrong coach about their intent to forfeit the match because of discrimination against their teammate.*

specify /spˈɛsɪfˌaɪ/
to state or describe something in detail, usually by providing specific information or criteria

Example: *The Ministry of Agriculture specified the schools they intended to work with for the poultry farm project.*

speculate /spˈɛkjʊlˌeɪt/
to form a theory or conjecture about something without form evidence
Example: *After seeing them in public together several times, many people speculated that she was being groomed to become the new princess of Scotland.*
to engage in risky financial transactions, typically with the hope of making a profit
Example: *Ryan speculated that if they engaged the new company ahead of their rivals, they may cash in big since they appear to be prospering at the moment.*
to ponder or consider a matter, often with curiosity or interest
Example: *The more I speculate over the information about the injured child, the less it makes sense.*
to meditate or reflect on a subject
Example: *Even when all the facts are given on a situation, the public will speculate if they want to.*

speed /spˈiːd/
to move or travel quickly
Example: *The motorcyclists speed down the road dodging in and out of traffic at a fast rate.*
to increase the rate or pace of something
Example: *Max turns the dial to speed up the process of whisking the eggs.*
the proceed advanced rapidly
Example: *Kate sped from the classroom to warn Jessie of the dorm inspection, but she was too late.*
to go beyond the legal or safe limit of speed, especially while driving
Example: *The campaign by the police department has seen many drivers charged for speeding along the highway.*

spell /spˈɛl/
to form words correctly by arranging letters in the proper order
Example: *At three, she can already spell three syllable words.*
to signify or represent by letters
Example: *Kindly spell your name for us.*
to indicate or signify something, often with a particular outcome or consequence
Example: *The model agency spelled out the terms and conditions of working with children to each parent or guardian who came to sign their children up for the job.*
to take turns performing a task or duty
Example: *We each took a spell at watching the baby while our parents were out.*

spend /spˈɛnd/
to use money or resources to buy goods or services
Example: *It is necessary to spend money wisely as both goods and services are expensive.*
to pass time in a particular way or place
Example: *I was fortunate to spend two lovely months with my mum in Tortola before she passed away.*
to exhaust or use up a resource, such as energy, effort, or emotion
Example: *Laura was spent from working through the night to finish the project.*
to allocate or devote time or effort to a particular activity or pursuit
Example: *Kiara will spend this summer learning to dive and other water sports.*

spike /spˈaɪk/
to drive a sharp object, such as a spike or nail, into something
Example: *According to historic reports, Jesus was spiked to the cross through his hands and feet.*
to increase suddenly and sharply, often referring to a rise in a graph or chart

Example: *Deaths due to accidents on the roads of Guyana have spiked considerably over the past six months.*
to add alcohol or drugs to a drink without the knowledge of the person consuming it
Example: *It is a common phenomenon at college parties to spike the punch bowl of drinks.*
to add flavour or season to food or drink
Example: *A dash of lime equally spikes the flavour of fried snapper and a cold Corona beer.*

spill /spˈɪl/
to accidentally cause a liquid or substance to flow out of its container and onto a surface
Example: *In her haste to open the door, she spilled wine down the front of her new dress.*
to divulge or reveal information that was meant to be kept secret
Example: *Six beers and a shot of fireball later, Marlon spilled the secret of his hit and run incident that had been weighing on his chest for years.*
to spread out or scatter in large quantities
Example: *Seeds were spilled onto the haphazardly prepared beds by the uncaring teens who just wanted the task to be over and done with.*
to flow or overflow beyond the confines of a container
Example: *Water spilled from the sides of the bucket that was left under the running pipe, in the otherwise deserted yard.*

spin /spˈɪn/
to rotate rapidly around a central axis or point
Example: *Kite flyers spin long pieces of polytene twine around a stick to use to fly their kite.*
the twist or turn something quickly
Example: *Spinning tops is a favourite pastime of many children.*
to give a biassed or slanted interpretation of information

Example: *Nicholas got cold feet and put a spin on what really happened, fearing harsh punishment from his boss.*

to manufacture or produce (tread, yarn, or fabric) by drawing out and twisting fibres

Example: *Is yarn still spun the way it used to be done several decades ago?*

to undergo a feeling of dizziness or disorientation

Example: *She started at the sound of his voice and sprang to her feet causing her head to spin.*

spit /spˈɪt/

to expel saliva or liquid from the mouth

Example: *Some women spit uncontrollably during the first trimester of their pregnancy.*

to eject or forcefully discharge something from the mouth or throat

Example: *Brenda spat the spoonful of bitter tasting food and asked what it was.*

to speak or express something and really or vehemently

Example: *Daniel spits his disgust at the way the sanctuary of God was desecrated by thieves over the weekend.*

spite /spˈaɪt/

to deliberately annoy, or friend, or hurt someone, especially in retaliation or out of malice

Example: *Her family spited for marrying an American by not attending the wedding.*

splash /splˈɑʃ/

to scatter or spray liquid in small drops or particles

Example: *Water splashed out of the pool as the bodyguard jumped in to rescue Dexta Daps from his ardent fans.*

to make a showy or extravagant display of something, often involving spending money

Example: *Tara has been splashing her children with money and expensive gifts to compensate for the messy divorce they were caught in the middle of.*

to attract attention or make a big impression
Example: *Trishanna splashed into the room in a bright floral outfit turning the heads of the men and causing jealous stares from the women.*

to move through water causing it to scatter or spray
Example: *The swim instructor splashes the water on the groups of children standing around the sides of the pool.*

splay /splˈeɪ/
to spread out or expand in different directions from a central point
Example: *The lone gunman splayed bullets from a bench in the middle of the cafeteria killing many twenty students and injuring seventy-five others.*

to cause something to spread out or extend in a splayed manner
Example: *The skins of several different animals lay splayed out to dry along the fences of the compound.*

to be spread out or positioned in a splayed manner
Example: *The desperate man splayed himself across the bonnet of his wife's car as she tried to leave.*

splinter /splˈɪntə/
to break or split into small, thin pieces
Example: *Cassie watched in horror as the vase with her mother's remains splintered into a million pieces.*

to divide or fragment into smaller groups or factions
Example: *The hike leader splintered the hikers and assigned a leader for each of these smaller groups.*

to cause a group or organisation to divide or fragment
Example: *Constant disagreements over the management of the business soon splintered the company, and the friends each went their separate ways.*

to develop a sharp, thin piece from a larger object
Example: *During survival skills session at camp, the leaders splinter the logs to create starters for the fire.*

split /splˈɪt/
to divide or separate into parts, often along a particular line or axis
Example: *The coconut vendor split the coconut into halves and gave us each a coconut spoon to eat the jelly with.*
to separate or sever from a larger group or entity
Example: *The Jones' children split from their parents' company and created a line of clothing of their own.*
to distribute something among different parties or individuals
Example: *The prize money will be split equally among the members of the group.*
to leave or depart from a place quickly or suddenly
Example: *The suspect had split by the time the cops arrived on the scene.*
the part or diverge along a particular direction or path
Example: *The part in the middle of her head split her hair evenly into two ponytails.*

splutter /splˈʌtɐ/
to speak or utter in a hasty, confused, or stuttering manner
Example: *Quesi's smooth rap was reduced to a splutter when the principal walked into the classroom.*
to emit or produce a series of short, explosive sounds, often when something is being cooked or when liquid is being expelled from the mouth
Example: *The fudge spluttered in the pot, warning us to stay clear or be burnt.*
the sputter or spurt out liquid or particles in an uneven or irregular manner
Example: *The hot thick syrup gurgled and spluttered as it was being poured from the flask.*

spoil /spˈɔɪl/
to damage the quality, appearance, or condition of something
Example: *The tenth and eleventh grade boys spoil their school pants by altering the legs of the pants, so they fit extremely close.*
to treat someone with excessive indulgence or leniency, often resulting in negative behaviour
Example: *Many parents are in the habit of spoiling their children; it is not a good practice.*
to impair or diminish the value of enjoyment of something
Example: *Count on Jane to spoil our fun every time she joins our girls' night out.*
to become unfit for consumption or use due to decay or deterioration
Example: *The fish we bought this morning has spoiled.*

spot /spˈɒt/
to see, notice, or identify something, often unexpectedly or by chance
Example: *Yesterday morning we spotted a red ibis on our way to New Amsterdam.*
to mark or identify a particular location or position
Example: *After we spotted the land we bought, we fenced it off to prevent the shifting of the boundary.*
to stain or mark something with spots or specks
Example: *Some of the shirts were spotted, while the others were tie dyed in preparation for a children's craft show.*
to provide sudden or temporary assistance or help
Example: *The committee spotted Chase as the most eligible for the role of drill instructor for the cadet's camp.*

sprawl /sprˈɔːl/
to lie or sit with the body and limbs spread out awkwardly
Example: *The dogs lay sprawled under the shade of the huge mango tree.*
to extend or spread out over a large area in a disorderly or untidy manner

Example: *Shacks and houses could be seen sprawled haphazardly all over Plastic City on the drone shot.*
to develop or grow in an uncontrolled or haphazard manner
Example: *Fruit trees could be seen peeping through the vegetation that sprawled across Thomas's plantation.*
to write or draw in a messy, careless, or sprawling manner
Example: *The doctor's orders were sprawled across the prescription in an unintelligible manner.*

spray /spreɪ/
to disperse liquid in small droplets or particles over an area
Example: *In the rainy season Jeyes Fluid is sprayed around the yard as a deterrent to snakes, rodents, and roaches.*
to emit a release of fine mists or stream of liquid
Example: *Spraying body splash on the body is the preferable way to cool down for some people, as opposed to powdering the body.*
to apply the liquid, such as paint or insecticide, in a fine mist stream
Example: *Spray the wall with even strokes of paint, or the finished product will be uneven as well.*
to cover or coat something with small droplets or particles of a substance
Example: *The gardener sprays the soil with weedicide to slow down the process of the regrowth of grass.*
to spread or scatter something over a surface or area in a haphazard manner
Example: *The children sprayed each other with the garden hose when they were sent to water the plants.*

spread /sprˈɛd/
to extend or distribute over an area or surface
Example: *The fire quickly spread from the bakery to the neighbouring houses.*
to become widely known or distributed

Example: *The Chronicle newspaper is spread through all the administrative regions of Guyana.*

the stretch or expand in all directions

Example: *The chair covers were spread to fit the entire chair nicely.*

to apply a substance thinly and evenly over a surface

Example: *The children were allowed to spread butter on their toast themselves.*

to promote or publicise something widely

Example: *I will spread the Good News everywhere I go.*

to cause something to be dispersed or separated

Example: *Heavy rains caused the embankment to wash away, and the river spread out much wider than we were comfortable with.*

spring /spr'ɪŋ/

to move suddenly or rapidly upward or forward

Example: *The robbers waiting in the underbrush sprang out into the path of the passing carriage.*

to originate or arise suddenly or unexpectedly

Example: *The next morning, a whole row of flowers had sprung up where there was none the previous day.*

to leap or jump forward with force or energy

Example: *Much quad-strength is needed to spring from the board into the pit in a long jump.*

to appear or emerge suddenly and forcefully

Example: *Bodyguards are expected to spring into action immediately on sensing danger in a situation.*

to release or let go of something suddenly and forcefully

Example: *The arrow sprang forward when the archer released the bow.*

to coil or twist tightly into a curled or wound shape

Example: *Her curls spring back into place every time she pulls them behind her ears.*

sprinkle /sprˈɪŋkəl/
to scatter or distribute small drops or particles of something over an area
Example: *D'Nae lightly sprinkled nuts and chocolate chips on the tops of her batch of cookies.*
to rain lightly or in small drops
Example: *The clouds lazily sprinkled drops of rain onto the parched ground, then stopped as suddenly as it had started.*
to apply or disperse something in a light, random manner
Example: *Sprinkle the seeds along the corners of the fence; they do not need to follow a particular pattern.*
to add a small amount of something as decoration or flavouring
Example: *Each child sprinkles a little glitter onto their painting and leaves it to dry.*
to distribute or spread something evenly over a surface
Example: *Before sticking the pizza into the oven, Keshia sprinkled some cheese over each pan.*

sprint /sprˈɪnt/
to run at full speed over a short distance
Example: *Kevon sprinted desperately alongside the kidnappers' van to get a glimpse of the driver's face.*

sprout /sprˈaʊt/
to begin to grow or develop new shoots, buds, or leaves
Example: *Adrian's kindergarten class exclaimed over the shoots sprouting from their containers where they had planted peas.*
to emerge or appear suddenly or unexpectedly
Example: *Kev had sprouted three beard hairs overnight and he was very proud of them.*
to grow or develop rapidly or abundantly
Example: *The corn had sprouted and were growing nicely before the swarm of locust descended on the farm.*

to show signs of growth or development
Example: *Treshel could not believe that the premature Baby Jasmine had sprouted into the squalling two-year-old she was holding.*

spur /spˈɜː/
to stimulate or encourage the growth, development, or action of something
Example: *The recent spike in the cost of living spurred many families to revive their kitchen gardens.*
to provoke or incite someone to action
Example: *Several onlookers spurred the two young men on to fight, but wisdom prevailed, and they both walked away.*
to urge or drive forward with sharp or pointed objects, such as spurs on a horse
Example: *Jason spurs his horse on as they near the finish line.*
to provide support or reinforcement to something
Example: *With their home crowd spurring them on, the Crusaders won the match 3-0.*
to press or push against something with a pointed object
Example: *Some jockeys are not in favour of spurring their horses with the metal spurs to make them run faster.*

spurn /spˈɜːn/
to reject or refuse disdainfully or contemptuously
Example: *The family watched as Andrew walked dejectedly into the yard, assuming from his demeanour that his marriage proposal had been spurned by Cindy.*

sputter /ˈspətɚ/
to emit a series of short, explosive sounds
Example: *Betsy sputtered, much to Alie's delight when he turned the key in her ignition.*
to speak rapidly and incoherently, often with difficulty

Example: *Chance sputters a comment and dashes from the room when Jessie's dad walks in.*

to spray or eject small particles or droplets in a scattered or uneven manner

Example: *The stranded group cheered loudly as the rusty pipe sputtered and coughed up some rusty water, before clean clear water poured in a steady stream from the tap.*

spy /spˈaɪ/
to secretly observe or watch someone or something, especially to obtain information

Example: *Cassandra admits to spying on her brother when his friends come over and reporting it to their mum.*

to discover or find out something by secretly observing or investigating

Example: *I had spied on the Alexander's for six months to find out where the husband worked, and to date I still did not know his occupation.*

to work as a spy or intelligence agent

Example: *Sam confessed that he spied for the government in his youth but claims that he's now retired.*

to catch sight of or notice something, often unexpectedly

Example: *Out of the corner of my eye, I spied the beautiful blue Saki come to rest on my bird feeder.*

squall /skwˈɒl/
to cry or wail loudly or harshly

Example: *The squalling baby reinforced my resolve to not have children of my own.*

to scream or shout angrily or vehemently

Example: *Squalling amongst the children in the home is not received well by their father.*

to experience a sudden, violent gust of wind, often accompanied by rain or snow

Example: *The wind squalled, ripping up a few zinc sheets and blowing down an old shack up the street.*

square /skw'eə/
to make something square or rectangular in shape
Example: *The cake decorator squared off the edges of the cake as she prepared to make a model of The White House.*
to bring into agreement or conformity
Example: *Indira and Ebrahim's parents were concerned that if they did not square off whose religion their children would follow before the wedding, they would encounter serious problems.*
to settle or resolve a debt or obligation
Example: *The men agreed that they had squared their debts and started a fresh game of poker.*
to adjust or make something level or perpendicular
Example: *The Ministry of Education aims to square education in the country by offering skill subjects and fine arts along with the regular academic subjects.*
to be in agreement or consistent with something
Example: *The professor ensures that his demands of his students square with his output he gives to his students.*

squash /skw'ɒʃ/
to crush or flatten something with force
Example: *Maxine squashed the fly with the fly swat.*
to suppress or quash something, such as a rebellion or rumour
Example: *The teacher squashed the rumours about Jamie being pregnant as soon as she heard them.*
to squeeze or press something into a smaller or confined space
Example: *Following several failed attempts, Coach Fox was finally able to squash the sleeping bags into the trunk of his car.*
to defeat decisively or overwhelmingly in a competition or game

Example: *Skeldon Line Path Secondary squashed Tagore Memorial in the match yesterday.*

to reduce or lessen the intensity or size of something

Example: *Wendy squashed some of the air out of the balloon to make it easier to tie.*

squat /skwˈɒt/
to crouch or sit with one's knees bent and one's heels close or touching the buttocks or the back of the thighs

Example: *James squatted for a long time with his eyes to the keyhole trying to count the kidnappers in the room.*

to occupy a property without permission, typically abandoned or unused

Example: *Homeless people in the Rose Hall Town community have started squatting in the abandoned houses in the community.*

to settle or inhabit a place temporarily, without legal permission

Example: *Many families who have been squatting on government land are being displaced and their shacks demolished.*

to lower oneself or one's body close to the ground

Example: *Squatting is a great exercise to build the thighs and calves.*

to settle or establish one's ilk in a particular position, especially in a low or crouching posture

Example: *I can squat for about 5 minutes before I need to change my position.*

squawk /skwˈɔːk/
to make a loud, harsh, and often piercing cry or something, resembling that of a bird

Example: *The parrot squawked loudly as the strange men approached her cage.*

to complain or protest loudly and vehemently

Example: *Megan squawked in protest as the guards led her off the football field.*

to transmit a signal or message using a two-way radio or communication device
Example: *The officer jerked awake as his radio set began squawking information from the chief that he had been waiting on.*

squeak /'skwik/
to make a short, high-pitched sound, often resembling that of a mouse or a rusty hinge
Example: *The doors in the house squeaked annoyingly every time they were opened.*
to speak in a high-pitched or barely audible voice
Example: *Frank could barely squeak a reply as doubled over in intense pain.*
to barely achieve something, especially by a narrow margin
Example: *The school's dance squad barely squeaked into the competition by the skin of their teeth.*

squeal /'skwil/
to make a high-pitched, shrill cry or sound, often in response to pain, excitement, or fear
Example: *The girls squealed loudly when Carlvin Burnette walked into the school's auditorium.*
to inform on someone or reveal a secret, often in a betraying manner
Example: *Afraid of the repercussions of their actions, Dan squealed to the police about the hit and run accident they were involved in the night before.*
to protest loudly or vehemently
Example: *The toddler kicked and squealed as he was removed from the bathtub by his dad.*
to emit a high-pitched, screeching noise, typically produced by tires or machinery
Example: *We heard the squealing of the brakes, then a loud explosion as the buses collided with each other.*

squeeze /skwˈiːz/
to apply pressure to something, typically with one's hands, to compress or force it into a smaller space
Example: *Morgan squeezed the sleeping bag into his camp luggage as they prepared to leave on their camping expedition*
to exert pressure or force in a tight space, often causing discomfort or construction
Example: *The minibus conductor squeezed another passenger into the seat already containing four passengers.*
to hug or embrace tightly
Example: *Mum squeezed Denise with joy when she stepped off the plane.*
to obtain something by applying pressure or influence
Example: *The police squeezed the information out of the suspect and hurriedly left to save the girl alone in the woods by the school.*
to fit or pack tightly into a space
Example: *Another bag of milk was squeezed into the hamper being sent to a needy family in Craig village.*
to extract or obtain something from someone or something with difficulty
Example: *The patient mother squeezed the coin out of the hand of the determined toddler to prevent him putting it into his mouth.*
to reduce or lower by applying pressure
Example: *Karl writhed in pain as the doctor squeezed the gas out of his tummy by massaging his lower abdomen with hard strokes of her palm.*

squint /skwˈɪnt/
to look with one or both eyes partly close to see more clearly or to avoid the glare of bright light
Example: *We squinted in the harsh morning light as the drapes were pulled open to reveal the day clean.*

to look or peer with suspicion or doubt
Example: *Pat squinted her eyes at Dan as he told the story of his encounter with the thief, as it just did not add up.*
to cause the eyes to partially close, often due to a physical condition or defect
Example: *An injury to his eyes causes him to squint whenever he is exposed to bright light.*
to be misaligned or not straight, especially when referring to the eyes
Example: *Andrew's disability affects his eyes and causes him to squint to see things clearly.*

squirm /skwˈɜːm/
to wriggle or twist the body from side to side, especially when feeling discomfort, embarrassment, or agitation
Example: *Francessca squirmed uncomfortably as he questioned her repeatedly about her family.*

squirt /skwˈɜːt/
to eject or discharge a liquid in a thin, fast stream
Example: *Nigel squirted water from the water gun at Adrian as they played around the pool.*
to eject or spray a liquid suddenly and forcefully, often in a targeted direction
Example: *Mrs. Sampson squirted a stream of water onto her plants, then retired upstairs to rest.*
to release or expel a liquid suddenly and in small amounts
Example: *The boys watched in awe as Jeremiah squirted streams of water in three directions from between his teeth.*

squish /skwˈɪʃ/
to crush or squeeze something, typically with a soft, wet sound
Example: *The children gleefully squished the water balloons as they ran and played in the park.*
to make a soft, wet sound when pressed or walked on

Example: *The wet grass squished under our feet as we walked across the lawn to the house.*
to compress or flatten something, often causing it to deform or lose shape
Example: *The floaties were squished to release the air from them to make them easier to pack.*

stab /stˈab/
to pierce or thrust with a pointed object, typically with force
Example: *Marcus stabbed the snake after it bit him on the leg.*
to injure someone by piercing them with a pointed object
Example: *The assailant had stabbed the man twenty- eight times causing him to bleed out on the spot.*
to cause a sudden, sharp pain or discomfort
Example: *A sharp pain stabbed Jessie as he tried to move his injured arm.*
to make a quick, forceful movement with a pointed object
Example: *Keyron stabbed at an imaginary foe with his spear, as he practised his martial arts.*

stabilise /stˈeɪbəlˌaɪz/
to make or become stable, steady, or firm
Example: *Two planks were placed on each side of the bridge to stabilise it as the children crossed to the other side.*
to maintain or restore balance or equilibrium
Example: *Jason will be taken off the life support machine as his condition has stabilised.*
to prevent or reduce fluctuations or changes in something
Example: *Now that the power supply has stabilised, I will repurchase my electronic items that were damaged.*
to make or become less volatile or uncertain
Example: *The deranged man was given several shots to stabilise his condition.*
to support or reinforce something to prevent it from moving or shifting

Example: *The men of the village will spend the next two weeks stabilising the homes of families that are on stilts to prepare for the hurricane season.*

stack /stˈak/
to arrange objects or items neatly on top of one another in a pile or vertical arrangement
Example: *The cases of beer were stacked in a high pile in the storeroom.*
to pile or heap things on top of each other in a disorderly manner
Example: *When the bell rang, the children hastily stacked their lunch bags and raced to line up for assembly.*
to organise or arrange items in a systematic way
Example: *The art supplies were stacked in alphabetical order in the arts and craft room.*
to accumulate or amass a large quantity of something
Example: *When news of the destruction done by the hurricane met the other islands, people rushed to stack up on non-perishable items.*
to line up or position objects or people closely together
Example: *Slaves were stacked like sardines and transported across miles of sea to serve on the sugar and cotton plantations in the Americas.*
to arrange data or information in a specific order or format
Example: *The new inventory system allows persons to stack information that was once tedious to collect, efficiently and with ease.*

stagger /stˈagɐ/
to walk or move unsteadily, as if about to fall
Example: *The drunken man staggered from the bar to his home amidst much jeering and laughing from the young men on the street.*

to move or proceed on steadily or unevenly, often due to shock, surprise, or exhaustion
Example: *The tired workers staggered onto the truck and flopped themselves down in preparation for the long journey home.*
to cause someone to feel shocked, surprised, or overwhelmed
Example: *The news of the death of her father staggered Susan, and she regretted not visiting him in the hospital.*
to arrange or set things in an irregular or alternating pattern
Example: *Three-year-old Kyle had built a shopping complex with his Jenga blocks using staggered lines for the fence and sides of his building.*
to vary or alternate in position or timing
Example: *The athletes were arranged in staggered positions for the 400m sprint race.*

stain /stˈeɪn/
to mark or discolour something with a spot or blemish that is difficult to remove
Example: *Wine had stained the front of her Panamaniac band tee shirt.*
to taint or tarnish someone's reputation or character
Example: *The rumours circulated by the jealous girls had only temporarily stained Rebbie's character as people soon realised, she was the opposite of what was described.*
to colour or dye something, often permanently
Example: *Following the demands of the school, Richie stained the sole of his sneakers black.*
to imbue or permeate something with a particular quality or feeling
Example: *His nasty attitude towards his wife stained his friend's view of her, and they treated her with disdain, though they barely knew her.*

stalk /stˈɔːk/

to pursue or follow someone or something stealthily, often with the intention of causing harm or capturing
Example: *The predators stalk its prey through the tall grass.*
to move in a stealthy or determined manner, often with an aggressive or menacing intent
Example: *He stalked angrily out of the room.*
to walk stiffly or haughtily
Example: *She stalked across the stage with confidence.*
to harass or intimidate someone persistently and menacingly
Example: *He felt as though he was being stalked by his ex-partner.*
to support or provide structural support for a plant, such as a stem or main axis
Example: *The stalks of the flowers reached towards the sunlight.*

stall /stˈɔːl/
to stop or cause to stop making progress, typically due to the lack of momentum, space, or time
Example: *The car's engine began to stall on the steep hill.*
to delay or procrastinate, intentionally or unintentionally
Example: *They stalled for time by asking irrelevant questions.*
to come to a standstill or halt, often temporarily
Example: *The negotiations stalled over disagreements about the terms.*
to cause an engine or machinery to stop running by depriving it of fuel or power
Example: *He accidentally stalled the lawnmower by pulling the cord too hard.*
to occupy or use a space, often temporarily, especially in a public area
Example: *Street vendors have stalls along the market street.*
to lose lift and begin to drop suddenly, often due to insufficient air speed or angle of attack
Example: *The aeroplane stalled as it attempted to climb too steeply.*

stammer /stˈamə/
to speak with involuntary pauses or repetitions of sounds, often due to nervousness, shyness, or a speech impediment
Example: *My brother stammers when he is nervous or excited.*

stamp /stˈamp/
to strike or press something, typically with the foot, with force
Example: *The worker quickly stamped the loose board in place as the supervisor came across to his section for inspection.*
to impress or imprint a mark or design onto something using a stamp
Example: *Report booklets must be stamped with the school's official stamp and signed by the relevant authorities before they are distributed.*
to affix a postage stamp or a similar label onto something as a mark of payment or approval
Example: *The class's favourite part of posting the letter was getting it stamped at the post office.*
to move or march with heavy steps, often to make a loud noise or to express authority
Example: *Nyasha stamped her feet loudly to attract the attention of her brother as he rode out of the yard, but he did not hear her.*
to declare or emphasise something forcefully or emphatically
Example: *Ms. Ram stamps her authority on the first day of class by formulating the rules of the class with her students.*

stand /stˈand/
to be on one's feet in and operate position, not sitting or lying down
Example: *She stood at the bus stop waiting for her ride.*
to occupy a particular position or location
Example: *The house stands at the end of the street.*
to be in a specified condition or state
Example: *His reputation still stands intact.*
to remain in existence or valid

Example: *The law stands as it was written.*
to take a particular position or viewpoint
Example: *He stands firmly against the proposal.*
to be in a particular situation or circumstance
Example: *The decision stands, regardless of the consequences.*
to tolerate or endure something without yielding or giving way
Example: *She stood the pain bravely.*
to represent or symbolise something
Example: *The dove stands for peace.*
to be ready or prepared for action
Example: *They stood ready to defend their homeland.*
to perform or participate in a particular role or function
Example: *He stood as best man at the wedding.*

stare /stˈeə/
to look fixedly or intently at something for a prolonged period, often with one's eyes wide open
Example: *Attempts to get his aunt's attention failed Adrian, as she stood staring as though in another world.*

start /stˈɑːt/
to begin or commence an action, activity, or process
Example: *Registration started for the new intake of students on the first Monday in July.*
to cause something to begin or commence
Example: *The gathering started reciting the National Pledge, signalling the commencement of the program.*
to originate or come into being
Example: *This year starts the Annual Talent Show Competition, slated for the last Monday of June every year, going forward.*

startle /stˈɑːtəl/
to cause someone to feel sudden shock, surprise, or alarm

Example: *Babies startle easily so be careful not to make loud sudden noises around them.*

stash /stˈaʃ/
to hide or store something, especially for future use or to keep it safe
Example: *The clever thief stashed the stolen cash in plain sight.*

state /stˈeɪt/
to express or communicate something in speech or writing; to declare or assert
Example: *Each new member of the club was asked to state their name and occupation.*
to formally or officially declare or announce something
Example: *Maria emphatically stated that she will not be renewing her contract with the company.*
to present or describe something in a specific manner or form
Example: *The textbooks given state exactly what must be done for this subject area.*
to affirm or attest to the truth or accuracy of something
Example: *She clearly stated everything she had overheard while occupying the guestroom, on the night of the murder.*
to lay down or establish a principle, rule, or law
Example: *The law states that minors cannot be tried as adults in a court of law.*
to specify or indicate something explicitly
Example: *The fire chief stated that citizens who tamper with fire hydrants will be prosecuted.*

station /stˈeɪʃən/
to place or position someone or something in a specific location
Example: *There were three guards stationed at the entrance to Castellani House.*
to assign someone to a particular task or duty

Example: *The Police Chief stations his most reliable officers in the neediest communities.*
to establish or set up a location for a particular purpose
Example: *A base was stationed at the Whim Community Centre for displaced flood victims.*
to stand or be located at a fixed point or position
Example: *A friendly guard was stationed at the entrance to Buckingham Palace yesterday.*
to provide with accommodations or facilities
Example: *The visiting students and teachers from the Hinterland region were stationed at the West Minister Secondary School for a period of three days.*

stay /stˈeɪ/
to remain in a particular place or position for a period
Example: *We were made to stay in the beach house until our luggage arrived.*
to continue to be in a particular state or condition
Example: *Horace had to stay with his teacher until his mum could collect him after work.*
to reside temporarily as a guest or visitor
Example: *We stayed at the Wronge's residence for a total of five days.*
to delay or postpone action
Example: *The parents were asked to stay pressing charges against the swim instructor until a thorough investigation was done by the school.*
to stop or halt someone or something from moving or progressing
Example: *The progress of the building project was stayed when the contractor's business burned to the ground.*
to wait for or anticipate something
Example: *Gabrielle stayed, expecting Frank to change when he discovered she was with child.*
to remain loyal or committed to a particular person, group, or cause

Example: *The family of the missing girl stayed committed to finding her, even after the police officers gave up hope.*
to support or uphold a decision, ruling, or judgement
Example: *Though unpleasant, my family stayed the ruling of the court and handed over the legal documents to the property to our father's new wife.*

steady /stˈɛdi/
to make or become firm, constant, or unwavering
Example: *Pollyann steadied her stance and refused to move out of the path of the oncoming vehicle.*
to prevent something from moving or shaking
Example: *The doctor ordered braces to help steady the legs of his patient suffering from cerebral palsy.*
to make or become calm or composed
Example: *Desmond's hand on her shoulder steadied Vanessa just when she thought she would explode in anger.*
to support or maintain someone or something in a difficult or challenging situation
Example: *The support of her family helps to steady Mandy and strengthen her resolve just when she feels like giving up.*
to bring to a desired level or state gradually or slowly; to regulate or control something
Example: *After several attempts, they were finally able to steady the heartbeat of the frightened child and prevent him from going into shock.*
to become constant or consistent over time
Example: *Jordie watched happily as his son steadied his steps as he walked towards him.*
to reassure or comfort someone
Example: *Babita felt steadied by her dad's bear hug, and she snuggled against him for a deeper hug.*

steal /stˈiːl/

to take (something) without permission or legal rights and without intending to return it or to pay for it
Example: *He steals even when it is not necessary; it was ingrained after years of stealing to eat.*

steer /stˈiə/
to guide or direct the movement over vehicle, vessel, or animal in a particular position
Example: *Jaden's dad allowed him to steer the car when they were driving along the quiet back road.*
to navigate or manage a course of action, often by providing guidance or leadership
Example: *The commanding officer gave valuable information meant to steer the young soldiers on a path to successfully completing their course.*
to influence or guide someone's actions or decisions
Example: *When we met her mother, we could tell that Myra had been steered into the modelling industry by her mother.*
to avoid or navigate around obstacles or dangers
Example: *The divers watched in suspense as Tommy cautiously steered the dinghy out from among the sharks towards the docks.*

step /stˈɛp/
to move by lifting one foot and put it down in another spot, typically in the sequence to move forward and backward
Example: *My baby sister steps gingerly towards us when we call her, as she is now learning to walk.*
to act or make progress
Example: *Troy stepped up his game and opened the taxi service he had spoken to us of.*
to proceed or advance in a process or series of actions
Example: *Vincent stepped forward with his plans to construct his home despite several setbacks.*

to take a particular measure or action in response to a situation
Example: *The neighbours of the woman being abused stepped in and reported the matter to the police.*

stick /stˈɪk/
to adhere or cling to something; to become attached
Example: *Stick three notebooks together for Home Economics from the beginning because it has three components.*
to remain in a particle position or state; to not move or change
Example: *Valerie seems to be stuck in the job of an office assistant despite her efforts to be promoted to Ms. Jace's personal secretary.*
to thrust or push something into or onto something else
Example: *Karen sticks the popsicle sticks together to form the fence for her craft house.*
to remain loyal or faithful to someone or something
Example: *They have stuck together even though they seldom see eye to eye on most issues in their lives.*
to continue doing or using something; to persist
Example: *Although Macy was experiencing severe difficulty on her job, she stuck it out until she was moved to a different department.*
to stay or be retained in a place
Example: *Harry was willing to try sticking it out as manager for another year, providing he was given a raise of pay and accommodations.*

stiffen /stˈɪfən/
to make or become stiff or rigid, often in response to cold, fear, tension, or stress
Example: *The hat and belt for her nurse's uniform were stiffened with a hard plastic material.*

stifle /stˈaɪfəl/

to prevent or restrain something from happening or developing
Example: *She tried to stifle her laughter during the serious meeting.*
to suffocate or smother someone or something by depriving them of ear or space
Example: *The heavy smoke threatened to stifle the firefighters' efforts.*
to suppress or hold back an emotion, feeling, or reaction
Example: *He tried to stifle his angle in front of his boss.*
to hinder or impede the progress or development of something
Example: *The regulations threatened to stifle innovation in the industry.*
to suppress or extinguish a sound or noise
Example: *She tried to stifle her sobs so as not to wake anyone.*
to dampen or deaden a feeling, quality, or enthusiasm
Example: *The negative feedback threatens to stifle their creativity.*
to oppress or crush someone's spirits or ambition
Example: *The lack of opportunities stifled her dreams of becoming an artist.*

still /stˈɪl/
to make or become calm, quiet, or motionless
Example: *The wind finally stilled, and the leaves ceased rustling.*
to cause or bring to a halt or stop
Example: *She stilled her racing thoughts and focused on the task at hand.*
to pacify or quieten someone or something
Example: *He stilled the crowd with a gesture.*
to make or become tranquil or serene
Example: *The lake stilled as the sun set, casting a golden glow over the water.*
to suppress or extinguish a sound or noise

Example: *She stilled her breathing to listen for any movement in the darkness.*
to allay or calm someone's fears or anxieties
Example: *Her soothing words stilled his worries.*
to control or restrain someone or something
Example: *He stilled his emotions and spoke calmly.*

stimulate /stˈɪmjʊlˌeɪt/
to encourage or induce activity, growth, or development, often by exciting or arousing someone or something
Example: *Jane uses oil to stimulate her hair growth.*

sting /stˈɪŋ/
to cause a sharp, sudden pain or discomfort, typically by piercing or pricking with a sharp object
Example: *Bees do not bite, they sting.*
to cause emotional pain or distress
Example: *Her mother's untimely death stung her.*
to feel a sharp, tingling sensation, typically due to cold, heat, or an injury
Example: *When I tried the salt and ice challenge, it started stinging my arm.*
to be bitten or attacked by an insect or small animal, typically resulting in a sharp, painful sensation
Example: *If you keep troubling that nest, the wasps will sting you.*
to feel a sense of loss or disappointment, typically due to failure or rejection
Example: *The betrayal stung her for weeks.*

stink /stˈɪŋk/
to emit a strong, unpleasant odour; to have a foul smell
Example: *The laundry began to stink in the washroom.*
to be of extremely poor quality or to be morally reprehensible
Example: *This movie stinks.*

stipulate /ˈstɪpjəˌleɪt/
to specify or dim and something as part of an agreement, contract, or condition
Example: *The contract stipulates that all football players must be in uniform during the game.*

stir /stˈɜː/
to mix or agitate something, typically with a spoon or similar utensil
Example: *Please stir that pot.*
to move or cost move slightly or gently
Example: *She stirred the chits in the hat.*
to provoke or stimulate a reaction or response
Example: *Do not stir the drama between those boys.*
to mix or blend emotions or thoughts, often resulting in excitement or arousal
Example: *Her emotions stirred as she saw her CAPE results.*
to incite or instigate trouble or onerous
Example: *Stop stirring the drama.*
to the store or disrupt a state of calm or tranquil
Example: *He came to stir up drama and disturb our peace.*

stitch /stˈɪtʃ/
to join or mend fabric or material with stitches
Example: *She stitched the torn seam of her dress.*
to inflict a sharp, piercing pain, typically in the side
Example: *He doubled over and paid as a stitch hit him during the race.*
to arrange or connect something in a neat or orderly manner
Example: *Jane stitched together a series of photos to create a panoramic view.*

stock /stˈɒk/
to supply or provide with goods, materials, or resources

Example: *When the new supermarket opened, I saw the owner stocking the shelves with some very unusual products.*
to have or keep a supply of something available for use
Example: *We need to keep stocking sugar because there will be a shortage soon.*
to keep a supply of animals, especially for breeding purposes
Example: *We must stock chickens for this upcoming Christmas season.*

stockpile /stˈɒkpaɪl/
to accumulate or gather a large supply of something for future use or emergency
Example: *Next month the Red Cross Society will begin to stockpile first aid equipment for the hurricane season.*

stoke /stˈəʊk/
to add fuel to a fire
Example: *The campfire is about to go out; please stoke it.*
to encourage and intensify a feeling, situation, or process
Example: *Sarah began to stoke her little sister's enthusiasm towards drum playing.*

stomp /stˈɒmp/
to tread heavily or forcefully with the feet, often to express anger, frustration, or emphasis
Example: *After being scolded the little girl stomped up the stairs.*

stoop /stˈuːp/
to bend the body forward and downward
Example: *She stooped low to avoid her family seeing her.*
to lower or debase oneself morally or socially
Example: *I never expected him to stoop that low.*
to descend from a higher to a lower level

Example: *After her parents abandoned her, her expectations of people stooped.*
to show signs of tiredness or fatigue
Example: *After the basketball game she stooped in frustration.*
to yield or submit to someone or something
Example: *I will accept defeat and stoop at their mercy.*

stop /stˈɒp/
to cease or halt an action, movement, or process
Example: *Stop that ball from rolling down the hill.*
to come to an end or a standstill
Example: *I will stop watching this movie if you do not stop speaking.*
to prevent or prohibit an action or activity
Example: *I stopped the police from arresting him.*
to pause or take a break from an activity
Example: *I do not feel appreciated so I will stop coming here.*
to stay or remain in one place or position
Example: *Stop moving right now!*
to block or fill a hole, gap, or opening
Example: *We must stop that water from flowing or the whole house will flood.*
to interrupt or disrupt the flow or continuity of something
Example: *Stop pouring the juice now.*

store /stˈɔː/
to keep or retain something for future use or reference
Example: *You need to store that cheese in the fridge, or it will go bad.*
to place or deposit something in a location for safekeeping
Example: *We should start storing food before the hurricane.*
to accumulate or gather a supply of something
Example: *I like to store antique bottles.*

storm /stˈɔːm/

to move quickly and forcefully, often with great energy or intensity
Example: *Avery stormed out of the building in frustration.*
to attack or assault a place with great force, especially in a sudden and violent manner
Example: *The man began to storm the cashier.*
to reach or express strong emotions, often in an unrestrained or tumultuous manner
Example: *When the girl finally got frustrated, she began to storm.*

stow /stˈəʊ/
to park or store something carefully and securely in a specified place, especially on a ship, aircraft, or vehicle
Example: *The auto theft stowed away the V6.*

straddle /strˈadəl/
to stand or sit with one leg on each side of something
Example: *She straddled the wild horse with ease.*
to extend across or cover both sides of something
Example: *She put her toddler to straddle her leg.*
to be in an ambiguous or intermediate position between two different situations, ideas, or groups
Example: *I am straddled between Argentina and Brazil for the World Cup.*

straighten /strˈeɪtən/
to make something straight or to become straight
Example: *Straighten your back or your posture will be bad when you get older.*

strain /strˈeɪn/
to exert oneself physically or mentally beyond normal limits
Example: *Her mother was afraid that she would strain herself trying to lift the heavy boxes.*
to stretch or exert force on something to the point of injury or damage

Example: *We were advised by the doctor to desist from straining to defecate.*

to separate solids from liquids by passing through a sieve, colander, or similar device

Example: *Bella strained the seeds and pulp from the lemonade drink and place it into the refrigerator.*

to put pressure or stress on something, often to the point of weakening or damaging it

Example: *The ropes tying the banana sucker strained dangerously every time the wind blew.*

strangle /strˈaŋɡəl/
to kill by squeezing the throat tightly to cut off airflow

Example: *The new murder victim had been strangled with her own shirt.*

to inhibit or suppress something forcefully

Example: *Tonya's mum tried to strangle the information from the distraught teen before the police arrived.*

strap /strˈap/
to fasten or secure something with a strap

Example: *The baby was securely strapped in the stroller.*

to beat or punish someone with a strap

Example: *Ms. Joyce strapped both boys for breaking the neighbour's window, after warning them about playing cricket in the yard.*

to bind or tie something with a strap

Example: *Father straps the bicycle chair onto the bicycle as he prepares to take the baby for a ride.*

stray /strˈeɪ/
to move away from the correct or intended path or direction

Example: *Dawn strayed from the tour group and found herself alone in a deserted corridor of the museum.*

to wander away from a familiar or safe please
Example: *The curious child strays around the unfamiliar property oblivious of the danger lurking within the grounds.*
to deviate from a set course or standard
Example: *The discussion in class can stray easily if it is not kept in check.*

streak /strˈiːk/
to move very quickly in a particular direction
Example: *Lightning streaked across the sky, terrifying the children with its suddenness.*
to mark with lines or stripes of a different colour or texture
Example: *On Alie's request, the children will streak lines on our family tent to identify it easily when it is packed with the others.*
to have a quality or feature in a prominent or distinctive way
Example: *The Daniels' siblings are streaked with wide flaring nose; our dad's trademark feature.*

streamline /strˈiːmlaɪn/
to make a process, system, organisation, or product more efficient and simpler by removing unnecessary steps or components
Example: *The digitalised records at all schools have helped to streamline several processes making record keeping efficient and effective in schools.*

strengthen /strˈɛŋθən/
to make something stronger or more powerful
Example: *My resolve to home-school my children has been strengthened with the recent spate of missing children being featured on social media.*

stress /strˈɛs/
to emphasise or gift particular importance to something

Example: *The team now understood the captain's reason for stressing on the need to walk with needle and thread.*
to subject to mental or emotional pressure
Example: *The young mother was stressed because she was out of diapers and milk for her children.*
to pronounce with emphasis or force
Example: *Jason stressed that he needed to be home by 8PM, or he would be pulled from the squad.*
to place physical force on something to test its strength or durability
Example: *Jess stressed the durability of the generator by letting it run for an entire day.*

stretch /strˈɛtʃ/
to extend or lengthen something beyond its normal length or dimensions
Example: *The seamstress stretched the fabric to be used for the costumes by adding black fabric to the floral fabric.*
to reach out or extend one's body or limbs to increase flexibility or relieve tension
Example: *Stretching is a great way to prepare your muscles for a more intense workout.*
to make something taut or tight by pulling or extending it
Example: *A rubber band was stretched across a piece of wood to fashion a make-shift slingshot for the children to play with.*
to extend the duration or time frame of something
Example: *The lecturer stretched the submission time to two more days to accommodate the students with internet issues.*
to make something longer or larger by adding to it
Example: *Mom stretches our skirts' waistband by adding a piece of dark elastic to it.*

stride /strˈaɪd/
to walk with long, decisive steps

Example: *Sam watched from the porch as her parents came striding up the driveway.*

to make significant progress or advanced confidently

Example: *The company strides to keep up with the demands of its customers.*

to overcome obstacles or difficulties with determination and confidence

Example: *Maggie now strides confidently, with her head held high, as she has obtained several passes at the CAPE examinations.*

strike /strˈaɪk/

to hit or deliver a blow with force

Example: *William strikes the ball over the boundary line, for six runs.*

to come into forcible contact with something

Example: *The angry woman struck the windscreen with a baseball bat.*

to cause sudden pain or discomfort

Example: *Tamica doubled over as pain struck her unexpectedly.*

to ignite or light a match or flame

Example: *Strike the match when the wind dies down so we can light a fire.*

to take industrial action by refusing to work as a form of protest

Example: *It is the legal right of any citizen to strike in protest of unfair salaries and working conditions.*

to impress or affect deeply

Example: *I was struck by her dishevelled appearance; then shocked to discover that it was my sister.*

string /strˈɪŋ/

to thread or arrange things in a line or series

Example: *I enjoy watching the children string beads together to create their own necklaces.*

to connect or tie together with a string or similar material
Example: *A pulley line was stringed from the back porch to the coconut tree, for us to hang our laundry in the sun.*
to stretch or extend something tightly between two points
Example: *They stringed him up between two poles and demanded answers about the missing children.*

strip /strˈɪp/
to remove clothing or covering from someone or something
Example: *Lisa has a habit of stripping off her clothes whenever she feels warm.*
to remove or peel away an outer layer or surface
Example: *The carpenter strips the chairs of the old wood.*
to deprive someone or something of possessions, rights, or status
Example: *The soldier was stripped of his accolades after speaking out on injustice.*
to dismantle or disassemble something into its component parts
Example: *The mechanic strips the vehicle to fix the problem.*
to remove or take away something essential or important
Example: *The heavy winds stripped the capital city of electricity.*

strive /strˈaɪv/
to make great efforts to achieve or obtain something
Example: *The students continue to strive for excellence.*

stroke /strˈəʊk/
to move one's hand or an object gently along surface
Example: *Mary stroked her cat until he fell asleep.*
to hit or strike something with a sweeping motion
Example: *He stroked the ball into the air.*
to caress or fondle someone or something gently
Example: *Mother gently strokes the baby's cheeks.*
to succeed or achieve something smoothly and effortlessly
Example: *He stroked through the five-kilometre to win the best prize.*

stroll /strˈəʊl/
to walk leisurely or casually, often without a specific destination or purpose
Example: *The new mom stroll down the road with her baby.*

structure /strˈʌktʃɐ/
to arrange or organise something according to a plan or system
Example: *The teacher structured the timetable to fit the academic needs of the students.*
to give form or shape to something
Example: *The house was structured to fit the size of the land.*
to build or construct something, typically a physical object or building
Example: *The bed was structured to withstand the six- hundred-pound man.*
to design or plan the layout or organisation of something
Example: *His essay was structured as instructed.*

struggle /strˈʌgəl/
to make forceful or strenuous efforts to free oneself from constraints or difficulties
Example: *The divers struggle against the current in search of the missing teen.*
to contend or fight against something difficult or challenging
Example: *The West Indies Cricket team struggles against England in the finals.*
difficulty or hardship in achieving something
Example: *Father struggles day to find a job.*

strum /strˈʌm/
to play (a string instrument such as a guitar or ukulele) by brushing the strings with one's fingers, usually inner rhythmic or casual manner
Example: *The old man strums his guitar as the day ends.*

strut /strˈʌt/

to walk with a proud, arrogant, or self-assured, often with exaggerated movements to display confidence or superiority
Example: *She struts around the class after being crowned the top student of the week.*

study /stˈʌdi/
to devote time and attention to learning about a subject or topic in a systematic and intentional manner
Example: *The students studied hard for their final exams.*

stuff /stˈʌf/
to fill something tightly or completely with the substance or objects
Example: *The suitcase was stuffed tightly.*
the cram something into a space or container
Example: *He stuffed his mouth with his remaining breakfast.*
to fill something with food or a filling
Example: *The turkey was stuffed with delicious fillings.*
to overeat or eat excessively
Example: *Her tummy stuff from overeating.*

stumble /stˈʌmbəl/
to trip or lose one's balance while walking or moving, often due to an obstacle or uneven ground
Example: *The man stumbled over the pile of wood.*
to make a mistake or encounter difficulty while speaking or acting
Example: *The professor stumbles through his presentation.*

stump /stˈʌmp/
to walk with a heavy or awkward gait, often due to physical impairment or injury
Example: *He stumped across the stage with his sprained leg.*
the travel around making political speeches or campaigning, especially during an election

Example: *The current president and his team stumped across the country soliciting supporters.*
to confuse or puzzle someone, making them unable to answer or respond
Example: *The teacher was stumped by the student's response.*
the challenge or pulls a difficult question or problem
Example: *The Mathematics exam stumps many students.*
to remove tree stumps from the ground
Example: *The city council used several men to stump the dead trees around the town.*

stutter /stˈʌtɐ/
to speak with involuntary pauses and repetitions of songs, syllables, or words, often due to a speech disorder or nervousness
Example: *Although he stutters, he managed to finish his speech.*

style /stˈaɪl/
to design or arrange something in a particular way, often according to a certain aesthetic or fashion
Example: *The old lady styled her hair in a unique way.*
to give a particular character or appearance to something
Example: *The wedding hall was styled in a garden theme.*
to create or invent something in a distinctive manner
Example: *The chef styled cake using his own invention.*

subdue /sʌbdjˈuː/
to overcome, bring on the control, or quieten by force or persuasion
Example: *I will subdue to her demands.*

sublet /sˈʌblət/
to lease or rent (a property) to someone else while one is oneself a tenant
Example: *We will sublet the apartment so we can afford it.*

submerge /səbmˈɜːdʒ/
to completely cover or immerse something on the water or in another liquid
Example: *If you submerge that shoe in that acid it.*

submit /səbmˈɪt/
to present or hand over something for consideration, decision, or action
Example: *Ensure you submit your assignments before 12:00 am.*

subside /səbsˈaɪd/
to become less intense, severe, or active
Example: *When our mother returned home, the argument began to subside.*
to decrease in intensity, violence, or force
Example: *The flooding began to subside when the sun came out.*

subtract /sʌbtrˈakt/
to take away or deduct one quantity from another
Example: *Subtract the price of your items from the total on the receipt.*

succeed /səksˈiːd/
to achieve a desired outcome or to accomplish a goal
Example: *If I do not succeed in my studies, I will always see myself as a failure.*

succumb /səkˈʌm/
to yield to a superior force or overwhelming pressure, to give in, or to surrender
Example: *Unfortunately, the dog succumbed to his injuries.*

suck /sˈʌk/
to draw into the mouth by creating a vacuum

Example: *The children happily sucked their lollipops.*
to draw in or take up by absorption
Example: *The sponge sucked up all the water that was left in the sink.*
to be very bad or unpleasant
Example: *This Wedding sucks.*
to be inferior or objectionable
Example: *I suck at playing tennis.*
to fail or be unsuccessful
Example: *I sucked at practice today.*

suffer /sˈʌfɐ/
to experience pain, distress, or hardship
Example: *I refuse to suffer in silence.*

suggest /sədʒˈɛst/
to propose an idea, recommend a course of action, or put forward a thought or opinion
Example: *I suggest we go to the market to buy our groceries.*

suit /sˈuːt/
to be appropriate or acceptable for someone
Example: *I think purple suits your skin tone much better than yellow.*
to be convenient or favourable
Example: *She is more suited for this position than you are.*
to meet the needs or requirements of
Example: *This cup suits the drink that is going in it.*
to adapt or adjust something to fit or match
Example: *You can season your food to suit your liking.*

sulk /sˈʌlk/
to be silent, morose, and resentful because of a perceived grievance or disappointment
Example: *Aliyah began to sulk after her mom told her no.*

summarise /sˈʌmərˌaɪz/
to give a brief statement or account of the main points of something
Example: *I do not want to hear all the details, please summarise your story.*

summon /sˈʌmən/
to call upon someone to be present, typically for a specific purpose or task
Example: *Summon the Priest to help with the exorcism.*

sunder /sˈʌndɚ/
to split apart, separate, or server forcefully
Example: *The wood sundered under the weight of the tractor.*

supervise /sˈuːpəvˌaɪz/
to oversee, manage, or monitor the activities or work of others
Example: *Shelly should supervise her brother in the kitchen.*

supplement /ˈsəpləmənt/
to add something extra to complete or enhance something
Example: *Ria added protein powder in her smoothie to supplement the nutritional value of the smoothie.*

supply /səˈplaɪ/
to provide or furnish something needed or desired
Example: *Your teacher will supply you with stationery for your project.*

support /səpˈɔːt/
to bear the weight of something
Example: *The branch is supporting the bird's nest.*
to hold up
Example: *Helen supports her grandmother as she tries to stand.*

to provide assistance, encouragement, or backing to someone or something
Example: *I will help to support her financially on her academic journey.*

suppose /sʌpˈəʊz/
to assume something to be the case
Example: *I suppose they are on their way.*
to expect something to happen based on evidence or reasoning
Example: *I suppose we will pool our funds to buy the food.*

surge /sˈɜːdʒ/
to move suddenly and powerfully forward or upward, often in a rapid and uncontrolled manner
Example: *The dog surged towards Leah on her motorbike.*

surmise /sɚˈmaɪz/
to suppose that something is true without having evidence to confirm it
Example: *She surmised that he was indeed being unfaithful to her.*
to guess or conjecture
Example: *Stop surmising and wait for me to give a definite answer.*

surprise /səprˈaɪz/
to cause someone to feel unexpectedly startled, astonished, or amazed
Example: *The amount of money in my bank account surprised me.*

surrender /sərˈɛndɚ/
to give up or relinquish control, possession, or power, typically in response to someone or something perceived as stronger or inescapable
Example: *It is better for me to surrender than to be brutally defeated.*

surround /sərˈaʊnd/

to encircle or encompass something completely
Example: *The ants surrounded the breadcrumbs.*

survey /sɚˈveɪ/
to examine or inspect something comprehensively, often with the intention of gathering information or understanding its characteristics
Example: *Tomorrow afternoon we will go and survey the plot of land.*

suspect /ˈsəsˌpɛkt/
to believe or think that someone is guilty of a crime or wrongdoing, typically without conclusive evidence
Example: *We suspect that she took the cheese.*

suspend /səspˈɛnd/
to temporarily stop or interrupt something
Example: *The police would quickly suspend your driver's licence if you were caught speeding.*

swab /swˈɒb/
to clean or apply something to a surface using a small piece of absorbent material, typically cotton on a stick
Example: *The forensics team thoroughly swabbed the murderer's van.*

swagger /swˈɑgɐ/
to walk or behave in a very confident, arrogant, or boastful manner
Example: *She swaggered down the hall.*

swallow /swˈɒləʊ/
to cause something to pass down the throat, typically through the mouth and oesophagus, into the stomach

Example: *If you do not swallow that medicine, we will have a problem Sir.*

swat /swˈɒt/
to hit or strike something, especially a flying insect, with a sharp blow, usually using the hand or a flat object
Example: *Swat that spider quickly!*

sway /swˈeɪ/
to move or swing gently back and forth or from side to side
Example: *The car began to sway from left to right.*

swear /swˈeə/
to make a solemn declaration or promise, often invoking a deity or something sacred
Example: *I swear I will do the shopping tomorrow.*
to use profane language or curse words
Example: *Do not you know it is rude to swear in the presence of your elders.*
to assert or affirm with great emphasis or conviction
Example: *I swear he was right there.*
the take an oath of allegiance or loyalty
Example: *I swear to always be honest with you.*

sweat /swˈɛt/
the action of excreting moisture from the pores of the skin, typically in response to heat, physical exertion, or emotional stress
Example: *Jerry's nervousness made him sweat profusely.*

sweep /ˈswip/
to clean or remove dirt, dust, or debris from a surface using a broom or similar tool
Example: *Sweep away the crumbs you left on that floor.*

to move or extend over an area with a wide, smooth motion
Example: *The birds swept across the sky with outstretched wings.*
to move forcefully or rapidly in a particular direction
Example: *The hurricane winds swept through the village flattening most of the houses.*
to cover or affect a large area or range
Example: *The covid pandemic swept through the world, causing many deaths.*

swell /ˈswɛl/
to increase in size or volume, often due to pressure, fluid accumulation, or growth
Example: *Her ankles swelled after walking all day up and down the stairs.*
to become filled with emotion, such as pride, joy, or anger
Example: *My father swelled with pride when I became a doctor.*
to bulge or protrude outward
Example: *The bicycle tire swells as air is being pumped into it.*
to rise or surge in intensity or force
Example: *The waves swell as the tide changed*

swerve /swˈɜːv/
to change direction suddenly or sharply, typically to avoid an obstacle or to veer off course
Example: *The bus driver swerved sharply from hitting the oncoming car.*

swill /swˈɪl/
to drink something greedily or in large quantities, often with the lack of refinement
Example: *During the break, players swill lots of water to quench their thirst.*
to rinse or clean something by pouring liquid over it
Example: *I swill water in my mouth after brushing my teeth.*

swim /swˈɪm/
to move through water using one's arms and legs, typically with a rhythmic motion
Example: *The old man swims every morning.*
to be immersed or floating in water without sinking
Example: *The swan swims gracefully across the pond.*

swing /swˈɪŋ/
to move back and forth or from side to side with a swaying motion
Example: *The chimes swing back and forth in the breeze.*
to move or cost move in a wide arc or curve
Example: *Lara swings the bat, hitting the ball for a six.*
change or fluctuate rapidly or dramatically
Example: *Mary's mood swings from happy to sad throughout the day.*

swipe /swˈaɪp/
to strike or pass with a sweeping movement
Example: *Karen swiped him across his nose with the racket.*
to steal or take something quickly
Example: *The man swiped the money quickly off the table before being seen.*

swirl /swˈɜːl/
to move or cost move in a twisting or spiralling motion, often creating a circular or twisting pattern
Example: *During the rain fall, the water swirls down the drains.*

swish /swˈɪʃ/
a soft, rustling or brushing sound produced by something moving quickly through the air
Example: *The horse swishes its tail as the mosquito bites into his skin.*

The act of moving with a whistling or hissing sound, often in a smooth and rapid manner
Example: *She swished her skirt gracefully as she piled across the stage.*

switch /swˈɪtʃ/
to change or exchange something for another, often involving a shift from one state, condition, or position to another
Example: *The lady switched the pants for a bigger fit.*

swivel /swˈɪvəl/
to turn or rotate around a fixed point, often horizontally or vertically
Example: *He swivelled his chair to get a better view of the football game.*

swoon /swˈuːn/
to fail or lose consciousness, often due to extreme emotion, excitement, or admiration
Example: *She swooned when she saw her high school crush.*

symbolise /sˈɪmbəlˌaɪz/
to represent or serve as a symbol of something else, often conveying a deeper or abstract meaning
Example: *The black on the national flag symbolises the strength of the people.*

sympathise /sˈɪmpəθˌaɪz/
to express or feel sympathy or understanding for someone's situation, feelings, or experiences
Example: *Her friends sympathised with her at the time of her mother's passing.*

Tt

tabulate /tˈabjʊlˌeɪt/
to arrange data or information in a systematic or tabular form, often in rows and columns for easy reference analysis
Example: *The judges are going to tabulate the scores to determine the winner of the contest.*

tackle /tˈakəl/
to deal with the problem or task
Example: *The team strategized and then proceeded to tackle the task ahead.*
physically confront or engage with an opponent
Example: *Players often tackle each other in rugby.*

tailor /tˈeɪlɐ/
to customise or modify something to suit a particular need, purpose, or individual
Example: *I will tailor this jacket to his liking.*

take /tˈeɪk/
to acquire or receive
Example: *Please take this book as a gift.*
to consume (medicine, food, etc.)
Example: *He takes his vitamins every morning.*
to grasp or seize
Example: *The thief took the person's bag and ran away.*
to capture or gain control of
Example: *The army plans to take the city by dawn.*
to travel by (a means of transportation)
Example: *We decided to take the train to the next city.*
to assume a position or role

Example: *Please take your seats, the show is about to start.*
to require or need
Example: *This task will take a lot of time and effort.*
to take a photograph or record
Example: *He took a photograph of the beautiful sunset.*
to react or respond to something
Example: *How did he take the news of the promotion?*

talk /tˈɔːk/
to communicate or exchange ideas, information, or feelings using spoken words
Example: *She will talk to her mother tomorrow.*

tally /tˈɑli/
to record, or keep score, often to ensure that figures or items are correct and accounted for
Example: *John will tally the race points.*

tame /tˈeɪm/
to domesticate an animal, making it less wild and more obedient or controllable
Example: *Jack tried to tame the horse, but it was too wild for him.*
to bring something on the control or making it less dangerous, intense, or difficult
Example: *I need to tame my hair before prom.*

tangle /tˈaŋɡəl/
to twist together into a confused mass, making something complicated or ensnared
Example: *The little girl played with the thread until it tangled.*
to become involved in a difficult or complicated situation
Example: *Rio got unexpectedly tangled in the drug operation.*

tantalise /tˈɑːntəlˌaɪz/
to tease or torment someone with the promise of something that is on obtainable or just out of reach
Example: *The kidnapper tantalised her with the steaming hot food.*

tap /tˈɑp/
to strike lightly
Example: *Please tap Mary on her shoulder.*
to draw liquid from a container
Example: *They tapped the tree in search of syrup.*
to access or utilise resources or reserve
Example: *The FBI agent tapped into the security footage to see the robbery.*
to make contact or establish communication
Example: *The waiter tapped me to let me know my date was here.*
to select or designate for a specific purpose
Example: *She tapped the numbers on the keypad furiously.*
to exploit or make use of secretly or dishonestly
Example: *The fake electrician tapped the phone in Jen's house to track her movements and set up the robbery.*

target /tˈɑːgɪt/
to aim or focus on something for action, investigation, or attack
Example: *He is targeting helpless senior citizens.*

task /tˈɑːsk/
to assign a piece of work or a duty to someone
Example: *She was tasked with organising the annual company retreat.*

taste /tˈeɪst/
to perceive flavour through the mouth
Example: *I wanted to taste the steak, but the smell of it made me change my mind.*

to sample or experience something
Example: *I will give him a taste of the job.*
to have a particular of flavour or quality
Example: *The taste of this juice is quite strange.*
to prefer or incline towards something
Example: *I have a taste for jazz music.*

tattle /tˈatəl/
to inform on someone's misdeeds
Example: *Sarah began to tattle to her older brother about her friend's behaviour at school.*

tattoo /tatˈuː/
to mark the skin with indelible ink, created a permanent design or pattern
Example: *She tattooed a strange mark on her arm.*

taunt /tˈɔːnt/
to provoke or insult someone with scornful or sarcastic remarks, often to provoke a reaction or elicit a response
Example: *She began to taunt me after I lost the bet.*

teach /tˈiːtʃ/
to impart knowledge, skills, or understanding to someone
Example: *We will teach you to ride a horse.*

tear /ˈtɛr/
to rip or pull something apart forcefully
Example: *That bear will tear you limb from limb.*
to move quickly or violently
Example: *She said she will tear herself away from that group.*

tease /tˈiːz/

to make fun of or provoke someone in a playful or unkind manner
Example: *The children teased the little boy when he fell off the swing.*
to tempt or entice someone, often playfully
Example: *He began to tease me in efforts to make me chase him.*

teeter /tˈiːtɐ/
to move or sway on steadily
Example: *The unsecure seat started to teeter beneath me.*
to be in a state of uncertainty
Example: *The impatient woman started teetering as she awaited her test results.*

telephone /tˈɛlɪfˌəʊn/
to communicate with someone using a telephone
Example: *Telephone the police immediately!*

tell /tˈɛl/
to communicate information
Example: *Tell me your name please.*
narrate a story
Example: *Her job is to tell the children a story before bed.*
give instructions to someone
Example: *Please tell your aunt to call me tomorrow.*

temper /tˈɛmpɐ/
to moderate or mitigate
Example: *He tried to temper his criticism with some positive feedback.*
to harden or strengthen (especially in metallurgy)
Example: *The blacksmith tempered the steel to make it more durable.*
to tune or adjust
Example: *You need to temper your expectations to avoid disappointment.*

tempt /tˈɛmpt/
to entice or lure someone into doing something, often something they might find attractive, but which might not be in their best interests
Example: *The Devil tried to tempt Jesus in the wilderness.*

tend /tˈɛnd/
to care for or look after
Example: *I will tend to your wounds when I am finished with mine.*
to be inclined or likely to do something
Example: *She tends to buy food there a lot.*
to move or direct oneself
Example: *The sheep tend themselves to the waterside.*

tense /tˈɛns/
the act of tightening or becoming rigid
Example: *Slugs get tense when you touch them.*
to make or become tense (in terms of mood or atmosphere)
Example: *The whole room got tense when they walked in.*

terrify /tˈɛrɪfˌaɪ/
to cause extreme fear or terror in someone
Example: *Haunted houses are not fun; they terrify me!*

test /tˈɛst/
to evaluate or access the abilities, knowledge, or quality of someone or something
Example: *Today we will test your upper body strength and your core strength.*

testify /tˈɛstɪfˌaɪ/
to give evidence or testimony, especially in a legal setting, often on the oath

Example: *I have been asked to testify against someone I know is innocent.*

thank /θˈaŋk/
to express gratitude or appreciation towards someone for something they have done
Example: *Grace will thank the mayor for his speech.*

thaw /θˈɔː/
to gradually become warmer and melt, especially after being frozen
Example: *Your sister said to take the beef out of the freezer to thaw.*

theorise /θˈɪəraɪz/
to formulate or suggest a theory or a set of principles to explain a phenomenon or set of facts
Example: *We began to theorise that our dogs were afraid of the dragon flies.*

think /θˈɪŋk/
to use one's mind to consider or ponder ideas, concepts, or possibilities
Example: *I must think about that before giving you a definite answer.*

thrash /θrˈaʃ/
to beat or hit repeatedly
Example: *His mother gave him a thrashing after she got off the phone with his principal.*
to move violently or uncontrollably
Example: *The waves thrashed against the beach.*
to defeat decisively
Example: *They thrashed our team mercilessly last weekend.*

thread /θrˈɛd/
to pass a thread through a needle or a narrow opening

Example: *Please help your grandmother to thread the sewing machine's needle.*
to move or make one's way through a narrow space
Example: *I suggest that the slimmest person should thread themself through the window and unlock the door.*
to interweave or follow a course
Example: *After turning left, continue threading on the dirt road.*

threaten /θrˈɛtən/
to express an intention to harm, punish, or cause distress to someone or something
Example: *The robber threatened to shoot her if she did not hand over her purse.*

thrive /θrˈaɪv/
to grow vigorously, prosper, or flourish
Example: *She will thrive in the medical field.*

throttle /θrˈɒtəl/
to choke or strangle
Example: *The intruder began to throttle the man in efforts to make him faint.*
to restrict or control the flow of something
Example: *Throttle the water flowing from that crack in the wall.*
to accelerate an engine
Example: *Sam throttled the engine, sending the car roaring down the open highway.*

throw /θrˈəʊ/
to propel something through the air by a rapid motion of the arm and wrist
Example: *You need to throw the ball to your teammate.*

thrust /θrˈʌst/
to push or drive with force
Example: *When he said that to me, I felt like he thrust a knife into my chest.*
to force someone or something upon another
Example: *She thrust the coat onto me angrily.*
to make a sudden, strong, forward movement
Example: *Jane thrust herself out of the car's way.*

thumb /θˈʌm/
to press, move, or turn something with one's thumb
Example: *Thumb that big red button.*
to hitchhike
Example: *We thumbed halfway across the country.*
to look through pages quickly
Example: *During the game Bible Search, we thumb through the Bible pages to find the verse our instructor calls out.*

thump /θˈʌmp/
to strike or hit something heavily, producing a dull, low sound
Example: *The waitress thumped on my back as I choked.*

thunder /θˈʌndɐ/
to make a loud, rumbling noise, typically associated with thunderstorms
Example: *His voice thundered through the halls.*

thwack /θwˈɑk/
to strike forcefully with a sharp, load blow
Example: *The girl thwacked the spider on her wall.*

tick /tˈɪk/
to make a light, clicking sound

Example: *The timer ticked loudly.*
to mark off items on a list with a check mark
Example: *I will pick up the groceries while you tick the items off the list.*
to function or proceed smoothly
Example: *The clock ticked loudly and evenly.*

tickle /tˈɪkəl/
to touch or prod someone lightly in a way that causes laughter or discomfort
Example: *Do not tickle my ear with that feather again.*

tidy /tˈaɪdi/
to organise or clean up a space, making it neat and orderly
Example: *While you cook, I will tidy the living room.*

tie /tˈaɪ/
to fasten or secure with a knot or string
Example: *Children learn to tie their laces at about age 4.*
to equal or have the same score as someone or something in a competition
Example: *He scored a goal when the game had a minute remaining and left the game tied.*
to form a connection or association
Example: *You need to make ties with a gang, so you will have protection in prison.*

tighten /tˈaɪtən/
to make something firmer, more secure, or less loose
Example: *He tightened the bolt on the bicycle to avoid it becoming loose while riding.*

tilt /tˈɪlt/

to incline or angle something in a particular direction, often unintentionally
Example: *She tilted the laptop, so that all the students were able to see the presentation.*

time /tˈaɪm/
to measure or set the duration of an event
Example: *His speech was timed for exactly one hour.*
to schedule or arrange and activity
Example: *The zoom meeting was timed for Wednesday at five o'clock.*
to choose the precise moment to do something
Example: *The comedian timed his jokes perfectly to amuse the audience.*

tingle /tˈɪŋgəl/
to experience a slight prickling or stinging sensation, often because of excitement, anticipation, or nervousness
Example: *He would often sense a tingle in his throat during singing.*

tinker /tˈɪŋkɐ/
to make small changes to something to repair or improve it, often in a casual or experimental manner
Example: *Tyrell enjoys tinkering with old computers to get them working.*

tinkle /tˈɪŋkəl/
to make a light, ringing sound, often associated with small, delicate objects, or falling drops of liquid
Example: *The chimes in the garden tinkle as the evening breeze brushes against them.*

tip /tˈɪp/

to tilt or overturn
Example: *The cat tipped the container to get to the rat.*
to give a small amount of money as a gratuity
Example: *The customers tipped the waitress for her kind service.*
to provide information or advice
Example: *The teacher gives the students tips before their Mathematics exam.*

tiptoe /tˈɪptəʊ/
to walk quietly and carefully on the balls of one's feet, typically to avoid being heard or to maintain balance
Example: *The ladies tiptoed in the church during the prayer.*

tire /tˈaɪə/
to become weary or fatigued
Example: *Mother was tired after climbing the long stairs.*
to exhaust the strength or patience of someone or something
Example: *He became tired because of the demands his boss placed on him.*
to become no longer useful or effective
Example: *The clothes were now tired after years of wearing.*

titter /tˈɪtɐ/
to laugh nervously, quietly, or in a restrained manner, often in response to something slightly amusing or embarrassing
Example: *The driver tittered at the passage who tripped in the aisle.*

toast /tˈəʊst/
to brown or heat bread in a toaster or over a fire
Example: *The bread was perfectly toasted.*
to raise one's glass and drink in honour of someone or something
Example: *Her dad toast to her success of becoming the youngest female pilot.*
to dry or warm oneself by a fire or other heat source

Example: *The children could not help but toasted their frozen hands in front of the fireplace.*

toddle /tˈɒdəl/
to walk with unsteady or wobbly steps, often characteristic of young children who are learning to walk
Example: *The calf toddled to its mother.*

toe /tˈəʊ/
to touch, kick, or move something with one's toe
Example: *Toe the ball to me Jack.*
to walk or stand on tiptoe
Example: *The children toed the line to avoid colliding.*

toil /tˈɔɪl/
to work extremely hard or laboriously, often involving physical or mental exertion
Example: *She toils from sunrise to sunset in efforts to make ends meet.*

tolerate /tˈɒləˌreɪt/
to allow or endure something that is unpleasant or undesirable without reacting negatively or taking action to stop it
Example: *Alcohol consumption will not be tolerated on this trip.*

toot /tˈuːt/
to sound a horn or whistle
Example: *Toot your horn so she will know we are here.*
to emit a short, sharp sound
Example: *Mike let out a toot after being startled by the fireworks.*

topple /tˈɒpəl/
to fall suddenly and often violently from an upright position

Example: *The bottle began to topple down the stairs.*

toss /tˈɒs/
to throw something lightly or casually, often with a quick, upward motion
Example: *Toss the frisbee to me.*

tote /tˈəʊt/
to carry or haul something, typically with some effort
Example: *You can help to tote the grocery bags.*

totter /tˈɒtɐ/
to walk or move unsteadily, often on the swaying motion, as if about to fall
Example: *The drunk man tottered out of the bar.*

touch /tˈʌtʃ/
to make physical contact with something
Example: *I touched her shoulder to get her attention.*
to affected emotionally
Example: *Her poem about cancer touched me.*
to handle or use something
Example: *Please touch the stop button on the washing machine.*

toughen /tˈʌfən/
to make something physically or mentally stronger, more resilient, or more resistant to stress or difficulty
Example: *He uses an extra bolt to toughen the hinge on the door.*

tour /tˈɔː/
to travel through a place or area for the purpose of exploring, sightseeing, or performing
Example: *They tour the amazon river in search of the missing child.*

tousle /tˈaʊsəl/
to make something, particularly here, untidy or dishevelled
Example: She tousled her hair in the wind making it messy.

tow /tˈəʊ/
to pull or drag something, typically a vehicle or boat, using a rope, chain, or other means
Example: The boy towed his little brother on his bicycle.

tower /ˈtaʊɚ/
to raise or reach a great height, especially in comparison to something else
Example: The bamboo tower over the hills, creating a beautiful arch.

toy /tˈɔɪ/
to handle or play with something in a casual or superficial way, often without serious intent
Example: She toyed with her pencil during the presentation on mammals.
to consider or flirt with an idea or possibility
Example: My parents toyed with the idea of moving to Japan.

trace /trˈeɪs/
to follow the outline or path of something
Example: Trace the letters on the page.
to find or discover by investigation
Example: The detectives traced the robbery back to the three girls.
to copy a design or drawing by following its lines
Example: The teacher instructed the children to trace the outline of their hands on the paper.

track /trˈɑk/
to follow the course or trail of something

Example: *The police officer used a device to track the fugitive.*
to monitor or keep a record of something over time
Example: *The employer tracks worker record punctuality daily.*
to locate or find someone or something
Example: *Father used a magnet to locate the missing key.*

trade /tr'eɪd/
to exchange goods, services, or assets, often in a business or market context
Example: *Father traded his car for a van.*

trail /tr'eɪl/
to follow behind someone or something, often at a distance
Example: *The dog trailed behind the owner as they left for work.*
to drag or let something drag along the ground
Example: *She trailed her finger through the sand while on the beach.*
to move slowly or lag behind
Example: *The new hiker trail behind the rest of the group.*

train /tr'eɪn/
to teach or develop skills or knowledge in oneself or others through practise and instruction
Example: *The coach trained the swimmer to dive.*
to prepare for a particle a task or activity
Example: *He trained hard for the upcoming race.*
to aim or direct something towards a particular goal or target
Example: *The photographer trained his camera to capture the night vision.*

traipse /tr'eɪps/
to walk or more wearily, reluctantly, or without any specific goal
Example: *After completing the marathon, the athletes traipsed wearily towards the crowd.*

tramp /trˈæmp/
to walk heavily or noisily
Example: *The boy tramped his feet along the corridor, causing great disturbance.*
to travel or walk long distances, especially on foot
Example: *The hunters tramp through the forest all night in search of a catch.*
the tread or stamp on something firmly
Example: *The boy tramped on the can to flatten it.*
to wander or travel about as a vagabond or itinerant
Example: *The homeless women tramp from city to city in aid of shelter.*

trample /trˈɑːmpəl/
to step heavily on something so as the crush, damage, or destroy it
Example: *The students trample on the flower patch until it is flattened.*
to treat with disrespect or disregard
Example: *The protesters trampled on photos of the elected president to show their disgust.*
the stamp or work heavily and noisily
Example: *The rescuers trampled through the rubbles in search of survivors.*

transcribe /trɑnskɹˈaɪb/
to write or type spoken words
Example: *The civil courts use highly skilled stenographers who transcribe the witnesses' testimonies during hearings.*
to make a written copy of something
Example: *Peter carefully transcribed all of grandma's letters.*
to convert music into written form or into another notation
Example: *Our music teacher transcribed Mozart's string quartet for piano last summer.*
to rewrite in a different language or alphabet

Example: *The school invested in a machine that transcribes all our textbooks into braille.*

transfer /ˈtrænsfɚ/
to move from one place to another
Example: *The child's car seat was transferred to another vehicle.*
to convey or pass from one person to another
Example: *My files were transferred to the human resource department.*
change from one vehicle, route, or mode of transportation to another
Example: *We transferred to the Atlanta airport.*
to relocate from one job, school, team, etc. to another
Example: *The doctor was transferred to a different hospital.*
to convey information, rights, or responsibility
Example: *He was transferred to the Chicago Bulls.*
to move funds from one account to another
Example: *The funds are transferred electronically.*

transform /ˈtrænsfɔɹm/
to change something significantly in form, appearance, nature, or character
Example: *The old warehouse was transformed into an art gallery.*

translate /trænsˈleɪt/
to convert text or speech from one language into another
Example: *We need someone to translate the Chinese into English.*
to express or interpret something in a different form or terms
Example: *Her portfolio is to translate the decision into a viable project.*

transmit /trænsˈmɪt/
to send or convey something from one person, place, or thing to another
Example: *The new technology allows for data to be transmitted via cellular phones.*

to spread diseases or infections
Example: *The disease is transmitted via physical contact.*

transport /ˈtrɑnspɔrt/
to carry or move something or someone from one place to another
Example: *The sapodillas were transported in small wooden crates.*

trap /trˈɑp/
to catch or confine someone or something, often by using a device designed for this purpose
Example: *The soldiers trapped the fugitive in the forest.*

travel /trˈɑvəl/
to go from one place to another, typically over a distance
Example: *Her job necessitates that she travels frequently.*

traverse /trɑvˈɜːs/
to travel across or through a particular area or to move or pass through something
Example: *The hikers traverse the forest in search of the waterfall.*

tread /trˈɛd/
to walk or step on something, often with a particular manner or with care
Example: *She tread carefully on the slippery tiles.*

treasure /trˈɛʒɚ/
to value something highly, to hold something dear, or to cherish it
Example: *I treasure our friendship.*

treat /trˈiːt/
to behave towards someone in a certain way

Example: *At the centre they try to treat everyone equally.*
to manage or deal with something
Example: *The situation must be treated with utmost care.*
to provide medical care
Example: *The baby was treated for dehydration.*

tremble /trˈɛmbəl/
to shake involuntarily, typically because of anxiety, excitement, or frailty
Example: *The girl clenched her fist as she trembled in fear during the earthquake.*

trick /trˈɪk/
to deceive or cheat someone by making them believe something that is not true
Example: *He tricked his friends into believing that he was kidnapped to obtain a large sum of money.*

trill /trˈɪl/
to produce a quavering or warbling sound, often associated with board songs or musical notes
Example: *She trilled a beautiful note on the piano leaving the audience in awe.*

trim /trˈɪm/
to make something neat or of the required size or form by cutting away irregular or unwanted parts
Example: *The barber trimmed the young man's hair for his graduation.*

trip /trˈɪp/
to stumble or lose balance
Example: *He tripped on Lego blocks that were scattered on the floor.*

to journey or travel
Example: *The journalist tripped through the city of Georgetown during the Mashramani celebration.*
to activate a switch on mechanism
Example: *He presumptuously tripped the fire alarm causing panic in the school.*
to cause someone to hallucinate or experience a mind-altering effect
Example: *The ecstasy drink tripped him out causing him to speak in an unfamiliar voice.*

triumph /trˈaɪʌmf/
to achieve victory or success, often with a feeling of great joy or satisfaction
Example: *Brazil triumphed three nil to reach the world cup finals.*

trivialise /trˈɪvɪəlˌaɪz/
to make something seem less important, significant, or serious than it really is
Example: *He has trivialised her concern about the group project making it seem as insignificant.*

trot /trˈɒt/
to move at a pace faster than a walk but slower than a run, typically by a four-legged animal
Example: *She trotted through the savannah, as she gazed on the blooming trees.*

trouble /trˈʌbəl/
to cause distress, difficulty, or inconvenience to someone or something
Example: *The taxi-driver disappearance troubled his family and the community.*

troubleshoot /trˈʌbəlʃˌuːt/

to systematically identify and resolve problems or difficulties in a system, process, or situation
Example: *He troubleshooted the laptop for hours until it began to work.*

trounce /trˈaʊns/
to defeat decisively or the beat severely in a competition or conflict
Example: *The West Indians Cricket Team was trounced by their opponents.*

trudge /trˈʌdʒ/
to walk slowly and with heavy steps, typically because of exhaustion or through difficult terrain
Example: *The campers trudge back to the campsite.*

trumpet /trˈʌmpɪt/
to proclaim or announce something loudly and forcefully
Example: *The principal trumpeted her views on after school care, in hope that the teachers will support her.*

trundle /trˈʌndəl/
to move slowly and noisily, often with a rolling or rattling sound
Example: *The golf car trundles around the court.*

trust /trˈʌst/
to have confidence in the reliability, truth, or ability of someone or something
Example: *The old woman trusted her neighbour to enter her house whenever she is away.*

try /trˈaɪ/
to make an attempt or effort to do something
Example: *The preschooler tried to colour within the circle.*

tuck /tˈʌk/
to put something into a small, confined space
Example: *Please tuck your shirt into your pants.*
to make something neat or secure by folding or tucking
Example: *She tucked the sheets over the mattress.*

tug /tˈʌg/
to pull something with a quick, sharp movement
Example: *The little boy tugged the girl's hair as he ran past her.*

tumble /tˈʌmbəl/
to fall suddenly and clumsily, often rolling or flipping
Example: *The bottle began to tumble down the stairs.*

tune /tjˈuːn/
to adjust a musical instrument
Example: *We called our instructor to tune our steel pans.*
to adjust a machine or device for optimal performance
Example: *The man tuned the lever so it would stop getting stuck.*
to adjust or regulate something to a particle standard or specification
Example: *Please tune the radio next to you.*
to adjust or adapt behaviour, strategy, etc., to a particle situation or requirement
Example: *She tuned her mind to be around her teachers.*

turn /tˈɜːn/
to change direction or position
Example: *Sarah will turn that chair to the right.*
to change state or condition
Example: *The weather started to take a turn for the worse.*
to rotate or spin
Example: *Turn the car to face the garage.*
to change focus or attention

Example: *The little girl turned her head quickly when she heard the fireworks.*
to reach a particular age or time
Example: *I will turn 54 years old in three days.*

tutor /tjˈuːtɐ/
to teach privately or in a small group
Example: *Abigail's mother asked me to tutor Abigail after school.*
to provide guidance or instruction
Example: *I help to tutor underprivileged children at the shelter.*

tweak /twˈiːk/
to make a minor adjustment
Example: *The DJ tweaked the knobs on his board.*
the pinch or twist slightly
Example: *The carpenter made some final tweaks to the screws on the wall.*

tweeze /twˈiːz/
to pluck or remove something, typically hair, using tweezers
Example: *The cosmetologist tweezed the pimples on her forehead.*

twiddle /twˈɪdəl/
to fiddle or play with something in a purposeless or nervous manner
Example: *She twiddled her earrings as she waited to go on stage and say her poem.*

twine /twˈaɪn/
to twist or entwine something around something else or together
Example: *Teone the wire into that post.*

twinkle /twˈɪŋkəl/
to shine with the flickering or sparkling light

Example: *Do not twinkle that light into my eyes again.*

twirl /twˈɜːl/
to spin or rotate something or oneself quickly
Example: *He twirled his dance partner six times.*

twist /twˈɪst/
to turn or bend something into a different shape
Example: *The clown twisted the balloon into a dog shape.*
to change direction suddenly
Example: *Our GPS said to twist down a two-lane road.*
to distort the meaning of something
Example: *Do not twist my words to give them your own meaning.*

twitch /twˈɪtʃ/
to make a small, sudden, and usually involuntary movement or jerk
Example: *The boy started to twitch in his sleep.*

twitter /twˈɪtɐ/
to make a series of high-pitched sounds
Example: *A bird is twittering at my window.*

type /tˈaɪp/
to write or input text using a keyboard or typewriter
Example: *Please type the letter I. have written.*

Uu

ululate /ˈʌljʊlˌeɪt/
to howl or wail loudly, often in a high-pitched manner, especially as an expression of grief, joy, or celebration
Example: *The villagers ululated in joy during the festival.*

unbend /ʌnbˈɛnd/
to relax, become less tense, or straighten out from a bent position
Example: *After a long day, she finally unbent and reclined on the sofa.*

unbind /ʌnbʌɪnd/
to release or remove something that is bound or tied
Example: *She unbound the ropes and set the bird free.*

unbuckle /ʌnbˈʌkəl/
to release or open a buckle, typically on a belt, strap, or fastening
Example: *He unbuckled his seatbelt after the car stopped.*

unbutton /ʌnbˈʌtən/
to undo or open buttons, typically on clothing
Example: *She unbuttoned her coat as she entered the warm room.*

unclasp /ʌnklɑ/
to release or open something that is clasped or fastened together
Example: *He unclasped the necklace and placed it in the box.*

unclench /ʌnklˈɛntʃ/
to relax or release a tightly held grip, typically of the hands or jaw
Example: *She unclenched her fists after the argument.*

uncoil /ʌnkˈɔɪl/
to unwind or straighten something that is coiled or wound up
Example: *The snake uncoiled and slithered away.*

uncover /ʌnkˈʌvɐ/
to remove a cover from something
Example: *He uncovered the dish to reveal the delicious food.*
to reveal or make known something that was hidden
Example: *The investigation uncovered the truth about the incident.*
to expose something that was previously concealed or unknown
Example: *They uncovered ancient artefacts during the excavation.*

uncross /ʌnkrˈɒs/
to change from a crossed to an uncrossed position
Example: *She uncrossed her legs and stood up.*
to disentangle or separate things that are crossed
Example: *He uncrossed the wires to fix the connection.*

uncurl /ʌnkˈɜːl/
to straighten out from a curled or coiled position
Example: *The cat uncurled and stretched lazily.*
to cause something that is curled to become straight or less curled
Example: *She uncurled the ribbon before using it.*

undergo /ˌʌndəgˈəʊ/
to experience or be subjected to something, typically something unpleasant or a process of change
Example: *He underwent surgery to repair the injury.*

understand /ˌʌndəstˈænd/
to grasp the meaning, significance, or nature of something
Example: *She understands the complexities of the situation.*

understate /ˌʌndəstˈeɪt/
to describe something as being less important, significant, or serious than it is
Example: *He understated the impact of the budget cuts.*

undertake /ˌʌndətˈeɪk/
to take on or commit oneself to a task or responsibility
Example: *She undertook the project with great enthusiasm.*
to begin or start something, especially a task or project
Example: *They undertook to renovate the old house.*

undo /ʌndˈuː/
to reverse the effect of an action or change
Example: *She wished she could undo her mistake.*
to unfasten or loosen something
Example: *He undid the knot with ease.*
to cancel or invalidate
Example: *The court undid the previous ruling.*
to ruin or destroy the effect of something
Example: *His careless remark undid all their hard work.*

undress /ʌndrˈɛs/
to remove clothes from oneself or someone else
Example: *She undressed quickly and got into bed.*

undulate /ˈʌndjʊˌleɪt/
to move with a smooth, wavelike motion
Example: *The flag undulated in the wind.*

unfasten /ʌnfˈɑːsən/
to release or loosen something that is fastened or secured
Example: *She unfastened her seatbelt after the plane landed.*

unfold /ʌnfˈəʊld/
to open or spread out from a folded or closed position
Example: She unfolded the map to find the route.
to reveal or disclose gradually over time
Example: The plot of the story unfolded slowly.
to develop or progress gradually
Example: The events unfolded as expected.

unfurl /ʌnfˈɜːl/
to spread out or open something that is rolled up or folded
Example: They unfurled the banner at the rally.

unhand /ʌnhˈɑnd/
to release or let go of someone or something that one is holding, typically forcefully or against their will
Example: The villain was ordered to unhand the captive.

unhook /ʌnhˈʊk/
to remove or release something that is hooked, typically from a support or attachment
Example: He unhooked the picture from the wall.

unify /jˈuːnɪfˌaɪ/
to bring together or combine multiple parts into a single, unified whole
Example: The leader unified the divided nations.

unite /juːnˈaɪt/
to bring together or join different parts, groups, or individuals into a single, unified entity or whole
Example: The new chief united all the tribes in the land.

unknot /ʌnnˈɒt/
to untie or loosen a knot

Example: *She unknotted the tangled rope.*

unlace /ʌnˈeɪs/
to untie or loosen laces, typically on a piece of clothing or footwear
Example: *He unlaced his boots after the hike.*

unleash /ʌnˈiːʃ/
to release or set free something powerful or intense, often with sudden or forceful action
Example: *The storm unleashed its fury on the coast.*

unlock /ʌnˈɒk/
to open or release a lock, typically with a key or combination, thereby allowing access to something that was previously secured
Example: *She unlocked the door to the office.*

unmake /ʌnmˈeɪk/
to undo or reverse the making or creation of something, typically by dismantling or destroying it
Example: *The sculptor had to unmake the statue and start over.*

unmask /ʌnmˈɑːsk/
to reveal the identity or nature of someone or something that was previously concealed or disguised
Example: *The investigator unmasked the true culprit.*

unpack /ʌnpˈak/
to remove items from a container, especially luggage
Example: *She unpacked her suitcase after the trip.*
to explore or analyse something in detail
Example: *The professor unpacked the complex theory during the lecture.*

unpin /ʌnpˈɪn/
to remove a pin or pins from something
Example: *She unpinned the notice from the bulletin board.*

unravel /ʌnrˈavəl/
to undo or separate the threads or fibres of something
Example: *She unravelled the sweater to use the yarn for something else.*
to clarify or solve something complex or mysterious
Example: *The detective unravelled the mystery of the missing jewels.*

unroll /ʌnrˈəʊl/
to straighten out or spread something that has been rolled up or coiled
Example: *She unrolled the yoga mat before the class.*
to unwind or release something that has been rolled or coiled
Example: *The hose unrolled smoothly as he pulled it across the lawn.*

untangle /ʌntˈɑŋgəl/
to separate or free something that is caught or twisted together, typically in a disorderly or confused manner
Example: *She patiently untangles the knots in the necklace.*

untie /ʌntˈaɪ/
to undo or loosen a knot or tie
Example: *He untied his shoelaces before taking off his shoes.*

untuck /ʌntˈʌk/
to remove or free something that was tucked into or under something else, typically clothing or bedding
Example: *She untucked the sheets from the bed.*

untwine /ʌntwʌɪn/
to separate or unwind something that is twisted or intertwined

Example: *He gently untwined the vines from the fence.*

untwist /ʌntwˈɪst/
to undo or straighten out something that is twisted or coiled
Example: *She untwisted the wire to straighten it out.*

unveil /ʌnvˈeɪl/
to reveal or make something known for the first time, especially if it was previously hidden or secret
Example: *The company unveiled its latest product at the event.*

unwind /ʌnwˈaɪnd/
to relax or become less tense
Example: *After a long day, she likes to unwind with a good book.*
to straighten out or untangle something that is twisted or coiled
Example: *He unwound the garden hose after using it.*

unwrap /ʌnrˈɑp/
to remove the wrapping or covering from something, revealing what is inside
Example: *The children eagerly unwrapped their presents.*

update /əpˈdeɪt/
to make something more current or up to date by adding new information, making revisions, or incorporating the latest developments
Example: *She updated the software to the latest version.*

upgrade /əpˈgreɪd/
to improve or enhance something, typically by replacing it with a better version or by adding new features or capabilities
Example: *They upgraded their old computer.*

uphold /ʌphˈəʊld/
to support, maintain, or defend something, especially a principle or belief, often by adhering to it or by ensuring its continuation
Example: *The judge upheld the previous court's decision.*

upset /əpˈsɛt/
to disturb or agitate emotionally; to make someone feel anxious, worried, or unhappy
Example: *The news of the accident upset everyone.*
to disrupt or overturn; to cause something to become disordered or chaotic
Example: *The sudden change in plans upset the schedule.*
to overturn or capsize, especially a vehicle or vessel
Example: *The boat was upset by the strong waves.*

urge /ˈɜːdʒ/
to strongly encourage or persuade someone to do something
Example: *He urged her to apply for the job.*

use /ˈjuz/
the action of employing something for a particular purpose or to accomplish something
Example: *She used the old jars for a new purpose.*

usher /ˈʌʃɐ/
to lead, guide, or escort someone, typically to a particular place or event
Example: *The host ushered the guests to their seats.*

utilise /jˈuːtəlˌaɪz/
to make use of something for a specific purpose or to put something to practical use
Example: *They utilised the available resources efficiently.*

utter /ˈʌtɚ/
to speak or express something aloud
Example: *She uttered a soft greeting as she entered the room.*

Vv

vacillate /ˈvɑsəˌleɪt/
to waver between different opinions or actions; to be indecisive
Example: *He often vacillates between different career choices.*

validate /vˈɑlɪdˌeɪt/
to confirm, prove, or support the truth or value of something
Example: *The scientist validated the results of the experiment.*

vanish /vˈɑnɪʃ/
to disappear suddenly and completely
Example: *The rabbit vanished from the magician's hat.*

vault /vˈɒlt/
to leap or spring over something, typically using the hands or a pole for support
Example: *She vaulted over the fence effortlessly.*

veer /vˈiə/
to change direction suddenly
Example: *The car veered off the road to avoid an accident.*

vent /vˈɛnt/
to express feelings, especially anger or frustration, openly and forcefully
Example: *He vented his frustrations after the meeting.*

venture /vˈɛntʃɐ/
to undertake a risky or daring journey or course of action
Example: *They ventured into the forest despite the warnings.*

verbalise /vˈɜːbəlˌaɪz/
to express ideas, feelings, or thoughts in words
Example: *She found it hard to verbalise her emotions.*

verify /vˈɛrɪfˌaɪ/
to confirm the truth, accuracy, or validity of something
Example: *He verified the information before sharing it.*

vex /vˈɛks/
to make someone feel annoyed, frustrated, or worried, especially with trivial matters
Example: *The constant noise vexed the residents.*

vibrate /vaɪbrˈeɪt/
to move rapidly to and from, typically in a repeating pattern
Example: *The phone vibrated in her pocket.*

view /vjˈuː/
to look at or consider something in a particular way or from a particular perspective
Example: *He viewed the painting from different angles.*

visit /vˈɪzɪt/
to go to a place, especially for a short period of time, often for a specific purpose or to see someone
Example: *She visited her grandparents over the weekend.*

visualise /vˈɪʒuːəlˌaɪz/
to form a mental image or picture of something in one's mind
Example: *He visualised his success before the competition.*

vituperate /vɪtjuəreɪt/
to criticise or blame someone in a harsh or abusive manner

Example: *The critic vituperate the actor's performance harshly.*

vocalise /vˈəʊkəlˌaɪz/
to express something with one's voice
Example: *She vocalised her concerns during the meeting.*

vociferate /vəˈsɪfɝeɪt/
to shout or cry out loudly, often with strong emotion or in protest
Example: *The protesters vociferate their demands.*

volley /vˈɒli/
to discharge or fire several shots, arrows, or other projectiles in quick succession
Example: *The soldiers volleyed their arrows at the enemy.*
to send or hit something forcefully and rapidly back and forth
Example: *They volleyed the ball during the game.*

volunteer /vˌɒləntˈɪə/
to offer to do something willingly and without being asked or obligated to do so
Example: *She volunteered to help with the event.*

vomit /vˈɒmɪt/
to forcefully expel the contents of the stomach through the mouth, typically because of illness or reaction to something unpleasant
Example: *He vomited after eating the spoiled food.*

vote /vˈəʊt/
to express a formal indication of choice, typically in an election or by ballot
Example: *She voted in the national election.*

vouch /vˈaʊtʃ/

to support or confirm the reliability, truth, or value of someone or something

Example: *He vouched for his friend's honesty.*

vow /vˈaʊ/

to make a solemn promise or commitment to do something

Example: *They vowed to always support each other.*

Ww

waddle /wˈɒdəl/
to walk with short steps, swinging from side to side, typically in a manner resembling the gait of a duck
Example: *The penguin waddled across the ice.*

wade /wˈeɪd/
to walk through water or another substance that impedes movement, often making it difficult to move
Example: *He waded through the shallow river to reach the other side.*

waft /wˈɑːft/
to move or cause to move gently and smoothly through the air, often referring to a scent or sound
Example: *The smell of fresh bread wafted through the kitchen.*

wag /wˈɑg/
to move or cause to move rapidly back and forth or up and down, often referring to a tail or finger
Example: *The dog wagged its tail happily.*

wager /wˈeɪdʒɐ/
to risk money or something of value on the outcome of an event or a proposition, such as a bet or a gamble
Example: *He wagered $50 on the outcome of the game.*

waggle /wˈɑgəl/
to move or cause to move with short, quick movements from side to side or up and down
Example: *The puppy waggled its ears in excitement.*

wail /wˈeɪl/
to make a prolonged, high-pitched cry of pain, grief, or anger
Example: *The baby wailed loudly when it was hungry.*

wait /wˈeɪt/
to stay in one place or remain inactive until something expected happens or someone arrives
Example: *She waited at the bus stop for her friend.*

wake /wˈeɪk/
to stop sleeping or to make someone stop sleeping
Example: *He wakes up early every morning.*

walk /wˈɔːk/
to move on foot at a regular and slow pace by lifting and setting each foot in turn
Example: *They walk to school every day.*

wallop /wˈɒləp/
to strike or hit someone or something very hard
Example: *He walloped the ball out of the park.*

wallow /wˈɒləʊ/
to indulge in something excessively, often a negative emotion or behaviour
Example: *She wallowed in self-pity after the breakup.*
to roll about or lie relaxedly in or on a surface
Example: *The pigs wallowed in the mud to cool off.*

waltz /wˈɒlts/
to dance the waltz, a graceful ballroom dance in triple time
Example: *They waltzed gracefully across the ballroom.*

wander /wˈɒndɚ/
to move or walk in a leisurely, aimless manner, often without a specific destination or purpose
Example: *He wandered through the park, enjoying the scenery.*

want /wˈɒnt/
to have a desire or a wish for something
Example: *She wants a new bicycle for her birthday.*

warble /wˈɔːbəl/
to sing or whistle with trills, melodic embellishments, or modulations in pitch
Example: *The bird warbled a beautiful song.*

warm /wˈɔːm/
to make or become warm; to raise the temperature
Example: *She warmed her hands by the fire.*

warn /wˈɔːn/
to inform someone in advance about a potential danger, problem, or undesirable outcome
Example: *He warned them about the slippery road ahead.*

warp /wˈɔːp/
to become bent, twisted, or distorted, typically because of heat, moisture, or pressure
Example: *The wooden door warped due to the humidity.*

wash /wˈɒʃ/
to clean something with water or a liquid
Example: *She washed the dishes after dinner.*

waste /wˈeɪst/

to use or expend carelessly, extravagantly, or to no purpose
Example: *He wasted his money on unnecessary gadgets.*
to fail to use or take advantage of something beneficial
Example: *She wasted her opportunity to speak up.*

watch /wˈɒtʃ/
to observe someone or something attentively, typically over a period
Example: *They watched the movie together.*

water /wˈɔːtɐ/
to moisten, sprinkle, or drench with water
Example: *She watered the plants every morning.*

wave /wˈeɪv/
to move one's hand or an object back and forth, typically to signal or greet someone, or to produce a ripple or undulating motion
Example: *He waved at his friend from across the street.*

waver /wˈeɪvɐ/
to hesitate or be indecisive; to show doubt or uncertainty
Example: *She wavered between accepting the job offer and staying at her current job.*

wear /ˈwɛɹ/
to have something on one's body as clothing or an accessory
Example: *He wears a suit to work every day.*

weave /wˈiːv/
to form fabric by interlacing threads or strands
Example: *She weaves beautiful rugs by hand.*
to create something by combining various elements in a complex way
Example: *The author weaves a compelling story with rich characters.*

wed /wˈɛd/
to marry or join in marriage
Example: *They wed in a beautiful ceremony by the sea.*

wedge /wˈɛdʒ/
to force something into a narrow space, often to secure or hold it in place
Example: *He wedged the door open with a piece of wood.*

weep /wˈiːp/
to cry or shed tears, especially as an expression of sadness, grief, or distress
Example: *She wept silently at the news of his passing.*

weigh /wˈeɪ/
to ascertain the weight of something by using scales or by comparing it to a known weight
Example: *He weighed the flour before adding it to the mixture.*

welcome /wˈɛlkʌm/
to greet someone in a warm and friendly manner, often upon their arrival
Example: *They welcomed the guests at the door.*

wend /wˈɛnd/
to travel in a particular direction, typically slowly or by an indirect route
Example: *They wend their way through the crowded streets.*

wet /wˈɛt/
to make something damp or moist with water or another liquid
Example: *The rain wetted their clothes as they walked.*

whack /wˈɑk/
to strike forcefully or suddenly with a sharp blow
Example: *He whacked the ball with the bat.*

wheedle /wˈiːdəl/
to use flattery or coaxing to persuade someone to do something or to obtain something
Example: *She wheedled her way into getting a discount.*

wheeze /wˈiːz/
to breathe with difficulty and with a whistling or rattling sound, often due to a respiratory issue
Example: *He wheezed after running up the stairs.*

whet /wˈɛt/
to sharpen or stimulate, often used in the context of sharpening a blade
Example: *He whetted the knife before using it.*
increasing someone's interest or appetite for something
Example: *The aroma of the food whetted their appetites.*

whimper /wˈɪmpɚ/
to make low, feeble sounds expressive of fear, pain, or unhappiness
Example: *The puppy whimpered when it was left alone.*

whine /wˈaɪn/
to make a long, high-pitched complaining cry or sound
Example: *The child whined about not getting a toy.*

whinny /wˈɪni/
to make a characteristic low, gently neighing sound, as a horse
Example: *The horse whinnied softly as it greeted its owner.*

whip /wˈɪp/

to move (an object) quickly or forcefully in a specified direction, often with a flexible implement or a sudden motion
Example: *She whipped the towel off the table.*

whirl /wˈɜːl/
to move or cause to move rapidly around and around
Example: *The leaves whirled in the wind.*

whisk /wˈɪsk/
to move or take (someone or something) in a particular direction suddenly and quickly
Example: *He whisked the documents off the desk.*

whisper /wˈɪspɐ/
to speak very softly or quietly, using one's breath rather than one's vocal cords
Example: *She whispered a secret to her friend.*

whistle /wˈɪsəl/
to make a high-pitched sound by forcing breath through a small opening between the lips or through a hole in a device
Example: *He whistled a cheerful tune while he worked.*

whittle /wˈɪtəl/
to carve or shape wood by cutting small pieces from it with a knife or other sharp tool
Example: *He whittled a small figure from a piece of wood.*

whoop /ˈwup/
to make a loud, excited, or jubilant cry, often as an expression of enthusiasm or joy
Example: *They whooped in celebration after their team won the game.*

widen /wˈaɪdən/
to make something broader or more extensive, or to become broader or more extensive
Example: *They widened the road to accommodate more traffic.*

wield /wˈiːld/
to handle or use (a weapon, tool, or power) effectively
Example: *She wielded the hammer with skill.*

wiggle /wˈɪgəl/
to move or cause to move up and down or from side to side with small rapid movements
Example: *The worm wiggled in the soil.*

wilt /wˈɪlt/
to become limp and drooping, as a plant from lack of water or heat, or to lose strength and energy
Example: *The flowers wilted in the hot sun.*

win /wˈɪn/
to achieve victory in a contest, competition, or conflict
Example: *They won the championship game.*
to gain something through effort or merit
Example: *She won the award for her hard work.*

wince /wˈɪns/
to make a slight involuntary grimace or shrinking movement out of pain or distress
Example: *He winced when he touched the hot stove.*

wind /ˈwaɪnd/
to move in or take a twisting or spiral course
Example: *The path winds through the forest.*

to wrap or twist something around a central point or object
Example: *She wound the yarn into a ball.*

windmill /wˈɪndmɪl/
to move or cause to move in a motion resembling the rotating blades of a windmill, often used to describe the action of arms or legs
Example: *He windmilled his arms to keep his balance.*

wink /wˈɪŋk/
to close and open one eye quickly, typically as a signal or gesture
Example: *She winked at him playfully.*

wipe /wˈaɪp/
to clean or dry something by rubbing its surface with a cloth or one's hand
Example: *She wiped the table after dinner.*

wish /wˈɪʃ/
to desire or long for something to happen or to be true
Example: *He wished for a better future.*

withdraw /wɪðdrˈɔː/
to remove or take back something, typically from a place or situation, or to retreat or pull back
Example: *She withdrew her savings from the bank.*

withhold /wɪðhˈəʊld/
to refuse to give something, to keep something back, or to retain something
Example: *He withheld his approval until the changes were made.*

withstand /wɪðstˈænd/
to resist or endure something without yielding or giving in

Example: *The building withstood the earthquake.*

witness /wˈɪtnəs/
to see or observe (an event, typically a crime or accident) take place
Example: *She witnessed the accident on her way to work.*

wobble /wˈɒbəl/
to move unsteadily from side to side with a rocking motion
Example: *The chair wobbled on its uneven legs.*

wonder /wˈʌndɐ/
to have a feeling of curiosity or doubt about something
Example: *He wondered if he had made the right decision.*

woo /wˈuː/
to try to gain the love or favour of someone, typically with a view to marriage
Example: *He wooed her with flowers and poetry.*

work /wˈɜːk/
to perform tasks or activities to achieve a particular goal or result
Example: *She worked hard to complete the project.*
to function or operate properly
Example: *The machine works efficiently.*
to exert effort or labour
Example: *He works in the garden every weekend.*
to have a particular effect or influence
Example: *The medication worked quickly to relieve the pain.*

worry /wˈʌri/
to feel anxious or concerned about something, typically something that may happen or is causing uncertainty or distress
Example: *She worried about her upcoming exam.*

worship /wˈɜːʃɪp/
to show reverence and adoration for a deity or religious figure
Example: *They worship every Sunday at the church.*
to regard with great admiration and devotion
Example: *She worships her grandmother for her wisdom.*

wrack /rˈɑk/
to cause extreme physical or mental suffering or pain
Example: *He was wracked with guilt after the accident.*
to ruin or destroy
Example: *The storm wracked the coastal town.*
to search or examine thoroughly
Example: *They wracked their brains for a solution.*

wrangle /rˈɑŋɡəl/
to argue or dispute angrily and persistently
Example: *They wrangled over the details of the contract.*

wrap /rˈɑp/
to cover or enclose something by folding or surrounding it with material
Example: *She wrapped the gift in colourful paper.*

wreck /rˈɛk/
to destroy or severely damage something
Example: *The hurricane wrecked many homes along the coast.*

wrench /rˈɛntʃ/
to twist or pull forcefully
Example: *He wrenched the door open.*
to cause emotional pain or distress
Example: *The news of the tragedy wrenched her heart.*
to move with a sudden twist or jerk

Example: *She wrenched her ankle while running.*

wrest /rˈɛst/
to forcibly pull (something) from a person's grasp
Example: *She wrested the book from his hands.*
to obtain (something) with difficulty or effort
Example: *He wrested control of the company after a long struggle.*

wrestle /rˈɛsəl/
to engage in a physical struggle, typically involving grappling and trying to throw or force one's opponent to the ground
Example: *They wrestled for the championship title.*

wriggle /rˈɪgəl/
to twist and turn one's body with quick, twisting movements
Example: *The worm wriggled on the wet ground.*

wring /rˈɪŋ/
to squeeze, twist, or compress forcefully to extract moisture
Example: *She wrung out the wet towel.*
to cause pain or distress
Example: *The heart-breaking news wrung her heart.*

wrinkle /rˈɪŋkəl/
to form creases or small folds on a surface, typically because of being compressed or crumbled
Example: *She wrinkled her nose at the unpleasant smell.*

write /rˈaɪt/
to form letters, words, or symbols on a surface with a pen, pencil, or similar tool
Example: *She writes a letter to her friend every week.*
to compose texts for communication or record-keeping purposes

Example: *He writes articles for a popular magazine.*

writhe /rˈaɪð/
to twist and turn, especially because of intense physical or emotional discomfort
Example: *He writhed in pain after the injury.*

Xx

xenograft /ˈziːnəˌɡrɑːft/
to transplant tissue or an organ from one species to another
Example: *The medical team successfully xenografted a pig's heart into the patient.*

xenotransplant /ˈziːnəʊˌtrɑːnsplɑːnt/
to transplant an organ, tissue, or cells from one species to another
Example: *Researchers are exploring ways to xenotransplant pig kidneys into humans.*

xeriscape /ˈzɪərɪskeɪp/
to landscape an area in a way that reduces or eliminates the need for irrigation by using drought-resistant plants and other techniques
Example: *They decided to xeriscape their yard to conserve water.*

xerox /zˈiərɒks/
to make a photocopy of a document using a Xerox machine or similar photocopier
Example: *She xeroxed the report for the meeting.*

x-ray /ˈɛks rˈeɪ/
to examine something with X-rays, typically to see inside it
Example: *The doctor x-rayed his arm to check for fractures.*

xylograph /ˈzaɪləˌɡrɑːf/
to carve or engrave on wood
Example: *The artist xylographed intricate designs on the wooden panel.*

xylophone /zˈaɪləfˌəʊn/
to play or perform music on a xylophone, a musical instrument consisting of wooden bars of different lengths that are struck with mallets to produce sound
Example: *She xylophone a beautiful melody during the concert.*

yank /jˈaŋk/
to pull something forcefully or abruptly
Example: *She yanked the door open.*

yap /jˈap/
to bark sharply or continuously, typically in a high-pitched tone
Example: *The small dog yapped at the mailman.*

yawn /jˈɔːn/
to involuntarily open one's mouth wide and inhale deeply, often because of tiredness or boredom
Example: *He yawned during the long lecture.*

yearn /jˈɜːn/
to have an intense longing or desire for something
Example: *She yearned for a vacation in the mountains.*

yell /jˈɛl/
to shout, often in anger, excitement, or to attract attention
Example: *He yelled for help when he saw the fire.*

yelp /jˈɛlp/
to utter a short, sharp cry, usually because of pain, surprise, or excitement
Example: *The puppy yelped when it stepped on a thorn.*

yield /jˈiːld/
to produce or provide something because of effort or work
Example: *The farm yields a good harvest each year.*

to give way to pressure, force, or influence
Example: *The door yielded under the heavy pressure.*
to surrender or give up
Example: *The soldiers yielded to the enemy forces.*
to give in to a demand or request
Example: *He yielded to her request for more time.*

yodel /jˈəʊdəl/
to sing or call out with sudden changes in pitch, alternating between low and high notes, typically in a traditional Alpine style
Example: *The performer yodelled skilfully during the show.*

yowl /jˈaʊl/
to make a loud, wailing cry, typically in distress, pain, or protest
Example: *The cat yowled when its tail was stepped on.*

Zz

zero /zˈɪərəʊ/
to adjust or reset to a starting point, typically to the number zero
Example: *He zeroed the scale before weighing the ingredients.*

zest /zˈɛst/
to scrape or cut out the peel of citrus fruit to extract its flavourful oils
Example: *She zested a lemon to add flavour to the cake.*

zigzag /zˈɪgzæg/
to move in a pattern resembling a series of sharp turns or angles
Example: *The bike zigzagged down the slope.*

zing /zˈɪŋ/
to move quickly with a high-pitched buzzing sound
Example: *The arrow zinged past his ear.*
to add excitement or energy to something
Example: *The spices zinged up the dish, adding excitement to its flavour.*

zip /zˈɪp/
to fasten or unfasten with a zipper
Example: *He zipped up his jacket before going outside.*
to move quickly or with speed
Example: *The car zipped down the highway.*
to compress files into a single, smaller file format
Example: *She zipped the files before sending them via email.*

zonk /zˈɒŋk/
to suddenly fall asleep or become unconscious due to fatigue or exhaustion

Example: *He zonked out on the couch after a long day at work.*

zoom /zˈuːm/
to move or travel quickly, often with a buzzing or humming sound
Example: *The plane zoomed across the sky.*
to focus in or magnify an image or view, typically using a camera or other optical device
Example: *She zoomed in on the photo to see the details.*

www.ingramcontent.com/pod-product-compliance
Ingram Content Group UK Ltd.
Pitfield, Milton Keynes, MK11 3LW, UK
UKHW020245240426
12048UKWH00026B/1617